INTRO

Welcome to Asheville. This city is traditionally known as the *Land of the Sky* which is one of the most contradictory, oxymoronic, yet awe-inspiring and naturally breathtaking descriptions imaginable.

Centered around an old historical downtown district and surrounded by the most beautiful mountains we've ever laid eyes on, Asheville's an easy place to fall in love with but a hard place to define.

Some folks call it *She-ville* because they claim it has more goddesses per capita than any city in ancient Greek mythology.

It was once dubbed *The Paris Of The South* which is pretty funny considering most people here probably kiss in French but can't speak much of it.

Call it what you will.
We just call it home.

TABLE OF CONTENTS

The Underground Asheville™ *Guidebook* did not accept any advertising dollars, gratuities, hot stock market tips, free drinks, backrubs, marriage proposals, kinky little favors, or other forms of bribery from persons or enterprises listed herein. (That doesn't necessarily mean we're above all that; it just means we didn't get any offers tempting enough to make us cave-in. But we're working on that.)

That isn't to say that this book is totally unbiased and clinically objective. *Au contraire!* As one of our staff put it "We are totally opinionated, unlike most guidebooks."

Of course we were unable to include everything we like. (But that ensures we have a built-in, pre-fab excuse to do a revised edition.)

Seriously though, folks, honest-to-Betsy...we didn't let anybody buy us out. (We've been saving ourselves for you, our adorable readers, and we're hoping you'll buy so many of these babies that we'll wind up mugging for Mom in front of the cameras on "Oprah" someday soon. Wouldn't that be a hoot?)

This guidebook is meant to . . .

THE GUIDE TO THIS GUIDEBOOK

You may use this as a standard reference
book to locate something specific. But
it was written for pleasure-reading.
If you have a particular interest,
you may prefer to turn to the section of the book that covers it
and read the whole chapter.
And if you like what you
find, you might decide to
sit down in an easy chair
and read the whole kit
and caboodle, cover
to cover. We'd be
much obliged if
you did.

. . . be a celebration of Asheville created around information valuable
to visitors and newcomers.
It contains listings of places you might like to go, it includes
introductions to people you might like to meet, it
has about 200 outstanding photographs, and it
contains at least one good banjo joke:

What do you get if you cross a chicken with a banjo player?
A self-plucking clucker.

Not only does this book contain tips on how to pack and prepare
for your journey to the mountains, it also includes
suggestions about how to quickly discover the things
you really enjoy in Asheville, so you can dive right into
your favorite scenes and start having fun. We understand
how frustrating it can be to piddle away your whole vacation asking people for suggestions and directions,
only to find out that the people you're asking are from
out of town and they're lost and clueless too. Hopefully
this book will help you find your niche in Asheville
and give you all the clues you need too enjoy your stay,
whether you're here for an afternoon or a lifetime.

We included **loads of information** about things like where to go to find the best lodging, restaurants, shopping, entertainment, and hiking spots. But this book also has **useful tips** about things like how to distinguish poison ivy from chewing tobacco and how to tell if a mountain lion is about to attack or just has a serious crush on you. Which reminds us, we even put a little heart-shaped symbol next to things included in the book which we think inspire romance.

We also threw in tidbits to help you figure out stuff like where to get your hair dyed a color that crayon manufacturers (not to mention your own mother) have never dreamed existed. And there are a few pages dedicated to those of you who are only visiting Asheville because you know *it's the one place in America where you can still enjoy a cappuccino while skinny-dipping in a clawfoot tub full of sourwoood honey.* Oh, you didn't know that about Asheville? See, you're already getting your money's worth out of this guidebook, and you're still on the first few pages.

We couldn't possibly include everything we wanted to tell you about Asheville in this one edition. We trust that you'll keep your eyes, ears, and minds open while getting to know the town, so that you can enjoy the same process of discovery that inspired us to write this book.

In between the places we listed in the guidebook are many awesome places we want you to experience. We'll try to

include them in the next edition, with one or two exceptions: Our favorite moonshine bar, which is disguised inside a double-wide trailer out in the sticks, and a hush-hush guest house with rose petal milk baths, feather massage, and intimacy galore, are top secret. Or maybe they don't exist at all and we just made that part up out of our imaginations. Yeah, that's it. Oh, well. Never mind.

We created many **self-guided tours**, which emphasize everything from architecture to Sunday brunch, and provided a **comprehensive index**. If we couldn't give you information directly, we tried to include the phone number of someone who can.

Of course we couldn't possibly include everything awesome about Asheville. We attempted to present a sampling, just to give you a flavor of what the area has to offer. Along the way, you'll encounter many wonderful things which aren't included, and you'll enjoy discovering them on your own.

You might even uncover things we don't know about, which really deserve to be included in the pages of this book. Our hope is that you'll add them on the **blank journal pages** we've provided throughout the book.

Finally, we tried our best to make this a **people-centered book**, *because we happen to believe that people are where love comes from, and that love is like apple butter . . . the more you spread it around, the sweeter life gets.*

The pictures in this publication are a book unto themselves, and you may find out as much about Asheville by looking at them as you could by reading the entire text.

Reprints of some of the photos and other artwork are available for purchase. Call the *Underground Asheville Guidebook* at 828.281.6210 or write to us at P.O. Box 1663, Asheville, NC 28802 or email to undergroundasheville@home.com with specific inquires.

THE UNDERGROUND GUIDE TO KID STUFF IN ASHEVILLE

Kid-friendly excursions in Underground Asheville are marked with a child's hand icon. Look for the icon when planning fun stuff for children to do in Underground Asheville.

This boy (with help from his little friends) did the research regarding which childrens' attractions to highlight in this guidebook. He chose to be photographed with his folding camping shovel because he likes to dig around and come up with cool places for kids to go and have fun.

THE UNDERGROUND GUIDE TO ROMANTIC ASHEVILLE

AMOROUS ASHEVILLE

Romantic readers can look for the heart-shaped icon when planning excursions intended to be more conducive for flirting, courtship, wooing, or downright seduction. Listings in the guidebook designated as such were chosen specifically because they have a reputation for a relatively high percentage of Cupid sightings. Remember to look before you leap and keep in mind that the publishers of this book usually don't when it comes to *les affaires de coeur*.

> The mind is just a suitcase. Don't put enough in it and you'll be lugging around dead weight. But overstuff it and it's liable to bust open and your underwear will spill out in the middle of the street.
>
> — *The Old Timer*

WEATHER

PACKING

DIRECTIONS

TRANSPORTATION

BEFORE YOU
COME
PREPPING FOR THE
JOURNEY

GRETCHEN BAER
TOURIST

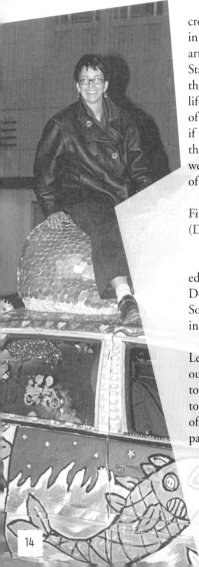

Gretchen and Tinuviel, two hapless travelers from Cape Cod, Massachusetts, en route to the annual Art Car Parade in Houston, Texas, blundered upon Asheville after their '88 Ford Tempo broke down and they were forced to revise...or shall we say, improvise...their itinerary.

They accepted that they would not be crossing any bridges into the new millennium in a four-door *objet d'art*. They would not be art car stars with limo-mural status in the Lone Star State. They would kick the tires, crank up the radio, and hit the on-ramp with enough life left in their jalopy to make it up to the top of the mountain. They could coast from there if they needed to. It's that kind of place. Or they could just hang around and be tourists, as we all are somewhere, sometime, in some state of mind or another.

First stop: Dollywood, USA.
(Dollywood or Bust!)

But a quagmire of endless traffic thwarted them again. Their plans to become Dolly's bosom buddies went by the wayside. So, by default (some say fate), they ventured into Asheville.

We spotted Gretchen's car parked on Lexington Avenue, surrounded by gawkers like ourselves. The irony of two tourists arriving in town and immediately attracting all the other tourists was irresistible to us. Usually that kind of attention is reserved for vehicles parallel-parked with one tire up on the sidewalk and

Gretchen Baer is Tourism personified.
To get where she's going, she doesn't
depend upon ordinary transportation.
She drives a four-door self-propelled tourist
attraction with bucket seats and whitewall tires.

14

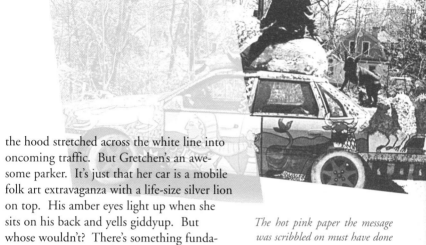

the hood stretched across the white line into oncoming traffic. But Gretchen's an awesome parker. It's just that her car is a mobile folk art extravaganza with a life-size silver lion on top. His amber eyes light up when she sits on his back and yells giddyup. But whose wouldn't? There's something fundamentally fetching about a woman whose ride sticks out like a ferris wheel in a funeral procession. So we left a note on the windshield which read, "We are publishing a cool book and want to include a photo of your cool car. Please call." She did.

We asked Gretchen Baer, our official Underground Asheville tourist...

What do you admire in a person?
Honesty and being genuine.

If you were going to live on a deserted island for two years, what three things (besides food and water) would you take along?
An African prince I know, many cases of Veure Cligvot, and lots of art supplies.

Do you have a recurring dream?
Yes. Hunkered down like outlaws in a haunted house with friends.

Do you have a favorite souvenir from this vacation?
Yes, a Dollywood tee-shirt.

The hot pink paper the message was scribbled on must have done the trick because within the hour we were taking turns riding shotgun, cruising downtown, scarves-into-the-wind, waving to our astonished friends from the cockpit of a gorgeously customized all-American made Henry Ford-invented and Goddess-inspired whacko-mobile. We experienced first-hand the raw power of ars gratia artis (art for art's sake). Our friends waved back from their own boring sedans, beige station wagons, and in one instance, the backseat of a squad car.

What is the strangest thing you encountered en route to Asheville?
Some of your roadside vistas, lunching with Dolly, and a billboard on the way to Dollywood that said, *Do you know where you're going?—God.*

What is your idea of the ideal way to spend your day while being a tourist?
Meeting artists, visiting their homes, seeing their art, or having a fun adventure.

What was the best thing about your first visit to Asheville?
Meeting the creators of this book.

If you could declare a holiday in Asheville, what would it celebrate?
Independence from Dollywood Day.

What was your favorite Asheville tourist sight?
The mythical Asheville tunnel. *

author's note: This refers to a cavernous space beneath Pack Square which some believe exists. The author, with the help of experts, researched this legend and determined that there may be a subterranean Asheville existing beneath our feet. We are in contact with persons who claim to live there, in an alternative, intentional community. The sequel to this guidebook will reveal our complete findings.

If you were to return to Asheville, what essential items would you be sure to bring?
Bright-colored clothes and postcards of my art car.

If you could only take one music recording on a road trip, what would you take?
The Carpenters Greatest Hits.

Are art cars an American phenomenon?
I don't think art on cars is, but junk glued on cars definitely is.

What's the coolest art car you know of?
I like the "Red Car" by Wayne Kosinki of Balitmore, MD. It's made of branches painted red and features a huge spinning wheel bigger than the car with shards of mirror glued all over it, dangerously.

What's your idea of the ideal type of vehicle to convert into an art-mobile?
Oldsmobile Ninety-Eight.

Do the aerodynamics of an art car adversely affect your gas mileage?
Yes. It cuts down on mileage. But, like high heel shoes, that's the price you pay for fashion.

What particular challenges are presented when operating an art car on our nation's highways?
Gawkers swerving into your lane to get a better view.

What one piece of advice would you give someone intending to become a tourist in Asheville?
Never say never.

Gretchen's former home, the art boat named "Dragonfly's Banquet," in the Atlantic Ocean near Cape Cod.

WEATHER CONDITIONS
FOR ASHEVILLE AND VICINITY

The following average temperatures were recorded in Asheville and at a nearby mountaintop elevation (approx. 3800 ft.). We provide both to give our readers an idea of the temperature fluctuations between the city and the summits.

Downtown Asheville		Higher Elevation
55	Spring	49
72	Summer	65
57	Fall	51
38	Winter	33

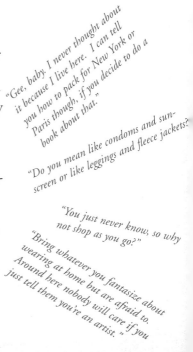

HOW TO PACK
FOR ASHEVILLE

Be prepared for wind and precipitation, especially at higher elevations. And expect sudden gusts of self expression and higher pressures to dance, particularly when exposed to live music downtown on weekends.

We got all sorts of evasive, ambiguous answers when we surveyed local wardrobe and travel experts on the subject of how to pack for a trip to Asheville. The following is a sampling of their suggestions, just to prove to you that we really and truly tried to find out:

"Gee, baby, I never thought about it because I live here. I can tell you how to pack for New York or Paris though, if you decide to do a book about that."

"Do you mean like condoms and sunscreen or like leggings and fleece jackets?"

"You just never know, so why not shop as you go?"

"Bring whatever you fantasize about wearing at home but are afraid to. Around here nobody will care if you just tell them you're an artist."

OUR PERSONAL SUGGESTIONS

We try to stay prepared for a variety of weather conditions, especially when traveling between downtown and the higher elevations. Pack as though you were going on two trips: one to the city, one to the countryside.

The temperatures can drop suddenly, especially on a mountaintop. If you plan to hike, it's essential that you carry warm clothes and/or an emergency blanket. Comfortable hiking, walking, and dancing shoes are a must. The hiking boots should be waterproof. A fleece jacket or vest is convenient for layering. Bring one in black and you can wear it out on the town at night if necessary. A waterproof windbreaker is handy, as are a hat, gloves, and scarf. A small backpack is convenient, so you don't have to tie your jacket around your waist when it gets too warm to wear. And it can double as a shopping bag or book bag when walking around town.

Of course Asheville is a good place to shop, whether you need a slinky red dress, some climbing gear, or a new banjo. So if you prefer, travel light and plan to shop on arrival. If your budget's maxed-out, we have some great thrift stores where you might find an impromptu wardrobe on the cheap.

We asked an old-timer: "If you could live at any place and any time in history, where and when would you choose to live?"
The old timer: "It might as well be here. And if it be here, it might as well be now."

AUTHOR'S NOTE

While writing this section, I got a phone call
from a neighbor. She asked me to leave an extra
pair of shoes on the back porch so she could lend
them to a friend for the weekend. "Okay, I can
handle that" I thought to myself. So far that day I'd
borrowed a tanktop, a laptop computer, and someone's ginger-ginseng moisturizer. I'd loaned out a
pair of shoes, some sunglasses, a car, and one rather
petulant black cat. I felt like I had at least broken
even for the week.

The phone rang again after a few minutes:
Someone was hyperventilating on the other end,
panting into the mouthpiece. But it turned out not
to be an obscene call —"Oh well, maybe next time
I'll get lucky" I thought. Instead, it turned out to
be yet another friend.

This one had been desperate to find a babysitter
within the next two hours. Everyone had told her
to call *moi*. And oh, yeah, the babysitter needed to
have no visible piercings except for maybe a nose
ring and absolutely no magenta or purple hair.

Those parameters slowed down the search a bit, but
not to worry. I thought of two people who fit the
criteria, no problem.

Well, at least that had been the case the last time
I had seen them, which was a few hours before.
But in a town like this, people and things change
with the slightest realignment of the planets. As it
turned out, one of my hot prospects had acquired a
major tattoo since then, but all her piercings
remained well-concealed in unusually intimate
places, so she got the babysitting gig and everything
worked out just hunky-dory for everyone.

No wonder it took so long to write a book about
this little town.

POSSIBLE CHAMBER OF COMMERCE RELOCATION

As we go to press, there is talk of moving the Chamber of Commerce to a location just a stone's throw from where it is now. If the C of C has moved, please adjust accordingly the directions in this book which begin or end at the C of C. Don't worry, it'll be a cinch. And if you get lost, what the heck? You're still at the Chamber of Commerce, which is probably the best place in town for wayward visitors to get directions.

From Boone, NC

Distance: 95 mi.
Driving Time: 1 hr. 45 mins.
Take **105-S** out of Boone, which turns into US **221 S**. Take this all the way to Marion. Be careful if the weather is bad, and watch out for road-hogging trucks on this scenic but dangerous stretch of road. At Marion, you will come to an intersection with US 70 W. Take a right onto **70 W** and continue on this road until you get to Old Fort. At Old Fort, 70 W turns into **I-40 W**. Take this until you get to **I-240 W**. Take **exit 4C** and turn left onto Montford Ave, then an immediate left onto Haywood Street. The Chamber of Commerce is directly on your left.

From Johnson City, TN

Distance: 60 mi.
Driving Time: 1 hr. 20 mins.
Take **I-181 S** for 16.8 mi., then at Unaka Springs, bear right onto **US 23** (going SW) for 25 mi. At Mars Hill, bear right onto **US-19 S** for 18.1 mi. until you get to the junction with I-240. Take **I-240E** and get in the left lane as soon as possible to get off at **exit 4C**. Take a right at the end of the exit ramp, and the Chamber of Commerce is directly on your right.

From Charlotte, NC

Distance: 114 mi.
Driving Time: between 2 and 2 1/2 hrs.
(depends on traffic / road works)
From Charlotte-Douglas International Airport, go out of the Airport and take Billy Graham Parkway to **I-85 S** towards Spartanburg. Take this until you see the sign for Asheville. Take **US 74W** to **I-26 W**, then take **I-240E** to **exit 4C**. Take a right at the end of the exit ramp and the Chamber of Commerce is directly on your right.

From Greensboro or Winston Salem, NC

Distance from Greensboro: 178 mi.
Driving Time: 2 1/2 hrs.

Distance from Winston-Salem: 144 mi.
Driving time: 2 hrs.

Take **I-40W**, then **I-240W**. Take **exit 4C**, then turn left onto Montford Ave, taking an immediate left onto Haywood St. The Chamber of Commerce is directly on your left.

From Waynesville, NC

Distance: 27 mi.
Driving Time: 30 mins.

Take **US 23 (NE)** for 1.6 mi. then bear right onto **US 19E** for 2.9mi. Turn right onto the I-40 connector then at **I-40 exit 27**, turn right onto **I-40 E**. Keep on I-40 until exit 46, where you make a left onto **I-240 E**. Take **exit 4C**, then take right at the end of the exit ramp and the Chamber of Commerce is immediately on your right.

From Great Smoky Mountains National Park

Distance: 80 mi.
Driving Time: 1 1/2 hrs.

Take **US 321 E** for 19.6 mi. Turn right onto Foothills Parkway E for 5.6 mi., then get on **I-40 E** and go a further 54.3 mi. to **I-240 E**. Take exit 4C. Take a right at the end of the exit ramp, and the Chamber of Commerce is immediately on your right.

LOCAL TRANSPORTATION

Asheville Transit
828.253.5691
The Asheville City Transit (A.C.T.) system operates daily from 5 a.m. until 7 p.m. There are two bus routes which continue until 9:30 p.m., except on Saturdays. Normal fares are 75 cents plus 10 cents for transfers, and discounts are offered for seniors and those with handicaps. Call for more information on schedules, routes, and fares.

Yellow Cab Co.
828.253.3311 or 828.252.1913
"The thinking fellow rides a yellow" is their motto. Taxis dispatched 24 hours a day, seven days a week.

All American Limousine, Inc.
828.667.9935
Owner Will Smith at All American offers a 1960 Caddy and three Lincoln Town Car limos for hire for sightseeing tours or a night on the town. Call for reservations and prices.

Euro Transport
828.254.2088
Thomas Brown offers limo service to and from the airport in cool-looking authentic London taxis which can hold up to seven passengers apiece. Call for reservations and prices.

In 1939 a Buncombe County resident entered the Guinness Book of World Records. "Big Boy" earned the international distinction of being the largest hog on record at a whopping 1904 pounds. "Big Boy" was nearly six feet high at the shoulder. Several eyewitnesses compared him in size and shape to a Volkswagen automobile. The couple who raised him told reporters, "Yeah, he's a big 'un. That's why we call him 'Big Boy'."

23

DEFENSIVE DRIVING
IN DYSFUNCTION JUNCTION

Keep in mind that this city is nicknamed Dysfunction Junction because of its reputation for logically-challenged intersections. We have traffic situations that force drivers to rely completely upon intuition. And we have drivers who have been in those situations who will never trust their intuition again for as long as they live. Which might not be too long, if natural selection has anything to say about it. It's no wonder that Asheville has evolved into a New Age Mecca where people let the spirit guide them. It's the only way to negotiate our traffic patterns, which resemble Celtic knotwork. Except Celtic knotwork doesn't involve newly ascended bliss-bunnies flipping you the bird while laying on the horn for dear life.

To be a defensive driver in Asheville you must not only predict what the other drivers are going to do, you

When used in the context of the Blue Ridge Mountains, the word Cherokee should conjure up the idea of American Indian affiliation. But nowadays some people hear it and think of the luxurious four-wheel drive yuppie gas-guzzlers which are ubiquitous on the Parkway. Automotive traffic has replaced the buffalo herds which once lived in these mountains and created pathways by pounding their hooves across the land. Their naturally created trails were used by Cherokee and other neighboring tribes as trading and hunting routes. Many of our modern-day country roads, city streets, state highways and even sections of the federal interstate system are based upon the original trails blazed by buffaloes and American Indians.

have to communicate with them telepathically and convince them to stop doing it before both of you hear that big crunching sound of cars turning into accordions and insurance rates ripping through the roof.

You will notice cars which have been in so many fender benders that the only thing holding them together is a collage of 20 or 30 bumper stickers. It's an alternative method of collision repair. The bumper stickers say things like "I'm A Chevy But I'm Channeling A Rolls," "My Other Car Is A Broom," or "Breastfeed Or Bust."

But don't get too distracted reading while you drive or you might miss some of our eccentric traffic signs. There are stop signs set so far back from the intersections they are warning you about that it is almost impossible to see the intersection from the stopping spot. One "Do Not Enter" sign in downtown was erected inside a 10 ft. high fence but you're supposed to heed it anyway. Our favorite stop sign has graffiti underneath the word "STOP" which reads "Talking On The Phone And Drive."

LEAF SEASON

What happens each autumn, to make the mountains and hillsides of Western North Carolina suddenly look like the tops of opened boxes of crayons?

The presence of *chlorophyll* (the green stuff that causes *photosynthesis*, which is that process you're supposed to know all about from grade school) in leaves begins to diminish so they lose their green complexion. When this happens, the leaf pigment underneath begins to show through. *Voila!* The leaves change colors depending upon the color of the underlying pigment.

The pigment has fancy scientific names: **Anthocyanans** make the leaves turn red. **Carotenoids** make the leaves turn orange, like a carrot. **Xanthyphylls** make the leaves turn yellow. **Tannin** is the pigment buried deepest in the leaf. It makes them turn tan, and that's when you know the party's over.

When you want to show off Asheville to visitors, what are the one or two places you make sure to take them?

"The first thing I do is take them up on a mountain so they can look down and see the configuration of the entire area. Most of the time that's up to the Grove Park Inn or to one of the overlooks up on the Blue Ridge Parkway. And the second place is downtown, because I think we have a wonderful, exciting downtown."

Asheville Mayor Leni Sitnick

L:ODGING

DOWNTOWN LODGING

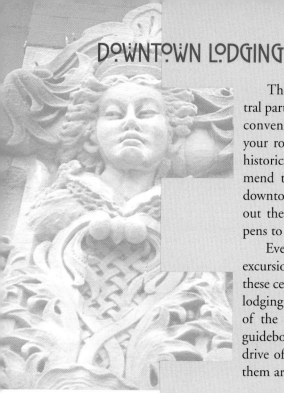

These are located in the central part of Asheville and offer the convenience of walking from your room into the heart of the historical district. We recommend them if strolling through downtown by day and hanging out there for the night life happens to be your cup of tea.

Even if you plan to take excursions into the countryside, these centrally located options for lodging are excellent. Almost all of the attractions listed in this guidebook are within an hour's drive of downtown, and most of them are closer.

For complete information about hotels, motels, inns, campgrounds, and other types of lodging in the Asheville area, check out these publications which can be ordered free of charge by phone.

The Accommodations Directory
Chamber of Commerce
828.258.6101

Lodgings Guide
North Carolina Dept. of Travel & Tourism
1.800.847.4862 or
1.800.VISIT.NC

Haywood Park Hotel & Promenade
One Battery Park Avenue
828.252.2522
1.800.228.2522

Suites priced from around $130 for single occupancy to about $295 for double occupancy. Luxury suites, wet bars, Spanish marble and ceramic baths, a fitness center, a non-smoking floor, lobby areas on each floor, fine dining, executive meeting rooms.

Right smack-dab in the middle of downtown's historical district at Battery Hill. The ever-popular New French Bar is attached to the hotel at street level. There are several shops inside the hotel, and the best shopping in Western North Carolina awaits you right outside the door.

Renaissance Asheville Hotel
One Thomas Wolfe Plaza
828.252.8211
1.800.333.3333

This centrally-located hotel is around the corner from the Thomas Wolfe Memorial. Our favorite feature is the sensational view of the mountains afforded by the penthouse restaurant on the twelfth floor. 8,100 square foot ballroom, fourteen meeting rooms, a deli, a sports bar and grill, and a fitness center. Guest rooms are decorated in a Queen Anne motif and have great views of the mountains and the city.

Best Western Asheville-Central
22 Woodfin Street
828.253.1851
1.800.528.1234

This downtown hotel is a little more affordable than some of the competition, but offers the same convenience of location along with oodles of amenities. It's just down the street from the Thomas Wolfe Memorial.

Okay, let's dispense with the flowery words and cut to the chase here: When my one-and-only Mama comes to visit, this is where she likes to stay. And only the best is good enough for Mama, who has always included "good value for the money" in her definition of "best" when it applies to hotels. She has always had a clean, comfortable, spacious room with great service and a great location.

Days Inn
120 Patton Avenue
828.254.9661
1.800.DAYS INN

This is one of the few less-expensive options for downtown lodging. It's centrally located to shopping, night life, restaurants, historical architecture, and everything else that the old town district has to offer. It's only about three blocks from the Chamber of Commerce, a block from Wall Street, and a hop, skip, and a jump from Pack Square.

Wolf Den
(A Hostel Style Alternative)
22 Ravenscroft Drive
828.285.0230

Call for pricing information. Last time we checked it was about $18 per person. This old home in the center of the historic downtown district is operated like a European hostel. Catering to the traveler who wants to feel like a local, not a tourist, the Wolf Den offers clean, comfortable lodging, linens, and use of the kitchen. A  great way to experience Asheville on a budget while staying in a place that has a warm, people-oriented atmosphere.

NEAR
DOWNTOWN LODGING

NATIONAL CHAINS

Here are a few of the "chain" motels and hotels in and around Asheville. If you call for a reservation, be sure to check the location. Some of these have more than one location in the area, and you might want to book the one closest to the attractions you plan to visit while in the region.

Comfort Inns	**Holiday Inns**
1.800.228.5150	1.800.465.4329
Hampton Inns	**Ramada Inns**
1.800.HAMPTON	1.800.2.RAMADA

TRADITIONAL AMERICANA-STYLE MOTELS

Back in the pre-yuppie era, Asheville wasn't nearly as cosmopolitan as it seems today. We used to come here in the '50s and '60s and stay in typical Asheville motor courts, while shopping for mountain souvenirs like salt and pepper shakers that looked like moonshine jugs, corn cob pipes, foot-long cigars, and hillbilly hats made from green felt with chicken feather plumes.

The outhouse motifs on restaurant matchbooks are long gone, but old-fashioned motels still exist. Although they have been modernized for comfort, the owners still uphold the tradition of mountain hospitality.

Here are two prime examples:

American Court Motel

85 Merrimon Avenue

828.253.4427   1.800.233.3582 Reservation Desk

This AAA Approved motel is a family business that's been running for years and years. The creators of this book stayed at the American while looking for their first apartment in town. It has all-American character and reminds us of the old fashioned Motor Courts that used to exist along Route 66.

Reasonable rates, all the basic comforts (including a Laundromat), convenient location (a few blocks from downtown and three miles from Biltmore House), and good, friendly folks.

The Mountaineer Inn

Tunnel Road

(I-240 take exit 6)

828.254.5331   1.800.255.4080 Reservation Desk

Just a stone's throw from downtown and, as the brochure proclaims, "conveniently located between two shopping malls, near thirty-three restaurants and steak houses and two cafeterias", this place is the real McCoy.

Every room has its own refrigerator. The old part of the motel features cedar paneling, the newer part has large rooms with "extra long beds" and "bedside panels" to control the TV and lights. The Mountaineer exemplifies the old style 1950s motel experience, except that the rooms have been updated with modern decor and amenities.

In other words, the people are all about Southern hospitality, the rooms are huge, and there is one designated as a bridal suite. A big curvaceous swimming pool is featured out front. Plus, the logo is a graphic depiction of a Lil' Abner era "hilly-billy" with his moonshine jug, felt hat, and flintlock rifle. So you can send your homeboys back in the big city a postcard of your hillbilly honeymoon destination and let them have a vicarious cultural escapade.

ROYAL ACCOMMODATIONS

Grove Park Inn Resort
290 Macon Avenue
828.252.2711   1.800.438.5800

This AAA Four Diamond resort hotel, with it's own 18 hole, award-winning golf course, indoor-outdoor tennis courts, sports center, and supervised children's programs, is an Asheville monument. Even if you don't stay there, you may want to visit the bar or restaurant to watch the sunset over Asheville from one of the best views in the whole wide world.

Designed with inspiration from the magnificent old lodge in Yellowstone Park, the Inn draws heavily from its own natural surroundings, figuratively and literally. Some of the boulders used to create the Inn weigh more than 10,000 pounds, and they were taken from the nearby mountains with their lichen and moss still intact. The walls of the hotel are almost five feet thick.

Tabletop scale model of the Grove Park Inn on display inside the Grove Park Inn.

Furnished with antiques from the Arts and Crafts era, the hotel is a virtual museum piece. The Great Hall at the Inn has two fireplaces, anchoring either side of the room. They are six feet high, six feet deep, and twelve feet wide. Those of you familiar with cutting and stacking a cord of firewood get a load of this: The fireplaces burn logs which are twelve feet long. But the Great Room they heat is almost 10,000 square feet large. It can accommodate 1,000 people at once, comfortably. That's a pretty good sized den.

Rent a room at the Inn and you may sleep on a bed once occupied by Daniel Day Lewis, Crystal Gayle, or Michael 'Air' Jordan. Other former guests (who may or may not fuel your fantasies) include Harry Houdini, Mikhail Baryshnikov, Debbie Reynolds, Eleanor Roosevelt, and Art Linkletter.

Additionally, Edison, Ford, Rockefeller, eight different presidents, a few kings and queens, and F. Scott Fitzgerald all stayed at the Inn.

Richmond Hill Inn
87 Richmond Hill Drive
828.252.7313   1.888.742.4554

Stately and elegant, this Inn has princely furnishings and spectacular views to compliment its high level of personal service. Gabrielle's is the Inn's own AAA Four Diamond restaurant. Built in 1889 on a hill overlooking the French Broad River, the grand Victorian mansion was the private residence of an ambassador and congressman. The Queen Anne style home has 36 uniquely appointed rooms.

LOCAL BED &
BREAKFAST LODGING

The Black Walnut Inn
288 Montford Avenue
828.254.3878   1.800.381.3878

This finely preserved Shingle style home was built in 1899 by Richard Sharp Smith who was the supervising architect at the Biltmore House. It was lovingly restored in 1992 as a bed and breakfast inn. Each room has its own private bath. Complimentary bicycles are available, as are VCRs. One room has a century-old armoire, fireplace, and clawfoot tub; another features a queen size sleigh bed, fireplace, and a new whirlpool tub. This house is included in the National Register of Historic Places.

The Blake House Inn & Sycamore Restaurant

150 Royal Pines Drive

828.681.5227   1.888.353.5227 Reservations

This 1847 Italianate / Gothic style mansion, situated underneath a magnificent sycamore tree, was once the summer home of wealthy lowland rice plantation owners. There are tunnels beneath the floorboards which used to serve as escape routes during the Civil War and which are believed to have been part of the Underground Railroad.

The house has been beautifully preserved and restored. It has twenty-two inch thick granite walls, heart pine floors, original English plaster moldings, and seven fireplaces. A full service dining restaurant is one of Asheville's best kept secrets. The dessert chef at the Sycamore Restaurant is one of the best we've ever encountered, in all of our gastronomical globe-trotting. Five spacious guest rooms, all with private baths, cable TV, and fine linens await those fortunate enough to reserve a room at the Inn.

A famous movie star's name is inscribed in one of the upstairs closets. It seems that her family used to live here and she left her inscription as a youngster. When you call for reservations they might do some name-dropping and give you a Hollywood historical tidbit to further attract you to the Blake House experience.

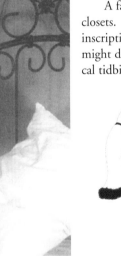

Blake House Inn

A Hill House Bed & Breakfast
120 Hillside Street
828.232.0345   1.800.379.0002

    This circa 1885 Grand Victorian "Painted Lady" offers exceptional vistas of the mountains and nearby downtown. Century-old trees and beautiful gardens enhance the one-acre grounds. The home has an original tin roof, which adds to its romantic charm during a rain shower. Our favorite feature of the Hill House is the interior woodwork and carpentry, which is stunning. This home is included in the National Register of Historic Places. Jacuzzis, fireplaces, and bedside breakfast. A cottage with a kitchen is also available.

The Lion & The Rose
276 Montford Avenue
828.255.ROSE   1.800.546.6988

    Located in historic Montford, this English style B&B is a simplified Queen Anne / Georgian style residence (circa 1898) listed on the National Register of Historic Places. It has been faithfully restored and decorated with antiques, Persian rugs, and period appointments. High embossed ceilings, golden oak, and classic leaded and stained glass windows create a charming old world atmosphere. The grounds are park-like, with century-old Sugar Maples that blaze in the autumn.

The Wright Inn & Carriage House
235 Pearson Drive
828.251.0789   1.800.552.5724

    This Victorian home is one of historic Montford's best examples of Queen Anne architecture. The totally restored Inn was built circa 1899 and is on the National Register of Historic Places. Period furniture, interior trim of handmade oak, and family heirlooms combine to create a warm yet elegant space within walking distance of Asheville's old town center. Bicycles and hair dryers are among the amenities provided.

COUNTRYSIDE
INNS & LODGES

Balsam Mountain Inn
Off US Hwy 73/23
Balsam, NC
828.456.9498

Located about a half hour's drive from Asheville, this old railroad inn was built in 1908 in a neoclassical Victorian style (the train track still runs by at the bottom of the hill). It was established as a place for lowlanders to escape the heat and refresh themselves in the crisp mountain air. The three story structure has two-tiered, 100 foot long porches and breathtaking views of 6,000 foot high mountain peaks (the Inn is at 3,500 ft. elevation). Ten foot wide hallways, large rooms with private baths or optional suites (with sitting rooms), a library, and an on-premises nature trail (the estate is twenty-six acres large) make this place unique. But the restaurant is the feature that most folks keep coming back to enjoy. Call for details and reservations.

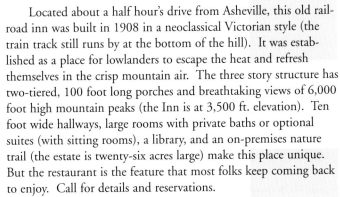

The Duckett House Inn and Farm
Hot Springs, NC
828.622.7621

This is a circa 1900 farm house on the banks of Spring Creek. A great secluded spot for relaxation, this B&B has six well-appointed rooms with shared bathrooms and a cottage available for families with children. The Inn offers picnic baskets and mountain bike rental. Delicious homemade breads are featured on the breakfast menu and a set vegetarian evening meal is available on the weekends. The creators of this guidebook stayed there to celebrate a birthday and had a delightful time. Call the friendly staff a few days in advance for dinner reservations.

Monte Vista Hotel
308 W. State Street
Black Mountain, NC
828.669.2119

   This inn, with its expansive porches and larger-than-life Southern ambience, is grand without being stuffy. It has high ceilings, a large Great Room with a big fireplace, and comfortably appointed guest rooms. The character of the place is expressed through its nineteenth century antiques and a long history of providing a soothing place for artists, tourists, and road-weary travelers to relax and enjoy the mountains. It's located right at the edge of the village of Black Mountain, which is a great little town for strolling around to shop or sample the local restaurants and music clubs.

Mountain Magnolia Inn and Retreat
Hot Springs, NC
828.622.3543

   This recently renovated circa 1868 treasure offers wonderful views, period decor, massage therapy and fine dining by reservation (Fri-Sun; one seating at 7:30pm). If you think rail travel is romantic, you'll be charmed by the noise of the passing trains, but if you are a light sleeper, the Inn's Garden House may be a quieter option. It can sleep families, groups or individuals, and has front porch rockers, a gorgeous back garden, kitchen and laundry facilities.

Mountain Magnolia Inn and Retreat (the historic Colonel James H. Rumbough House)

ALTERNATIVE
COUNTRYSIDE ACCOMMODATIONS

Hot Springs Spa and Campground

315 Bridge St.
Hot Springs, NC
828.622.7676   1.800.462.0933

Hours
In Season: Mid-Feb to Nov 30: 9am-11pm
Off-Season: Dec 1- Mid Feb: weekends only 11am-11pm,
weather permitting

Call in advance during winter schedule. Reservations recommended. Full hook-up RV camping available all year round. Seasonal tent camping with partial hook-ups and hot showers available. See our write-up in the Health and Beauty section of this book for details about the naturally heated mineral baths on the premises. Refer to the overnight hiking section for the scoop on Hot Springs township, which is a great vacation destination.

Pisgah Inn

Milepost 408.6 on the Blue Ridge Parkway
828.235.8228

This is the premier place to stay if you want to be close to hiking trails in the Pisgah National Forest. Located at a 5,000 ft. elevation at the entrance to Mount Pisgah, the Inn offers breathtaking views from each room. Rooms have private balconies or porches overlooking Pisgah Ledge and the mountain ranges in the distance. The Inn has a restaurant with hearty fare at reasonable prices.

If you plan to stay in the month of October, which is the peak season for enjoying the fall colors, reserve a year in advance. September is the slowest month for the Inn, but it is recommended that you reserve rooms at least four to six weeks in advance. Six to eight weeks in advance for other months. This Inn is operated as a private venture under the auspices of the Park Service (It's technically a "concession" of the Park Service).

> You can live in my heart as long as you want. All I ask is that you clean up after yourself.
>
> — *The Old Timer*

"I don't go to restaurants that often, but when I do I tip heavy, and I don't tip at the end of the meal, I give them the tip as soon as they bring the menu. Thataway, I know I'm gonna get good service. Works every time.

— *The Old Timer*

AMERICAN

ITALIAN

JAPANESE

MEDITERRANEAN

MEXICAN & CARRIBEAN

MIDDLE EASTERN

PIZZA & BREW

SOUL FOOD

SOUTHERN HOMESTYLE

VEGETARIAN

CAFES

SUNDAY BRUNCH

RESTAURANTS & CAFÉS

AMERICAN & CONTINENTAL CUISINE

23 Page

1 Battery Park Ave.

(Inside the Haywood Park Hotel)

828.252.3685

This fine-dining destination serves delicacies like free-range chicken, Long Island duck, a variety of game, mountain trout or Maine lobster. Start out with the vegetarian borscht or rock shrimp appetizer, and don't forget 23 Page's excellent wine list. The menu changes seasonally.

This is one of the most elegant restaurants in town, with the average entree going for around twenty-five bucks. The good news for those a little light in the wallet is that the restaurant has recently added a less expensive bistro menu which is fantastic.

Sycamores
at the Blake House Inn

150 Royal Pines Drive
Skyland

828.681.5227

Lunch Tue-Sat 11am-2pm
Sun Brunch 11am-2pm
Dinner Tue-Thu 5:30-9pm
Fri-Sat 5:30-10pm

This lesser-known (and reasonably priced) restaurant is one of the best in Western North Carolina and some of its dishes could compete with the finest restaurants in the Southeast. Situated inside a beautifully preserved and restored circa 1847 Gothic Italianate mansion, it has two elegant dining rooms and a broad porch available when weather permits. Inside you can reserve a table by the fireplace or view the gardens from a great window table. The menu includes mountain trout, delicious pasta dishes, vanilla rubbed lamb, and filet bernaise. The desserts are the among the best we've sampled in our lives.

Blake House Inn

ITALIAN

La Caterina Trattoria
5 Pack Sq.
828.254.1148
Lunch Tue-Sat from 11am,
Dinner daily from 5pm,
Sunday Brunch Noon-3pm

This upscale restaurant, which consistently offers the best Italian cuisine in Western North Carolina, is conveniently located in Pack Square and has both indoor and outdoor seating in season.

La Caterina has one of the best Italian wine selections in Asheville. Owners Victor and Robbin Giancola sell many wines at just a little above cost, believing that customers should be able to enjoy the best wines to complement their delicious Southern Sicilian offerings.

Their delicious ravioli and fettuccine are made in-house. Chefs here create a menu that changes daily, and it includes hearty, filling delicacies such as Gamberie Fagiolini (fresh shrimp sautéed with cannellini beans, with tomato, rosemary and penne pasta). For lighter fare try their incredible salads, such as the Insalata Finocchio (a fennel slaw with roasted peppers and zesty lemon vinaigrette). How do you say "yum" in *Italiano*?

Vincenzo's Restorante
10 North Market St.
828.254.4698
Mon-Thu 5:30pm-10pm, Fri-Sat
5:30pm-11pm, Sun 5:30pm-9pm
Bar open daily from 5pm "until"

Vincenzo's chef Woody Dawson may come from Burnsville, NC, but his classical culinary training elevates this Italian restaurant's fare to a distinctly European standard. The focus of the menu is Northern Italian, but Woody brings his French culinary skills to bear in the form of other continental delicacies such as Coquilles St. Jacques. Woody describes his menu as Milanese with Venetian and Florentine accents, just in case any readers out there know what that means.

The ambience of the dining room is relaxed, but it's a good place to wear some snappy duds if you feel like it. Check out the original molding of the dining room's ceiling. The downstairs bar area is more casual, and features a full bar, a smaller, but equally delectable menu, and live music (mostly low key jazz).

JAPANESE

Heiwa Shokudo
87 North Lexington Ave.
828.254.7761
Lunch Tue-Sat 11:30am-2:30pm, Dinner 5:30pm-9:30pm

   Specializing in <u>healthy, organic fare</u> (the <u>miso, tofu and brown rice</u> are all organic), this is one of Asheville's favorite restaurants. The gigantic <u>bowls of noo</u>dle soup — with your choice of udon or soba noodles — are more than a meal in themselves. We like the Medicine Man (corn, crab, shiitake and wakame), the Geisha (broccoli, shiitake, carrot and beansprouts) and the Executive (shrimp, salmon, scallops and wakame) in particular.

   Sushi is a specialty here, with exotic specials every night, along with seventeen kinds of sushi handrolls on the regular menu. Tuna, salmon and chicken (broiled, teriyaki-style or deep fried) show up in at least twenty different dishes on the menu, along with vegetable tempura and vegetable itame. For an appetizer, try the wakame seaweed salad with spicy sesame dressing or the miso soup. The green tea ice cream is simply luxurious. Take out available.

MEDITERRANEAN

The Golden Horn Restaurant
48 Biltmore Ave.
828.281.4676
Tue-Thurs Lunch 11:30am-3:30pm, Dinner 5-9pm
Fri-Sat Lunch 11:30am-3:30pm, Dinner 6-10pm

   This stylish, comfortable restaurant is owned by Gary and Suzi Mehalick, who managed to miraculously revamp the building's interior in an astonishing six weeks. Apparently they didn't take any siestas during that time. The name Golden Horn refers to the harbor of Istanbul (once Constantinople) which served as a trading crossroads between eastern and western lands. Here exotic eastern spices were traded with the seafood and vegetables of the Med, leading to a unique cuisine.

   The Golden Horn's chef, Andrea Nathansen, serves flavorful creations from the sun-drenched shores of the Mediterranean that are a nice change from some of the pasta-based dishes that seem to characterize downtown Asheville menus. Of course, there is pasta on their interesting menu (which changes daily), but do try sumptuous and unusual dishes such as their Moroccan Shrimp ("Fresh shrimp sautéed with apricots, roasted red peppers, garlic, sherry, scallions, topped with cashews and served over basmati rice") Need I say more?

MEXICAN & CARRIBEAN

Rio Burrito

11 Broadway
828.253.2422
Mon-Fri 11:30am-7:30pm

Andrea and Jack are a gregarious, likable duo who just happen to run one of downtown Asheville's healthiest, most economical and most time-efficient (Translation: it doesn't take eons to get your order, to stay or go) restaurants.

Rio Burrito features burritos, burritos, burritos. The huge, over-stuffed, California-style burritos are filled with healthy ingredients of your choice: low-fat pinto or black beans; steamed rice; fresh tomato salsa, hot or mild; grilled veggies; grilled shrimp, steak or chicken; and extras like the popular cilantro-onion relish. The place boasts daily special burritos like salmon with mango chutney salsa or Thai chicken with peanut sauce and cucumber relish.

Salsa

6 Patton Ave.
828.252.9805
Lunch 11:30-2:30, Din
9:30 daily except closed on S

Salsa is one of the
acclaimed of Asheville's restaurant
but not one of the most expensive.
It was recently featured in <u>Southern Living Magazine</u>.

This is the best place in town to find out how art and cooking combine. Chef Hector Diaz blends Puerto Rican, Carribean, and out-of-this-world cuisines to create some of the best dishes of any restaurant in the United States. He uses ingredients like organic local produce, exotic roots and vegetables, fire-roasted peppers, and smoked goat's cheese to transform centerpieces like fresh mountain trout and wild boar meat into works of mouth-watering art.

The Bohemian-flavored restaurant is small, lively, and simply but colorfully decorated with a Latin folk art motif. Here is where you can spot Hollywood celebrities as well as local politicians, artists, business leaders, and miscellaneous eccentrics like this author. The chef's trademarked sauces sell internationally. This place is popular, often busy, and well worth the wait to get a table.

Musician Scott Kinnebrew (founder and CEO of the notoriously popular Papa Roux Records Co.) was sighted hanging out downtown with the young and glamorous artist, model, and underground celebrity Kathryn L. Crawford. Don't they understand that's how rumors start?

in a friendly setting, try Jerusalem
natives Frank Badr and his sister
e you are guests in their home. The
great prices. Their creamy hummus,
nd-made pitas are the best in town.
Don't miss ____ either. Catering to vegetarians and omnivores alike, this unpretentious place comes highly recommended. Jerusalem Garden also offers a catering service for office parties and will set up special parties at the restaurant if you desire.

NATIVE AMERICAN

Spirits On The River
571 Swannanoa River Road
828.299.1404

Tue 5pm-9pm, Wed-Thu Noon-9pm, Fri-Sat Noon-10pm, Sun Noon-9pm

<u>Southern Living Magazine</u> said "The flavors of the forest are at Spirits On The River" and we agree. Owners Flip and Ann Bell operate the region's best-kept cuisine secret. This hideaway on Swannanoa River Road is housed in a relatively nondescript building and is easy to miss, even if you're looking for it. But those who discover it keep coming back, and word-of-mouth keeps spreading the secret far and wide.

A maze of Indian artifacts, books, jewelry and carvings greet visitors as they head through the rustic main dining room to the riverside deck, which is decorated with flaming torches atop river cane poles. On a clear night the moon shines across the flowing water, where the sound of the river accompanies the restaurant's Native American music. Sometimes there are live performances of traditional American Indian music, drumming, and dance.

The menu is unique and exotic: Buffalo, rattlesnake, gator, trout, quail, and pheasant. And *Spirits* offers an excellent selection of vegetarian items. Whatever featured entree you choose, try the Sacred Seven Salad and raspberry vinaigrette dressing, and pure wild rice or a twice-baked potato. For dessert sample the authentic Indian frybread with smooth-flowing honey or ice cream on top.

PIZZA & BREW

Asheville Pizza & Brewing Company

675 Merrimon Ave.
828.254.1281

Daily 10:30am-10pm

Asheville Pizza & Brewing Company is a true, one-stop entertainment Mecca. Here, you can grab a gourmet pizza, enjoy a refreshing on-site microbrew, catch a popular dollar movie, watch the "X-Files" or "Southpark" on an honest-to-gosh movie screen; and listen to a red-hot band like Southern Culture on the Skids.

This movie - theater - pizza - parlor - brew - pub - nightclub offers something for everyone, including free weekend movies for children to give Mom & Dad a break.

SOUL FOOD

Rabbit's Motel & Restaurant

110 McDowell St.
828.253.9552

Opens around 5pm most evenings

Rabbit's is the premier authentic soul food kitchen of Asheville. Established more than half a century ago, the cozy little restaurant still serves up original-recipe BBQ, pigs feet, pork chops, catfish, greens, potato salad, and other southern soul dishes. The beer is inexpensive and ice cold, and the last time we were there you could still order *Thunderbird* by the glass for a buck or two. The folks who run Rabbit's are among the nicest people you could ever meet, and everything they cook tastes as good or better than homemade.

SOUTHERN HOMESTYLE

Hot Shot Cafe

7 Lodge St.
828.274.2170

Daily 7am-3pm

The Hot Shot is something like grandma's kitchen. Old-fashioned, country breakfasts (served with the hands-down best biscuits and gravy in town) are the staple of this legendary Asheville diner, but the lunch menu's none too shabby either, offering comfort dishes like the meatloaf and mashed potatoes combo.

VEGETARIAN

Laughing Seed Café

40 Wall St.

828.252.3445

Daily 11:30 am-10pm (closed on Tue)

The Laughing Seed Cafe is a vegetarian's dream. All-vegetarian, mostly vegan fare that in no way resembles the bland sprouts-and-plain-tofu of veggie restaurants in times gone by.

They serve delicacies such as the Smokey Mountain Blue Plate (vegetarian meatloaf, potato salad, steamed veggies with sesame ginger sauce, roasted corn relish and cornbread); Low Country Roll-Ups (sweet and tangy tofu barbecue wrapped in tortillas with cheese and tahini mustard sauce); and the Island Fantasy (yams, plantains, squash, corn, garlic and pinto beans, flavored with chipotle peppers and apricots and topped with spicy tofu sloppy joe and five-alarm salsa). Pizza, nachos, quesadillas and various spiced-up, beans-rice-and-steamed-veggies dishes also. The juice bar offers luscious, exotic smoothie concoctions, and the desserts are fabulous.

Max & Rosie's Most Excellent Cafe & Juice Bar

52 N. Lexington Ave.

828.254.5342

Mon-Sat 11am-6pm Sun Noon-5pm (winter hours may vary)

Rosie is a macrobiotic chef, Max is a painter and jeweler. Try the Middle Eastern plate, rice and mushroom quesadilla, or Rhiamedear rice salad (a mound of brown rice with avocado and seasonal vegetables on a bed of lettuce). Cappuccino, espresso, fresh squeezed lemonade, raspberry ice tea, side dishes of tofu, hummus and pita bread, bagels.

Max & Rosie make you feel loved with *Hangover Helper* tonic, *Cure the Cold* juice, *It Takes Two To Mango* and *Ring Around The Rosie* smoothies, and *Get A Healthy Buzz* doses of vitamin powder, spirulina, ginseng, or fresh garlic. Because this establishment is located in a half-basement with windows at street level, it has a reputation as the best place in town for leg-watching...especially when the weather's warm. But the choicest tables are on the sidewalk, with a panoramic view of colorful Lexington Ave. Delivery available in the downtown area.

Don't be offended if your server neglects to bring water to your table in an Asheville restaurant. Recently, it's become somewhat of a tradition to serve water only by request, in order to conserve our precious supply which has been threatened by a lack of rain and by the clear-cutting of area forests. But in Europe it's almost always standard procedure, so consider it part of Asheville's old world charm.

TAPAS

Melanie's Food Fantasy

32 Broadway Ave.
828.236.3533
Tue-Sat 8am-2:30pm
Sun. brunch 10am-2pm

Eating here is such a treat for the body and soul that we considered listing this little restaurant under the Health & Beauty section of this guidebook. But it could just as easily be under Soul Food, because Melanie cooks (and looks) like a Southern angel and everything she serves is good for the spirit.

Belgian Waffles, Greek or Mexican Omelets, and fresh ginger tea are enough motivation to convince even honeymooners to get up and out in time for breakfast. Try the Eggplant and Tomato Melt and a Very Berry Smoothie for a sublime yet substantial lunch. Experience Melanie's homemade breads and pies and put your mother's best baking to shame. Better yet, bring your mother to Melanie's and order the Daily Special or a Peasant Lunch to reassure her that not only are you eating right, you're also managing your budget like a pro.

Zambra

85 Walnut St.
828.232.1060
(Call for hours. Open hours were not decided at the time of publication, although Zambra will initially be open at nights, beginning around 4pm.)

As we go to press, this new restaurant and *tapas* (not to be confused with *topless*) bar is about to open on Walnut St. in the space beneath Malaprop's Bookstore. The Moorish / Spanish style restaurant will serve the typical Spanish bar fare known as tapas (gourmet appetizer-snacks) along with what promises to be the best wine selection in Asheville.

With an interior by Madaras Designs, paintings and murals by artist Sally Bryenton, and the culinary genius of owner and chef Hector Diaz (who was recently featured in <u>Southern Living Magazine</u>), we expect Zambra to steal the show. The opening of this place may single-handedly redefine the Asheville restaurant scene by importing a European dynamic previously unknown in this neck 'o the woods.

The lovely and talented Valerie Sells at Melanie's Food Fantasy.

CAFÉS

BeanStreets Coffee

3 Broadway

828.255.8180

Mon-Tue 7:30am-6pm, Wed-Fri 7:30am-Midnight, Sat 9am-midnight, Sun 9am-3pm

(Thursday is open mic night)

Sightings of celebrities like Mary Louise Parker and Andie McDowell aren't nearly as common as visions of Asheville's local character spectrum, but this is a still a funky place to people-watch. Expansive streetside windows and a large but cozy smoke-free environment make this a favorite hangout of both locals and tourists. Check out the interior eclectica like the mannequin's foot protruding through the ceiling or the circa 1940s hair dryer in the corner, while enjoying the house blend and a piece of melt-in-your-mouth carrot cake. Extensive list of gourmet coffees, teas, snacks, and light breakfast and lunch items. Chair massage and a chess table available too.

Double Decker Coffee Company

41 Biltmore Ave.

828.255.0441

1.800.299.0991

Mon-Thu 7am-9pm
Fri-Sat 7am-11pm, Sun 9am-5pm

This coffee shop is an authentic bright red two-decker British bus. The upstairs tables offer a playful ambience with an interesting view of Biltmore Ave.

It's an age-old tradition that social and political change arises over espresso in cozy cafes. Adding to that history, the owners endured what can be described as an epic battle of endurance with the city bureaucracy in their struggle to get a permit to open for business. Many local residents support the independent enterprise on political principal alone, because they consider this coffee shop a symbol of the little guy winning against the impersonal forces of big business and powerful city government.

Serve up caffeine with scones in a romantic setting from sunrise to sunset and you'll inspire all sorts of social movements and loyal support, Lovey.

Al Reed is Mr. Hospitality at the A & SD Doggs Enterprise's hot dog stand on Battery Hill, where Asheville goes for traditional American fare served "all the way." Hot veggie dogs are offered too. The stand operates 10:30 am til 6pm, Mon.-Sat, weather permitting. It's a favorite with locals and tourists alike.

Gold Hill Espresso & Fine Teas

64 Haywood St.
828.254.3800

Mon-Fri 7:30am-7pm
Sat 8am-7pm, Sun 9am-2pm

Cappuccino, latte, more than forty kinds of tea by the cup or in bulk, light lunch, and some of the best bagels in town. A stylish tea room with marble-top tables, a good selection of newspapers to read, and interesting art exhibits which change every few weeks. If you happen to be writing a book, this is a good place to go to do your editing over a bowl of soup and a sandwich. We can vouch for that.

TIPPING TIP:

We recommend tipping 15 to 18 percent at a bare minimum, and 20 percent or more for excellent service. And tipping is customary not only in restaurants but at coffee shops, bars, and other venues offering counter service. The prices in town are affordable enough to allow heavy tipping and many of the service workers are struggling artists who deserve our support.

Treat them with generosity now and maybe after they get discovered and famous they'll give you an autograph or a lock of hair for your memorabilia wall back home.

Malaprop's Café

(inside Malaprop's Bookstore)
55 Haywood St.
828.254.6734

Several people we asked said that Malaprop's is the one place they would be sure to take a first-time visitor to Asheville, because it is one of their all-time favorite destinations. That's mighty high praise in a town that boasts such awesome attractions as Biltmore Estate and the Blue Ridge Parkway. We highly recommend a visit to this local cultural treasure.

If you need to rendevouz with someone on the west side of downtown, this is the place to do it. It's highly visible on Haywood St. and if one of you is running a little late, the other won't mind because the book-browsing, buttermilk chocolate cake sampling, and people-watching make for great entertainment. We like to order a Brain Freeze and a Dr. Suess (Translation: A frozen espresso milkshake concoction to die for and a peanut butter and jelly croissant) and sit by the window on a sunny day, reading a new book or writing postcards.

Old Europe Coffee Bar

Flat Iron Building
18 Battery Park
828.252.0001
Mon-Thu 9am-10pm
Fri 9am-Midnight
Sat 10am-Midnight, Sun 10am-9pm

Writer Constance Richards and artist Vadim Bora at Old Europe Coffee Bar.

Zoltan Vetro, this café's Hungarian owner, has earned the right to name his upscale coffee shop "Old Europe." This is the closest thing you will find in Western North Carolina to a truly European coffee house and patisserie. They also serve beer, wine, spirits, and sandwiches and provide chess sets for more cerebral customers. They make the best key lime pie in town.

Old Europe's laid-back daytime ambience becomes more lively at night, when the outdoor tables fill up with hipsters on summer evenings. The cafe has become a favorite hangout for local business owners, artists, and various types of wannabe Hungarians. It seems to bring out the European in all of us.

One time, I was sitting in Old Europe nursing a frothy cappuccino, when some random guy came up to me and started an absurd conversation in French. Presuming he was in fact, a native of Gaul, I replied in my rusty textbook Francais. When he asked which part of France I was from, I knew there was something fishy going on, and it turned out that this Mediterranean prince was actually from rural Buncombe County. It's a small world, after all.

Vincent's Ear Coffee House

68 N. Lexington Ave.
828.259.9119

This basement cafe (with a cool upstairs lounge) also has a wonderful outdoor patio with shade trees and chess tables. Great selection of coffee drinks, sandwiches, and desserts (as well as beer and wine) at really reasonable prices. A perfect place to stop and hang out awhile if you're on lower Lexington hitting the antique stores, vintage clothing boutiques, and skateboard shops.

Vincent's has a reputation for bringing some of the most unique music to town, where it's performed in the small brick basement to standing-room-only audiences.

Here's a hotdog of a fish story for you to tell your friends back home:

In 1952, Asheville resident Charlie Randall caught a forty-five pound catfish in the French Broad River, using a hot dog as bait. The fish was larger than his grandson.

SUNDAY BRUNCH IN ASHEVILLE

Had a busy Saturday night and want to let someone else wash the dishes? Let Asheville's eateries take care of your cravings with some tasty fare that transcends the greasy spoon breakfast scenario. Sunday breakfast / brunch opportunities exist at the following locations:

Model of Grove Park Inn

For a special treat, (for your palate, but perhaps not your pocket book) try the Grove Park Inn's famous breakfast buffet or brunch. The Grove Park Inn is worth visiting just to experience a taste of the lives of the rich and famous, and to admire the unusual architecture. The brunch might cost you the same as dinner at a fancy restaurant, but should keep you satisfied all day. With extensive selections of breakfast food, meat and fish entrees, roasts, great veggie side dishes and delectable desserts, this buffet is quite overwhelming, and it's hard not to overeat. If you exercise as little self-restraint as this author, the rest of your Sunday will be highly unproductive, as possible post-brunch activities will be confined to devouring the <u>New York Times</u>. Don't plan a big hike after this brunch unless you have a good siesta first.

Blake House Inn

Another belly-busting delight is to be found at Sycamore's restaurant, located within the historic Blake House Inn in Skyland. Start the day off with a sparkling mimosa and some complimentary fresh-baked bread and herbed butter. Enjoy Sycamore's pre-Civil War dining room, with its original plaster moldings, while choosing from unusual breakfast fare such as revamped grits dishes or sizzling catfish bake. For those more interested in the lunch side of brunch, they also offer fabulous pasta dishes. Don't forget to leave room for a diet-defying dessert. All of chef Kevin Rice's dessert selections are incredible,

53

but one mouthful of the chocolate creme brulee will set off chocolate cravings that will last long after your visit.

If you prefer a healthier, lighter brunch, try Laughing Seed Café in downtown Asheville. The Seed offers delicious vegetarian and vegan entrees as well as more traditional eggs 'n' biscuit type fare for its Sunday brunch. Of course, the biscuits are made with no lard, and the sausage is actually soysage, a soy product. So if you don't delight in tofu-beast-based dishes stick with the delicious fluffy omelets and a side of delicately seasoned home-fries (made with sweet and white potatoes).

Also on the healthy side is Melanie's Food Fantasy. Brunch is from 10am-2pm and features fresh crepes with fruit or vegetable fillings topped with a light and creamy hollandaise sauce, as well as veggie omelets, home-baked bread, granola and waffles loaded with honey, yogurt and fruit. Follow Melanie's fabulous breakfast with a fresh-made fruit smoothie, or order one to go.

Melanie's Food Fantasy

If you are a real bread-head, head on over to Blue Moon Bakery for some authentic crusty French and Italian bread that is good enough to eat all on its own. The coffee is good and the ambience light and airy. The bakery also offers a menu of light lunch fare. *Vegetarians: Be careful to ask if an item is truly vegetarian, as many items contain meat stock in true French fashion.*

If it's warm outside and you feel like eating outdoors, The New French Bar is your place for Sunday brunch. Eating here has obvious advantages for late-risers recovering from the night before, as brunch runs from 11:30am-4pm and offers large Bloody Marys. Indoor seating is also available inside this stylish watering hole, if the weather is chilly. Elegantly presented menu offerings include Eggs Benedict and other dishes that elevate the humble hen's egg, bagels with flavored cream cheese, and substantial crepes.

For the only shrimp omelet in town, go to the easy-going Grove Street Café for brunch. This building looks like an old school house from the outside, but resembles a 1980s Charleston scene on the inside. Twin flags - Stars and Stripes and the Rainbow Flag - adorn the exterior. As you might expect, the cafe is friendly and the brunch crowd is a fun, diverse mix.

John Beckorage, who runs the Grove Street Café, was blown into Asheville from Charleston, SC by Hurricane Hugo. He lost three businesses there to the devastating hurricane and re-located in Western North Carolina, opening the cafe in 1995. We're glad he did. The cafe serves up such delights as seafood omelet (with shrimp, salmon, mushroom and Swiss), banana stuffed French toast, romantic blueberry waffles and banana nut hotcakes. The raspberry sorbet, served with a dollop of cream and finished off with a shot of raspberry Schnapps, is not to be missed. Call for reservations, because the place is extremely popular.

If you are in Weaverville, or feel like an easy 15 minute drive North of Asheville (on Hwy.19/23 North), there are a few excellent brunch options. One is the Four Cent Cotton Café, so named for an old Appalachian fiddle tune originally performed in the late 1920s by Gib Tanner and the Skillet Lickers. Four Cents' skillet-lickin' brunch is well worthwhile. I still have good gustatory memories of their mushroom marsala omelet, and I hear the fruit-smothered waffles and pancakes are everything that sweet breakfast food should be. They serve Sunday brunch 11am-3pm.

New French Bar

They are also open for lunch and dinner Tue-Sat from 11am-9pm.

Another Weaverville eatery is the Raven Moon Café. It is housed in Preservation Hall,

the oldest commercial building still in use in Western North Carolina, built in the mid 19th century. Follow in Thomas Edison's footsteps (who once drank tea here) and head over for a leisurely brunch. Not into tea drinking? Wash down a breakfast quesadilla with one of Raven Moon's excellent gourmet organic coffees instead. Veggie and omnivorous options offered, including some intriguing vegan French toast with mango and bananas. Sunday brunch is served 11am-3pm. Their other hours are 6:30am-11:30am (breakfast); 11:30am-2:30pm (lunch), 5:30pm-9:30pm (dinner). They have a thriving evening scene with live acoustic music every night. Their popular open mike night is Wed., so bring your musical talents and share them.

Would you care for a little fresh ground history with your gastronomy? About forty years ago the space at 5 Pack Square was occupied by a popular eatery named Gross Restaurant. Nowadays one of our personal favorite restaurants is in the same location. It's got an Italian name we can't pronounce, much less translate. But our gut instinct tells us it doesn't mean "gross."

SUNDAY BREAKFAST / BRUNCH INFO:

Grove Park Inn
290 Macon Ave.
828.252.2711
Breakfast Buffet: 6:30am-10:30am
Sunday Brunch: 11:30am-2:30pm $$$

Sycamore's
Blake House Inn
150 Royal Pines Drive, Skyland
828.681.5227
Sunday Brunch: 11am-2pm $$

Laughing Seed Café
40 Wall St.
828.252.3445
Sunday Brunch: 10am-2pm $$

Melanie's Food Fantasy
32 Broadway Ave.
828.236.3533
Sunday Brunch: 10am-2pm $

Blue Moon Bakery
60 Biltmore Ave.
828.252.6063
Sunday hours: 7:30am-4pm $$

The New French Bar
1 Battery Park Ave.
828.252.3685
Sunday Brunch: 11:30am-4pm $$

Grove Street Café
11 Grove Street
828.255.0010
Sunday Brunch: 11am-2:30pm $$

Four Cent Cotton Café
18 Main St.
Weaverville, NC
828.958.2660
Sunday Brunch: 11am-3pm $

Raven Moon Café
Preservation Hall
Main St.
Weaverville, NC
828.658.8777
Sunday Brunch: 11am-3pm $

PRICE LEGEND:
$$$- pricey, but worth it.
$$- reasonable
$- great value

The Hop Ice Cream Shop
507 Merrimon Ave.
828.252.8362

Tue-Thu Noon-9pm, Fri-Sat Noon-9:30pm, Sun Noon-8:30pm

This is vintage '50s ice cream done right. The frozen delights taste like the original recipe, not some pseudo-homemade replica of what ice cream used to be. This is the kind of ice cream that inspired American teenagers in the 1950s to compose authentic rock 'n roll...while giving them the nutritional stamina to dance to it all night long. Cruise up in your T-Bird ragtop and they'll serve you through the window, or sit down and listen to a few vintage tunes while sharing a two-straw malted with your sweetheart. Plus frozen yogurt and sorbet to diet and die for.

One resident was overheard saying, "Asheville used to be the kind of place where you don't shop til you drop, you just shop til you get bored." That's changing fast, so put on your walking shoes, grab a tote bag, and pack an extra credit card if shopping is your psychotherapy of choice.

Downtown Asheville is not just a business district; it's a community.

When a resident who worked downtown was seriously injured and hospitalized by an accident, the hospital bills were predictably astronomical. But the person didn't have medical insurance so a friend decided to organize a benefit, by walking from merchant to merchant in downtown Asheville, requesting items that could be used in a raffle. The proceeds were used to defray the medical expenses.

More than 60 individuals or businesses contributed to the effort in just 48 hours. Donations of goods and services continued to be made right up until the hour of the raffle.

One innovative donor offered "a homecooked meal" for the person holding the winning raffle ticket . . . another offered to create a work of art. And some winners declined their prizes, asking instead that the items be raffled again in order to raise more money.

> I like to sit down with somebody over a
> cup of coffee and talk about whatever it
> is we just can't talk about.
>
> — *The Old Timer*

> The best things in life
> always cost the most.
> It's the worthlessness
> that's free.
>
> —*The Old Timer*

ANTIQUES

ARTS & CRAFTS

BAKERIES

BOOKSTORES

CAMPING SUPPLIES

CANDLES

CARDS & GIFTS

CIGARS

CLOTHING & SHOES

DRUGS/LAUNDROMATS

FLOWERS

GROCERIES

HEALTH & BEAUTY

INTERNATIONAL

JEWELRY

MUSIC

SHOPPING

TOYS

VINTAGE & THRIFT

WINE & BEER

BONNIE CONTRERAS
BONNIE'S LITTLE CORNER

Bonnie's Little Corner — the little shop with the giant cigar store Indian standing watch, on the busy corner fronting Pack Square — has been a downtown institution for going on a decade now. Owners Bonnie and Hector Contreras started out with a few boxes of cigars and a few cartons of cigarettes, throwing in candy and soft drinks for good measure. These days, Bonnie's carries a mindboggling variety of domestic and exotic imported cigarettes and an extensive line of fine cigars (the shop's trademark), plus pipes, incense, keychains, wine, beer (singles are a specialty), juices, candy, rolling papers, and a host of other "corner store" staples.

Proprietress Bonnie notes she might soon start "carrying canned goods and toilet paper, so it'll be more like a little European shop that has everything." And the store has the best Cuban coffee this side of Miami.

Spend half an hour at Bonnie's Little Corner and you'll literally encounter representatives of every cross-section of Asheville's population. Bonnie herself is part philosopher, part psychologist, part spiritual adviser and part physician. She warmly engages customers from every walk of life with equal concern ("You should really get that little growth on your neck looked at," she worriedly told a downtown worker who'd stopped in for a can of juice the day we interviewed her).

"We want to serve our people who live and work downtown, not just tourists," Bonnie emphasizes. "And I always tell people my motto is 'Come in and enjoy the sweet Southern hospitality,' because I'm really just a sweet Southern belle."

We'll let the Southern belle speak for herself:

What makes Asheville home to you, as opposed to just a place to live?
I think it's the warmth. I think it comes from the mountains. I'm from Alabama and there's quite a lot of difference down there. They say home is where the heart is, anyway, and my heart is here.

Bonnie & Hector Contreras, owners of "Bonnie's Little Corner" store.

What's the best thing about being a downtown merchant?

I'm a people person, so I really enjoy the variety of people I get to meet. We get everybody. Our little down-on-their-luck alcoholics love me to death and I treat them with just as much respect as somebody rich. You have to love people, and I do. And when it comes to people downtown, especially our kids, I really enjoy them. We've had, like the man that does the Quaker Oats commercials, Wilford Brimley, in here. And when they were filming the movie "My Fellow Americans" downtown here with Jack Lemmon and James Garner, the stunt men and the crew hung out in my store a lot. I get to meet everybody.

What's your notion of the perfect way to spend a day in Asheville?

Being a crafts kind of person, my perfect day would be to go to some pottery places and artsy places that would inspire me to get my hands a-goin'. But going to outdoor places like Lake Lure and Chimney Rock would be real good, too.

If you had to live on a deserted island for two years, what three things (besides food and water) would you take along?

Something that I could work on with my hands like pottery or knitting, something crafty. And my bikini. Let's see. You know, I think actually I'd take nothing. If I were stranded on an island, just the peace and serenity of being there would be enough.

If you were a tourist in Asheville and ended up lost, where would be the best place to do it?

Oh, I would say downtown. If nothing else, you could just watch the people, especially in the summertime.

If you became famous because of some personal attribute, what do you think it would be?

I would hope it would be my hospitality.

ANTIQUE SHOPPING

Downtown Asheville offers wonderful antiquing. The historic district where Walnut St. connects Broadway St., Lexington Ave., and Rankin Ave. is especially populated with antique stores. Some of them carry high-end 18th and 19th century imports while others offer early American collectables. And there are those that specialize in fulfilling our demand for nostalgic junk.

In one hour of perusing the antique stores in the blocks around Walnut Street (downtown), the author discovered a smorgasbord of items for sale including: A woman's vintage Panama hat, vintage cashmere sweaters, an unusual antique two-seater school desk circa 1888, a handmade antique chaise lounge from the Grove Park Inn, a 50 caliber black powder rifle with scope, an authentic hand-painted English pub sign, a "Dump Nixon" political protest button, a three-quarter size Stella brand guitar in good condition, a set of Russian laquered eggs featuring hand-painted images of the Beatles, and a fossilized walrus jaw ("I am the walrus, you are the egg man!").

Also fantastic collections of old postcards and magazine covers, and of course the quintessential rare find: An entire skunk skin, tanned with fur intact.

Asheville Antiques Mall
43 Rankin Ave.
828.253.3634
Mon-Sat 10am-5pm
Sun: Noon to 5pm (Jun-Dec)

You have to visit this place to understand it. It's more than an antiques mall, it's a museum of vintage Americana eclectica. Don't miss the section of collectible postcards and print ads. Take your time, the place is loaded with surprises.

Lexington Park Antiques
65 Walnut St.
828.253.3070
Mon-Sat 10am-6pm
Sun 1pm-6pm (Jun-Dec)

This sprawling warehouse of antiques and what-nots is one of the best we've ever encountered. If they don't have it, chances are you can live without it. They usually have a great selection of women's vintage clothing and gobs and gobs of antique houseware and furniture. Don't expect to do this joint in under an hour, it's too vast for a quick cruise-through. But it's worth the time invested, especially if you're searching for something specific...or nothing in particular.

Preservation Hall Antiques & Architectural Salvage
23 Rankin Ave.
828.251.2823
Mon-Thu 10am-6pm,
Fri-Sat 11am-6pm
and by appointment

This warehouse of architectural salvage recycles doors, mantles, windows, household hardware, and all sorts of other amazing stuff found in and around Asheville. Some of the pieces date back well over a century. This place is a treasure chest for those trying to renovate or restore old interiors and an inspiration for decorators who have a little creative vision.

ANTIQUE JEWELRY & SILVER

The Gilded Lily Ltd.
One Battery Park Ave.
(inside the Haywood Park Hotel)
828.236.0006
Mon-Sat 10am-5pm

The Gilded Lily specializes in antique and estate jewelry and silver and is a reliable source for interesting, exceptionally rare items of jewelry and silver.

ANTIQUES IN BILTMORE VILLAGE

The Antique Tobacco Barn
75 Swannanoa River Road
828.252.7291
Mon-Thu 10am-5pm
Fri-Sat 9am-5pm

70,000 square feet of antiques at reasonable prices. It's the largest selection in Western North Carolina, with nearly a hundred dealers under one roof.

Fireside Antiques & Interiors
32 All Souls Crescent
828.274.5977
Mon-Sat 10am-5pm (Sundays during the Christmas season only)

Specializes in 18th and 19th century English imports, porcelain, oil paintings, and interior design.

Village Antiques
755 Biltmore Ave.
828.252.5090
Mon-Sat 10am-5pm

The region's premier dealer of 18th and 19th century French antiques. English imports too. Stunning selections worthy of inclusion in any collection.

ARTS & CRAFTS

Earth Guild

33 Haywood St
828.255.7818
Mon-Sat 10am-6pm

Here you will find one of the most authentic resource centers in the country for celebrating mountain arts and crafts. Earth Guild covers an alphabet's worth of handcrafts including basketry, beads, candlemaking, dyes, knitting, knotting, leatherworking, papermaking, polymer clays, pottery, rug-making, spinning, weaving, woodcarving, and yarns. Not a craftsperson? Not to worry. They'll teach you in their extensive workshops offered year around. They have the books, tools, materials, and mentors galore.

Folk Art Center and Allanstand Craft Shop

Milepost 382
Blue Ridge Parkway
828.298.7928
Daily 9am-5pm Jan-Mar.
Daily 9am-6pm April-Dec

The Allanstand was the first craft shop in the nation, established in 1895 by Frances Goodrich. Once located in downtown Asheville, the Allanstand is now part of the Folk Art Center on the Parkway. Here you can still find superlative examples of crafts in a variety of media, including pottery, wood, glass, fiber, metal and jewelry.

Craftspeople represented at the Folk Art Center are all members of the Southern Highlands Craft Guild, an educational non-profit organization comprised of some seven hundred craftspeople from the mountain counties in nine southeastern states. The center blends traditional work such as quilting masterpieces with more contemporary pieces such as fabulous raku pottery.

World Market Place

10 College St.
828.254.8374
Mon-Sat 10am-5pm

This is a great store for native crafts from around the world. Profits support low-income artisans in more than thirty countries. (See the *International Shopping* category for more information.)

BAKERY

Blue Moon Bakery and Cafe
60 Biltmore Ave
828.252.6063
Daily 7:30 am-4pm

This European-style bakery is the sole reason that one world traveler decided to make Asheville her permanent home. Gourmet breads by the loaf and an assortment of pastries sure to boggle the mind and seduce the tongue are the mainstay. But this is also a favorite place for light lunch, brunch, or breakfast. Come early for fresh bread; the locals sometimes buy it all by mid-afternoon.

City Bakery
88 Charlotte St.
828.254.4289
Mon-Fri 7:30am-6pm,
Sat 7:30am-3pm (Closed Sun)

This warm little shop serves up scrumptious carrot cake, focaccia, scones, muffins, cookies, breads, Danish pastry, and more. There is a small bar with stools for those who want to hang out and have a cup of tea or coffee with their morning muffin.

BOOKSTORES

Captain's Bookshelf
31 Page Ave.
828.253.6631
Tues-Sat 10am-6pm

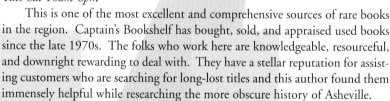

This is one of the most excellent and comprehensive sources of rare books in the region. Captain's Bookshelf has bought, sold, and appraised used books since the late 1970s. The folks who work here are knowledgeable, resourceful, and downright rewarding to deal with. They have a stellar reputation for assisting customers who are searching for long-lost titles and this author found them immensely helpful while researching the more obscure history of Asheville.

In many respects, this store is like a mini-museum of literature. You can browse through dozens of signed, first edition books in mint condition. And the prices, even for the highly collectible copies, are reasonable. What else do you demand of a first-rate book dealer? If you haven't yet cultivated a penchant for the printed word, an hour spent perusing the shelves might change your perspective forever. And if you happen to be a bookworm, this place will tickle you silly.

Downtown Books and News

87 N. Lexington Ave.

828.253.8654

Mon-Sun 8am-6pm, (Summer only Fri-Sat 8am-8pm)

Lose an afternoon perusing the bulging stacks of this awesome second-hand book store, with its extensive selection of fiction and non-fiction works. Conveniently categorized and lovingly cared for by the friendly staff, the books range in topic from erotica to business to Native American lore and foreign language learning tapes.

Downtown Books and News also stocks a wide selection of international and domestic newspapers, periodicals, 'zines, and comics, including "Weirdo: a graphic journal for the rootless, alienated nihilist, postmodern existentialist masses." Something for everyone, it seems. The store is the only one in town that has a "customer wish list" which acts as an active book-searching service. Essentially, Downtown Books and News is a store that is defined by its customers, as its stock is made up of a collection of books that Ashevilleans read, then trade. It represents the reading tastes of the community.

If you want to trade or sell your books to the store, come by between 10am and 4pm Thurs-Sat. Please heed the sign kindly made by one highly literate customer that reads: "Please do not annoy, torment, pester, plague, molest, worry, badger, harry, harass, heckle, persecute, irk, bullyrag, vex, disquiet, grate, beset, bother, tease, mettle, tantalize or ruffle the staff of Downtown Books and News."

While you are there, introduce yourself to the resident feline, named "Retail" who wandered into the store in 1991 and never felt like leaving. One visit and you will understand why.

Malaprop's Bookstore and Cafe

55 Haywood St.

828.254.6734   1.800.441.9829

Mon-Thurs 9am-9pm, Fri-Sat 9am-11pm, Sun 9am-6pm

More than just a bookstore, Malaprop's has become downtown Asheville's unofficial cultural center and meeting place. It's a great place to people watch. Enjoy a coffee and bagel in the cafe while you write a poem or card to a friend. Look at art in their mini-gallery space while your children are kept amused by kid's storytelling hour. Or share your own heartfelt scribblings at one of Malaprop's women's poetry evenings.

Malaprop's is a strong supporter of local artists, writers and independent publishers, and the store has a generous selection of titles in stock. Choose from books in sections such as About Women / Men, Judaica, Conscious Living, Myth, Ancient Cultures, as well as from more traditional sections such as Art, Psychology, Business, and Children's Books.

Can't decide what to buy from a mind-boggling collection of erudite tomes? Pick up Malaprop's own quarterly newsletter in which staff members' insightful book reviews are printed. It also lists upcoming events that Malaprop's regularly hosts, such as musical concerts and book readings / signings by popular authors (who recently included Bill Bryson, Allan Gurganus, Gail Godwin and Charles Frasier). If you are something of a literary critic, or want to learn more about literature, join Malaprop's **Book Club**, which meets to discuss a different book every month. Malaprop's offers a 10% discount on each month's book selection. Ask Malaprop's staff about Book Club dates.

Cafe of Our Own (women's poetry readings) every 3rd Sat, 7:45pm sign up time. Readings start at 8pm.

Children's Story Hour (with Rachelle), every 2nd Sat at 10am.

The Reader's Corner
31 Montford Ave.
828.285.8805
Mon-Fri 11am-7pm, Sat 10am-6pm, Sun 1-6pm

This second-hand bookstore is conveniently situated at the entrance to historic Montford neighborhood. It's one of our favorite places to go treasure-hunting. Every time we visit we come away with wonderful books, in excellent condition, at great prices. Reader's Corner sells a good selection of books (reasonably priced from a dollar up), as well as second-hand CDs and vinyl. Don't neglect the "Occult and Miscellaneous Weirdness" and "Gen-Xploitation" book sections, where you can peruse such obscure titles as "Undercover with Vampires in America Today" and "How to Mutate and Take Over the World" (We're still trying to master the technique). Once we found a valuable old blues record on the original Chess label, for about five bucks. Several times we've found great (slightly used) CDs at deeply discounted prices.

Insomniacs may really enjoy the store's after-hours "honor system" shelves. Instead of tossing and turning in your lonely hotel room, wrestling with the idea of turning on the TV, even though you KNOW you will only be assaulted by Infomercials, head on over and browse the 10c and 25c paperbacks left outside the store. Your small donation goes to our stellar local public radio station (WNCW) and you will find something to help lull you into the torpor you desire. This author actually found one of her all-time favorite novels in this manner. But if what you truly desire is a book to put you to sleep, choose a snoozer such as <u>A Doctor Speaks on Sexual Expression in Marriage</u> (yawn).

Ask them about their book-trading policy. This is a great place to unload the books taking up space on your shelves before your next house move.

Before you leave, don't forget to pay some attention to the inordinately large shop cat, Pobidiah (Pobie for short), who loves attention and has an incredible sense of rhythm. Many customers swear they have witnessed him tapping his puffy tail in time to Cole Porter records.

CAMPING SUPPLIES & OUTDOR OUTFITTERS

Black Dome Mountain Sports

140 Tunnel Road
828.251.2001
Mon-Sat 10am-8pm, Sun 1pm-5pm

This store specializes in gear and clothing for climbing, backpacking, camping, running, hiking, snowboarding, and snowskiing. Good selection of maps and outdoor books.

Diamond Brand Camping Center

Hwy. 25, Naples, NC
(I-26 at exit 13, then half a mile south)
828.684.6262
Mon-Sat 9am-6pm, Sun 1pm-6pm

Quality camping equipment, canoes, kayaks, climbing gear, touring skis, maps, hiking boots, trail information, and sportswear. Excellent service.

The Enchanted Forrest

235 Merrimon Ave.
828.236.0688
Mon-Sat 10am-5:30pm, Sun 1pm-4pm

This second hand consignment store sells great outdoor equipment including everything from kayaks to backpacks. They have the best return policy on hiking boots we've ever heard of. (See our write-up under the *Vintage & Thrift* category, for more details.)

Mast General Store

15 Biltmore Ave.
828.232.1883
Mon-Thu 10am-6pm
Fri-Sat 10am-8pm, Sun 1pm-6pm

Mast General Store started out in Valle Crucis, NC as a mercantile general store serving a rural county. The outfit grew into a corporate chain with locations in several mountain towns. The Asheville venture is a big department store with top-of-the-line outdoor and casual clothing, old timey housewares, and excellent-quality hiking and camping gear.

CANDLES

Guinevere's
28 N. Lexington Ave.
828.252.6536
Mon-Sat 10:30am-6pm

This colorful shop sells Celtic inspired gift items like cards, bedspreads, and writing journals, but the mainstay is candles made skillfully and artfully on the premises. Our favorites are the ones that float. You can light them and set them in a dish of water, a bathtub, or the swimming pool at your hotel for a romantic alternative to land-based lighting.

Mountain Lights
1 Walnut St.
828.253.0080
Mon 11am-6pm, Wed-Sat 11am-6pm (Closed Tue & Sun)

Pamela Brown Chandler re-establishes the art of hand dipping candles right before your eyes. Her wax palette continually evolves, resulting in a multitude of spontaneous colors. She offers long-burning mandala candles, beeswax lanterns, antique tin and Mexican tile-inlaid crosses with Mexican church candles, Moroccan lanterns, tackboard sconces, handmade paper lanterns, wrought iron candleabras from The Netherlands, and a great little selection of Chinese hanging votive lanterns. She also carries a whacky line of electric lights which are functionally whimsical.

CARDS & GIFTS

The Loft
53 Broadway
828.259.9303
Mon-Sat 10am-6pm, Sun 1pm-4pm (Except Jan-Apr when hours are Mon-Sat 10am-5pm)

Lost objects become found treasures at this shop. Lovely rustic picture frames made from recycled barnboard, rusted steel, and painted sheet metal. Handmade paper, soap, and candles. Functional furniture made funky by an artist's touch.

M'Press Cards & Eclectica
61 Haywood St.
828.236.2282
Mon-Sat 10am-7pm

Come here to buy those cards you've been meaning to write and you'll be inspired to send one to everyone in your address book. The shop supports local artists and carries the best selection of locally created greeting cards, especially photographic cards of the region.

This offshoot of Malaprop's Bookstore carries tasteful, radical, wonderful stationery and giftwrap. They have postcards, greeting cards, make-your-own-card supplies, journals, sketch pads, ink pens, ink pads, calligraphy pens, stickers, heart-shaped paper punches, sealing wax, handmade paper, fridge magnets, lapel buttons with printed slogans like "What part of meow don't you understand?", wood blocks for printing, goddess tee-shirts and more.

Rainbow's End, Inc.

10 N. Spruce St.
828.285.0005
Mon-Thu 10am-6pm
Fri-Sat 10am-7pm, Sun 1pm-5pm

Rainbow's End offers every kind of "diversity rainbow" accessory you can imagine from coffee mugs to handmade pillows. Fun selection of bumper stickers, candles, greeting cards, posters and prints, books, videos, tee-shirts, and jewelry items. This exceptionally "gay-friendly" store also offers a small but comprehensive community-resource section with free newspapers and brochures about area events, organizations, and tourist attractions.

CIGARS

Bonnie's Little Corner

1 Pack Square
828.252.1611
Mon-Thu 11am-10pm
Fri-Sat 11am-Midnight
("Sunday we take a day of rest to revise ourselves for the next week.")

Bonnie's sells all sorts of tobacco products, snacks, drinks, and candies. The best thing in this store is not for sale though, it's free: Bonnie's personal charm and hospitality.

The Cuban coffee is the only genuine cup of it we've found since we left Miami and the poster of Marilyn Monroe is the sexiest one we've ever seen. It's not for sale, although many people have offered lots of cash for it.

CLOTHES & SHOES

Benomran Designer Clothing

22 College St.
828.252.6660
Mon-Fri 9am-6pm, Sat 10am-6pm

Many men's clothing stores send their suits to Benomran for alterations. Owner Yousef Benomran offers expert tailoring and fast turn-around time. Buy an oversized vintage overcoat at a thrift store and let him transform it into a custom fit, or design your own vest and have Benomran's create it from scratch. A friend of ours had a new lining masterfully created for an old leather jacket, for under fifty bucks. The store also offers brand-name men's clothes, including the popular Kangal line of hats.

Constance Boutique

62 Haywood St.
828.252.4002
Mon-Fri 10-6, Sat 11-6, Sun 12-5
(Except during the months of
Jan/Feb/Mar)

A women's wardrobe expert was asked by the author for sensible suggestions regarding how to pack for a trip to Asheville. The spontaneous reply was "Wear a bikini for swimming and a trenchcoat to keep you covered on the plane. Upon arrival, go and get everything else at Constance."

Fullfill your boutique dreams or just redefine them at this elegantly understated cache of snazzy threads. Constance Ensner, who has an inimitable eye for style, travels frequently to select elegant, distinctive, and deliciously fun clothing and accessories for her shop. For more than fifteen years she has quietly and consistently validated the notion that, whereas fashion can be bought, style can only be discovered.

Constance offers a full line of creations from Tocca, Bonnie Strauss, Cynthia Rowley, and Eileen Fisher. Exquisite cut velvet gowns...Italian shoes... accessories from Hobo and BCBG...silk, cashmere, linen, and leather. *{Note to men: Although Constance Boutique may be a "woman thing," a gift from here for that special woman in your life has the potential to upstage chocolate truffles, roses, and your earnest attempts at poetry. The giftwrap alone has a reputation for inciting cardiac pitapats. }*

Mystic Eye

30 N Lexington Ave.
828.251.1773
Mon-Thu 11am-6pm
Fri-Sat 10:30am-6pm
Sunday by appointment

This women's clothing store sells beautiful art-to-wear in natural fibers and exotic colors. Owner Laura Petritz works with a local seamstress to create her own hand-dyed designs in silk and rayon. The result is a sexy range of outfits with a wonderfully subtle color palate and highly "pettable" texture. If you go shopping without a girl friend, Laura or her friendly staff will help you decide which dress really makes your hips look smaller. Personal dressing consultations are available by appointment. The store also stocks interesting jewelry and cards.

Native Expressions

32 N Lexington Ave.
828.255.7996

Mon-Sat 11am-7pm
(Winter 11am-5:30pm)

With an interesting selection of women's clothes, a small men's section, and an attractive plus-size section in bright African hues, this store has something for everyone. It features clothing in linen, cotton, hemp and silk from Africa, Peru, India, Indonesia and beyond, along with a small selection of jewelry, hats and drums.

Open Door Boutique

35 Haywood St.
828.254.8056

Mon-Sat 10am-5:30pm
Sun 12:30pm-5pm

This colorful women's clothing store always seems to have something that fits just right. Whether your body type is Rubenesque, or more like a Modigliani nude, you are sure to find something to flatter you. It's easy to spend a couple of hours trying on their eclectic and comfortable selection of cotton, linen, hemp and tercel creations. They also stock incense, Indian bedspreads, drums, hair accessories and affordable silver jewelry.

Tops for Shoes

27 N. Lexington Ave.
828.254.6721

Mon-Sat 10am-6pm

This long-established Asheville institution has an extraordinary ability to deliver stylish, comfortable, hard-to-find footwear at excellent prices. One Scottish visitor found a special type of old fashioned shoelaces she had been unable to locate in the major shopping districts of the United Kingdom. A local gent with a chronic condition of aching feet found the most comfortable pair of shoes he's ever owned—made in Denmark—at a price worth bragging about. Recommended as a visitor's first stop in Asheville in order to guarantee a pleasant walking tour of our rigorous terrain.

DRUGS

Asheville Discount Pharmacy

57 Haywood St.
828.258.8511

Mon-Fri 9am-5:30pm, Sat 9am-1pm

Underground guidebooks were invented to list establishments of this type. This store is culturally diverse, centrally-located, discount-priced, and serves an essential function in the community. The pharmacy can fill your scripts at a discount while you browse an impressive collection of natural herbal remedies including cayenne-goldenseal, uva-ursi leaf, and damiana leaves. If you get a bit peckish they carry potato chips, potted meat, canned chicken & dumplings, and soda pop. Their most exotic feature is a wall covered with about three hundred hair pieces (weaves and braids) in every style and color. It seems that the friendly folks who run the place have a smile (and a hairpiece) for everyone.

LAUNDROMATS

Dutch Girl Laundromat

954 Merrimon Ave.
828.253.4741

Daily 7:30am-10pm
(last load curfew 9pm)

This place is what every Laundromat ought to be. Large capacity double and triple load washers (you can wash a sleeping bag or a quilt in one) and big toasty dryers. Change machines which always have spiffy new coins in them and are pretty good about not rejecting your currency just because it happens to have an old-age wrinkle. Large clean counters for folding and sorting. Drop-off service available. Convenient to supermarkets so you can shop as you wash.

Montford Laundromat

233 Montford Ave.
828.253.9893

Sun 8am-6pm, Mon-Fri 7am-9pm
Sat 8am-9pm

A small but excellent little Laundromat in the heart of historic Montford (close to downtown). Double and triple loaders, efficient dryers, a change machine, and an attendant on duty at all times. Clean, comfortable, and well-lighted. Neighborhood grocery store next door. Fluff and fold service available.

FL:OWERS

Bloomin' Art
60 Haywood St.
828.254.6447
Mon-Sat 10am-6pm
(Open Sun 1pm-5pm Oct-Dec only)
This florist shop has been serving Asheville for more than a decade. Fruit baskets, cut flowers, and designs made to order by Beth Stickle.

Perri Ltd. Floral Decor Studio and the Perri Institute
65 1/2 N. Lexington Ave.
828.281.1197

Wonderful folks to do business with and a beautiful selections of flowers year-round. Phone orders accepted by credit card payment.

Perri Crutcher is a dreamer and artist whose medium of choice is flowers. If you don't experience the beauty, artistry, elegance, inspiration, healing power, and Southern charm this individual expresses through flowers, then your visit to Asheville is indeed incomplete. As one observant resident stated "This store is the quintessential Asheville shopping experience."

Perri is a charming ambassador of Mother Nature who even decorates the public counter at the local post office with a generous vase of flowers. That might not seem so extraordinary until you consider that Jackie O. herself used to buy Perri creations to decorate the night table in her own bedroom.

He's been designing for more than 15 years and has worked with the world's top floral designers. He opened his shop in a narrow alleyway and soon expanded into two adjacent storefronts. But, as he says, "the heartbeat of the shop is the alley."

GROCERIES

BaBa Riche Gourmet Foods
2 Hendersonville Rd.
(inside Trevi Restaurant)
828.253.8118
Mon-Sat 11:30am -2:30pm and
reopens from 5pm-9pm
Sun 5pm-9pm (Except Jan-Mar when
Sat hours are 5pm-9pm only)

Barbara Laibson (aka "BaBa") sells the best peasant bread—along with assorted herb and cheese loaves—in the city, baked daily in the kitchen of Trevi, the acclaimed Italian restaurant which her husband Richard (aka "Riche") operates. BaBa Riche, located inside Trevi, carries a stupendous array of gourmet foods...oils, vinegars, pastas, coffees, teas, jams, jellies, preserves, confections and custom gift baskets.

BaBa Riche offers over 100 chocolate products including chocolate body paint ("The dessert's on me tonight, honey"). If that's not hot enough for you, try one of the fifty-six different gourmet hot sauces.

Downtown Food Market
75 Haywood St.
(Inside the Vanderbilt Apt. Building)
Mon-Fri 8am-5:30pm
Sat 8am-Noon

In downtown new-age Asheville you can channel your bygone gerbil and have your aura mapped faster than you can find basic staples like flour, milk, and canned beans.

If the metaphysical shopping opportunities of Asheville become a tad too other-worldly for you, then stop in here and get a carton of eggs with a reality check thrown in for free. This little convenience store (hidden inside an old apartment building next to the Civic Center) is one of those scarce-as-hen's-teeth places in cosmopolitan downtowns where one can purchase staples such as potatoes, cold cereal, toilet paper, and five-cent candy.

French Broad Co-op
90 Biltmore Ave.
828.255.7650
Mon-Fri 9am-8pm, Sat 9am-7pm
Sun Noon-6pm

For years, this has been the only real grocery store in downtown Asheville. Operated as a food co-op, this is where local residents come for local organic produce and a great selection of herbs, alternative medicines, and bulk staples like pasta, honey, and whole wheat flour. They have the best mountain-grown potatoes we've ever tasted, excellent handmade soaps, and a great selection of essential oils, moisturizers, and shampoos.

On Saturday mornings during the warmer months the co-op parking lot becomes a tailgate farmers' market. It's small, with only about a dozen vendors, but the produce and the prices are hard to beat.

The Fresh Market

944 Merrimon Ave.
828.252.9098
Mon-Sat 9am-9pm, Sun 11am-8pm

This is part of a regional chain of gourmet grocery stores with an extensive produce section, a complete bakery, and free gourmet coffee while you shop. Convenient to one of Asheville's best laundromats in case you want to shop while your clothes take a spin.

Earth Fare

Westgate Shopping Center
(Near intersection of I 240-West and Patton Ave.)
828.253.7656
Mon-Sat 8am-9pm, Sun 9am-8pm

A gigantic supermarket specializing in organic produce and health-food, featuring microbeers, imported cheeses, and a big vitamin/mineral/medicinal section. Earth Fare has a deli and mini-cafeteria for those too hurried to cook.

HEALTH & BEAUTY

Ananda Hair Studio

22 Broadway Ave.
828.232.1017
Tue-Sat 9am-6pm

Ananda Hair Studio has eight designers who are good listeners with fast scissors and extraordinary design and color skills. Ananda focuses passionately on the art of hair, using products from Bumble & Bumble (one of NY's leading hair salons), Schwazkopf (the world's oldest hair color line which developed the first herbal hair treatment and the first botanical hair color), and Phytologie (a French line and the leader in plant-based botanicals).

Ananda advertises its location as "beautiful downtown Asheville" and their one-stop urban beautification program expands one client at a time. Prices of cuts reflect degree of difficulty, not gender discrimination, and the scalp massage even includes a bit of aromatherapy. Dream-inducing chair massage is also available on the premises. Schedule in advance for an appointment, although if they have a last-minute cancellation they will try to work you in on short notice.

[Note: Ananda also houses an interesting art gallery — the exhibits change every 6-9 weeks.]

The Liquid Dragon Tattoo Art Studio
73 Broadway, 2nd Floor
828.251.2518
By appointment Mon-Sat Noon-7pm
Sun 1pm-6pm

Liquid Dragon offers tattoos, body piercing, cover-ups, repairs, free consulations and the confidence that you're dealing with a studio that has won praise from satisfied, pierced, dermagraphically enhanced, walking works of art. Centrally located.

Well Groomed Barber Shop
145 Biltmore Ave.
828.254.5155

Walter Wells' motto for his barber shop is "It pays to be well groomed" and here you can enjoy being groomed without paying so much that you get fleeced in the process. Nice folks with great barber skills and years of experience.

Joc King's Barber & Style Shop
484 Merrimon Ave.
828.254.4164

This traditional barber shop is a local institution where folks have been getting old fashioned service for generations. Stop in for a style or cut and experience the reason why customers sometimes want to come back for a haircut before their hair has time to grow out, just to sit, visit, and be treated the ole timey barber shop way.

L'eau de Vie Hair, Body, and Skin Care
20 Battery Park Ave.
Suite 203
828.258.9741 Salon
828.252.0761 Retail Center

This oasis within the historical Flat Iron Building offers the full Aveda Concept line of haircare, skincare, pure-fumes, custom blending, cosmetics, and bodycare. Complete hair care, massage, foot reflexology, facials, waxing, make up application, manicure and pedicure...in an atmosphere so relaxing and refreshing browsing is a vacation in itself.

Studio Chavarria
12 1/2 Wall Street
828.236.9191

Guadalupe Chavarria is a hair designer and color stylist whose skills have earned him an international clientele and a local reputation for creative excellence. His private studio was created around the desire to give elegant personal service and undivided attention to his clients. Call ahead for an appointment because he's in high demand.

Mendhi by Katie

828.255.9170

By appointment only

This local artist (whose drawings and paintings are featured in this guidebook) also creates traditional henna tattoo temporary body adornment (Mendhi). The designs last about two weeks before washing off. And Katie is a delightful person to experience, while you're being decorated.

Heavenly Hairstyles by Johanna

650 1/2 Hendersonville Rd.

828.274.9594

Tue-Sat 9am-6pm, Fri 9am-7pm

Johanna Hair Care Product line for all types of hair. Johanna can weave, cut, curl, color, or relax your hair, and her shop is conveniently near the hotels in Biltmore Village...which is one reason she has clients from places as distant as Texas and Bermuda. Call for an appointment although she can accomodate some walk-ins.

Jolie De Shea

295 West Haywood St.

828.254.0231

Open Tue-Sat

Hair weaving, relaxing, curling, design, and color. This is one of the most popular design studios in Asheville, and as their advertising explains, they "specialize in ethnic hair care." Walk-ins are welcome. There is also a small boutique on the premises.

Full Circle Salon

34 Wall St.

828.251.1722

Tue-Sat 9am-6pm

The premise is as simple as their Zen-esque circular brushstroke logo: They do hair, only hair, and everything to do with hair (except waxing it off). With five of the city's best designers this studio focuses on making you feel great about your great-looking head of hair. They have a stellar reputation for style, creativity, and consistency. They use and carry a full line of Rusk and Aveda products.

Sky People Tattoo

828.253.1294

"Tattoos are visible ambassadors of the mind" according to Sky People's owner/artist Kitty Brown who has a Masters of Fine Arts degree from the Maryland College of Art. As soon as she opened her practice, "Miss Kitty" became a household name to those in Western North Carolina who derma-decorate.

Kitty, who has "made art her life," specializes in photo-realism, art nouveau, Celtic, floral, and fine line styles. She says "The tattoo is a unique art form in which the canvas decides what will be painted, and the artist lends the skill required to make the image as beautiful as possible." She has a particular talent for creating designs which are specific to her clients' needs, and her regional reputation as a cover-up tattoo artist is unchallenged.

Miss Kitty at work.

INTERNATIONAL SHOPPING

A Far Away Place
11 Wall St.
828.252.1891
1.888.452.1891
Mon-Tue 10am-5pm, Wed-Sat 10am-9:30pm, Sun 11am-5pm

Clothing, jewelry, recorded music, musical instruments, and artifacts from more than fifty countries are presented in this unusual store. It looks more like a gallery than a shop, and is worth a visit just to browse amongst the folk art. South American, Mexican, African, and Indian arts, crafts, and artifacts. The owner is a world-traveler who believes in supporting native artisans and the cultures they represent. The store sponsors cultural presentations in Asheville on a regular basis; call for a schedule of upcoming events.

Artzy World
32 Biltmore Ave.
828.285.0209
Mon-Sat 11am-5:30pm

Drums and other musical instruments, clothing, artifacts, masks, and jewelry imported from several countries on the continent of Africa. This colorful little shop has beadwork, embroidery, wood block printed cloth, and handcrafted leather accessories. Conveniently located at the top of historic Eagle Street.

Cosmic Vision
34 N Lexington Ave.
828.285.0073
Mon-Sat 10am-6pm

Cosmic Vision is a non-profit venture. Besides selling stylish, exotic, and artistic-looking clothing and handicrafts at really great prices, most of the store's proceeds go to aid projects in developing nations through AMURT (Ananda Marga Universal Relief Team).

The store's customers, the store's Brazilian coordinator, and a team of dedicated international volunteers form a team that helps to fund projects such as hurricane disaster relief in Nicaragua and school building / food distribution to undernourished children in Haiti. There is an interesting photo documentary-type display on the walls of the shop, which is intended to show customers where the profits go.

My Native Ireland
12 Battery Park Ave.
828.281.1110
Mon-Thu 10:30am-6pm, Wed-Sat 10:30am-10pm, Sun Noon-5pm

Drop by to visit this light and cozy shop and vicariously experience Dublin through the spirited personality of proprietor Annmarie McConnell.

Annmarie's love of her homeland is celebrated through exotic items including spectacular antiques; world famous Aran knitwear designed with trellis, blackberry, cable, or honeycomb stitches; caps and hats knitted or woven from luxurious wool; raku sculpture from Dublin; blackstone carvings from Kilkenny; linen shirts for men and christening dresses for children (made by members of the Irish Linen Guild); and even British chocolate bars.

Jewelry handcrafted from rare Irish coins, stone replicas of the Irish river gods, carvings from beautiful pieces of nine thousand year-old bog oak, and handmade bone china from Belfast combine to transform this wee shop into a virtual Irish museum. But may the buyer beware: Irish magic enchants many an unsuspecting shopper.

Spend too much time in My Native Ireland and you may find leprechauns dancing across your brain, as this writer can attest.

World Market Place
10 College St.
828.254.8374
Mon-Sat 10am-5pm

The World Market is a non-profit 10,000 Villages store which helps low-income craftpersons in over thirty developing nations by providing a market for their work. For every $1200 in retail sales from the store, a family of four in a developing nation can have food, health care, education and housing for one year. When you consider that the majority of the world's population subsists on less than a dollar a day, your purchase really can make a difference.

After paying the rent, utilities and only two modest salaries (all other employees are volunteers), the World Market Place gives all profits back to the artisans. Any left-over money goes to local charities. The store sells very reasonably priced hand-crafted items such as baskets, jewelry, pottery, chess sets, Christmas ornaments and cards, masks, wood carvings, and handmade paper. Buy "guilt-free gifts" that give twice: First to the lucky recipient, and secondly to the artisan you support. Teach children about the world by buying them beautiful dolls from Vietnam (whose proceeds go to Vietnamese street children) or a board game from Indonesia called "Congklak."

Caffeine junkies can stock up on organic, shade-grown, gourmet Equal Exchange coffee. The money from your coffee purchase will go directly to Third World farmers instead of to the large companies who exploit them. Shade-grown coffee is grown using sustainable agricultural methods that preserve the soil for future generations and avoid deforestation. As their educational pamphlet says: "Equal Exchange is like drinking a cup of justice, and justice can taste outstanding."

JEWELRY (HANDCRAFTED) & GEMSTONES

Blue Goldsmiths

4 All Soul's Crescent
Biltmore Village
828.277.2583
Mon-Sat 10am-5pm

Jewelers Lynn Daniel and Susan West expanded their successful wholesale business in 1997 to open this retail store. Lynn describes her work as being inspired by nature and she enjoys creating asymmetrical designs. Conversely, Susan's passion lies in diamond setting and her designs are more technical and geometric. Both artists like to work in all four gold colors (often in the same piece) and only use hand-cut stones which bring out the true radiance of precious stones.

Filled with their unique wearable art pieces, as well as the work of other women artists, Blue Goldsmiths is a delight to visit. Browse for original, one-of-a-kind gold and silver pieces or have Lynn or Susan brainstorm a new design from an existing piece. Trust your wedding or commitment ring design to their discerning eyes. Gay or traditional couples are welcome to work together with the artists to celebrate their bond with custom-made wedding or commitment rings.

Cast In Stone

19 Patton Ave.
(Inside Kress Emporium)
828.252.4653
Mon-Thu 10am-6pm
Fri-Sat 10am-7pm, Sun Noon-5pm
(Closed Sundays Jan-Mar)

Asheville was lucky enough to snag Cast in Stone's jewelers Melissa Grosse and Gary Whitaker from their native Wisconsin. Melissa, a graduate of University of Wisconsin's BFA program, has a litany of impressive awards to her name. She stunned the craft world by winning first place awards at the prestigious Wisconsin Jewelers Association Design competition three years in a row from 1995-1998. Gary learned his trade in a more traditional manner, "watching the old guys and asking too many questions." Gary started working with gold as an apprentice; polishing, sizing, soldering and modifying other people's designs. These experiences served as a good stepping stone for designing his own pieces.

You can see Gary and Melissa at work at their mini-studio at the Kress Emporium, where they hand-forge exquisite 14-carat gold fittings for exotic gems such as opals, mandarin garnets, crazy lace agate, and black tiger's eye. They specialize in custom work, starting off with a series of sketches that the customer chooses from, then making a wax model of the piece before the final casting. Their work uniquely blends artistic prowess and functional wearability. They also offer repairs, periodic appraisal clinics with an expert gemologist, and free cleanings.

Jewels That Dance

63 Haywood St.

828.254.5088

Mon-Sat 10am-6pm

Jewels That Dance comprises a stylish store and the working jewelry studio of self-taught local artist Paula Dawkins. A pleasant place to shop, Jewels That Dance feels more like a gallery, with its bright airy feel, elegant display cases and sculptures. Featuring work from local and nationally renowned jewelers, Jewels That Dance offers contemporary and classic treasures in platinum, gold, silver, gemstones and diamond. Want to set that loose stone that Grandma left you in her estate? Let the knowledgeable staff pick out a setting for your heirloom. Jewels That Dance also offers custom work, jewelry appraisals and repairs

MUSIC

Almost Blue Records

92 Patton Ave.

828.285.0808

Mon-Sat 10am-7pm

Chock full of new and used CDs, Almost Blue offers downtown's most extensive music selection. The shop focuses on roots music of the folk, bluegrass and alternative-country sort. Excellent inventory of jazz, blues, and rock. Functions as a ticket office for concerts held at several Asheville venues. Great music bar in the basement, aptly named The Basement.

KarmaSonics Music & Video

14 Haywood St.

828.259.9949

Mon-Thu 10am-7pm
Fri-Sat 10am-9pm, Sun Noon-6pm

This store has a cosmic inventory of new music and perhaps the best selection of used CDs in the city. If you hear a local band you fancy, come here to find the band's CD; the store has a huge collection of locally grown music for sale. The fellows who run this store are well known for their support of local musicians, and they have great in-store concerts from time to time. If you are looking for something which is out of stock or just too wierd for conventional record stores to carry, ask them to order it. They are a resourceful store for finding rarities.

Whizz Records
32 Biltmore Ave.
828.255.9333
Mon-Thu 11am-7pm
Fri-Sat 11am-9pm, Sun Noon-5pm

The author of this guidebook has found some of his favorite rare CDs at this shop, but really and truly, old-fashioned vinyl records are the thing here: New and used and in every conceivable genre. You'll find such gems as Julie London's "Calendar Girl," Hank Williams' classic "Sing Me a Blue Song," and a somewhat inexplicable release called "Musical Cocktail Party With Cedric Dumont, His Orchestra and His Shaker." The selection is heavy on surf, lounge, garage punk, "post-punk," and rockabilly. Whizz also carries 45s. This is the store where you'll find what the others stores don't have.

TOYS

Enviro Depot
18 Haywood St.
828.252.9007
Mon-Thu 10:30am-6pm
Fri-Sat 10:30am-7pm, Sun Noon-5pm

This is the store where kid-friend-ly meets enviro-friendly. Educational, fun, challenging games; creative, col-orful, nature-inspired toys, and the best selection of stuffed animals and hand puppets.

The Toy Box
740 Merrimon Ave.
828.254.8697
Mon-Sat 10am-6pm

This little store, living up to its name, is chock full of goodies just like a toy chest. Award-winning and educational toys, art, science games, and other incredibly imaginative playthings. The best selection of kid-inspiring toys under one tiny roof that we've ever seen.

VINTAGE & THRIFT STORES

The Enchanted Forrest

235 Merrimon Ave.
828.236.0688
Mon-Sat 10am-5:30pm
Sun 1pm-4pm

This consignment shop runs the gamut from sexy dresses to rugged hiking gear. When the author visited, owner Forrest Hogestad had just sold out of red kayaks and was writing up the sale of a stunning spagetti strap evening dress (cut across the bias) to a young woman visiting from Alaska...who stopped in to pick out a pair of already-broken in but like-new hiking boots.

Enchanted Forrest has a three-day return policy on their merchandise, and they don't give you store credit, they give you a full refund of your money. The owner encourages customers to "Wear those hiking boots for a weekend and if they don't fit properly, bring them back the next day." She gets consignment items from the best women's boutique in town, from the sales rep of a major outdoor clothing and equipment manufacturer, and from wardrobe buyers for motion picture companies who want to unload everything after an Asheville film shoot. On one recent visit, the author found the following items: Givenchy® scarf $3, Vasque® hiking boots in great condition $20, LL Bean® Maine Hunting Shoes $18, North Face® wool jacket $35, Two person tent $45. (*Note: The owner is a former restaurant critic with insightful recommendations for exciting places to dine in the Asheville area.*)

Hip Replacements

72 N. Lexington Ave.
828.255.7573
Mon-Sat 11am-7pm, Sun 1pm-5pm

Ultra-hip and ultra-friendly. This funky shop caters to the young Bohemian crowd and pretty much anybody else who appreciates a 1973 polyester button-down shirt emblazoned with images of "All-American Vacation Spots." They have great lace party dresses from the '40s. The author found a bright red suede vintage 1950s baseball jacket for fifteen bucks. They carry cherry-condition Hawaiian shirts with real wooden buttons, and have platform shoes for sale or rent.

A few new items have made their way into Hip Replacements' stock, like platform boots, fishnet tights, leather jackets and women's underwear. They offer the "Cookie Puss" line of glittery, fluorescent nail polish, lipstick and false lashes. Jewel-toned and fluorescent wigs in long and short bobs are a staple of this shop. Great selection of sunglasses. The shopping bags are hand-painted and decorated and one customer bought something at this store just to get the cool bag.

Never underestimate the potential of thrift store shopping in a resort town where the population is relatively transient from season to season. Those who move tend to travel light, and those who stick around can buy their cast-offs for next to nothing.

Iee's Buys
58 Lexington Ave.
828.252.2329

Tue-Sat 11ish-7ish, Sunday 1pm-6ish (Open late some Fridays. Generally open "Until the weird people come by.")

Pronounced "Eyes Buys" this quirky second-hand store is named after owner Annmarie Riley's aunt, who always let Annmarie rummage around in her pocket book. A rummage through Iee's Buys will turn up unexpected treasures such as a 1950s Boonton plastic tableware set, a 1950s "Easy" brand washing machine with a plastic leg protruding from it, a fantastic collection of vintage hats, magazines from the 60s, and old pre-loved toys that will put a smile on even the most jaded shopper's face. This place really makes you feel good about any pack-rat tendencies you may have. It is the ultimate hoarder's paradise.

Annmarie describes her store as "A variety store of emotion-evoking antiques and uniques." Her goal is really to have fun and make people smile. This is the woman who, as a child, would squirt chocolate pudding at her friend with a water pistol for laughs. Now Annmarie finds gentler humor and fun in the unusual items of her store. She thinks it is important to preserve everyday items such as kitchen equipment and brushes for posterity. It is not uncommon to see customers get that misty-eyed look and say things like "Oh, I remember my grandmother had one of these." Annmarie also does computerized astrological charts and interpretation.

Interplanet Janet
68 Lexington Ave.
828.259.9274

Retro gear plus new clothing and accessories from Tribal, Freshjive, Alien Work-shop, Cosmic Girls, and Custo Barcelona are available at Interplanet Janet, which has been Western North Carolina's hippest way-cool store forever and ever. It's the cat's meow. Trek on over to the world of Interplanet Janet.

Rags

1-C Walnut St.

Daily 2pm-6pm
(Subject to change)

Ann Carpenter's collection of vintage and pre-owned clothes is one of the best kept secrets in western North Carolina. She doesn't have a phone and can't promise she'll be always be there but that's part of the intrigue of discovering this treasure chest of beautiful, classic, sometimes-funky bargains. Her cup runneth over with lovely duds and she is one of the most hospitable, charming women in town. Give yourself enough time to browse the merchandise while having a chat with one of Asheville's beautiful people.

Salvation Army Thrift Store

45 Rankin Ave.

828.254.5308

Mon-Sat 9am-4pm

This is a huge store with everything from portable eight track tape players to vintage lingerie. One shopper found a fifteen dollar coat in excellent condition that originally sold for over a grand. Another found a great sofa for fifty bucks and got the store to deliver it for a small fee.

WINE & BEER

Asheville Wine Market

65 Biltmore Ave.

828.253.0060

Mon-Sat 10am-6pm

This place carries pricey vintage year Burgundy but the folks are just as enthusiastic to help customers with only a few bucks to burn. "We taste many mediocre wines...so you won't have to!" is their motto. AWM has a great selection of affordable wines which really and truly taste expensive. All wine regions are represented, artisan producers are featured, and they have everyday low prices as well as monthly specials.

Shopping Tip: If you're on a budget (and who is not when it comes to wine?) buy those bottles described as "Amazing Value," and "AWM Best Buy." There is a special rack near the entrance where the AWM Top 10 Best Buys are displayed.

Weinhaus

86 Patton Ave.

828.254.6453

Mon-Sat 10am-6pm

One of the best selections of domestic and imported beers in the area, along with an excellent variety of wines from every major region. Weinhouse has good prices and great service at a convenient downtown location.

SHOPPING EXCURSION ON
BATTERY PARK HILL

Start at the Chamber of Commerce with one of their small maps of downtown and head down Haywood St. toward the Basilica and Civic Center. When you get to the St. Lawrence Basilica, hang a right onto Haywood St. and you will find yourself easing into the one of the best sections for shopping in town.

On one side of the street you'll encounter Gold Hill, a coffee shop where you can read The New York Times, enjoy the best bagels around, and have a great pot of tea. Next door is Constance Boutique, a stylish women's clothing and accessories store. Most of us would expect to encounter this kind of shop only in more cosmopolitan cities like New York, Atlanta, or the Lost City of Atlantis. It's dreamy.

Across the street is Jewels That Dance, a jewelry gallery and working studio, M'press, a unique card and eclectica shop, and Malaprop's Bookstore, an Asheville cultural repository based around books and the folks who read and write them. Continue along Haywood St. and you'll pass the Chocolate Fetish, where the name implies everything and then lives up to it.

On the corner is The New French Bar, where bohemians meet to procrastinate over cocktails and business travelers pause for a game of cell phone tag over lunch. Nearby is Earth Guild, home of everything you need to be crafty and creative. Across from The New French Bar is Enviro Depot, where kid-friendly meets environmentally friendly. To the west along Battery St. is the A & SD Doggs Enterprises hotdog stand where folks in Asheville go for portable lunch. This sidewalk cart serves up hot dogs (veggie dogs too) with everything on them including a satisfying portion of hometown hospitality.

Further along is A Far Away Place which is one of those "typically unique" Asheville shops where you can browse until the cows come home and still not quite get enough. At the end of the street is the majestic Grove Arcade, America's first shopping mall. It is under restoration as we go to press. When it opens, it will transform Battery Hill into a self-contained market village with more activity per square foot than any other downtown block.

Below Battery Park St. is Wall St. See our *Wall Street Shopping Guide* for a step-by-step description of what it holds in store (or stores). One level below Wall St.(look for the signs to College St. Shops for a shortcut through the building) is College Street, where World Market Place, International Link, and Jack of the Wood pub offer a quick blitz through global shopping, global socializing, and local brew.

AUCTIONS

Johnny Penland Auctions
155 Craven Street
828.253.7712

Auctions every Fri 6pm
Previews every Thurs 9am-4pm
Call for details and procedures.

Estate, household, and consign-ment items as well as antiques are the mainstay at Penland Auctions. Johnny and his son Tommy operate a class act with a down home feeling. These auc-tions are not only entertaining but can be rewarding to buyers and sellers alike.

You never know what you'll find, but chances are you'll discover something that will have you bidding like a pro. And you'll enjoy the thrill of doing something quirky on a Friday night.

AUCTIONS:

To find out about area estate auctions, look for announcements in small-town newspapers and trade rags, on windows or bulletin boards in grocery stores, or on fliers stapled to telephone poles. Or just ask folks at feed stores and gas stations in rural communities.

Estate auctions take place in farming communities around Western North Carolina all summer long and into early autumn. Most are held on Saturday mornings under a canvas tent erected in front of the house being auctioned. Larger or more expensive items are sold first. These might include the house itself, large pieces of furniture, or kitchen appliances. Then everything else in the estate is auc-tioned off, from lawn mowers and apple butter kettles to old mason jars full of ten-penny nails.

Refreshments are usually sold in the back of the tent and often include goodies like pimento cheese sandwiches, hotdogs, boiled peanuts, pound cake by the slice, and soda pop. Most of these country auctions require no entrance fee; all you have to do is sign up and get a number in order to bid. At some auctions, profes-sional antique dealers dominate the bidding at first and then drop out early to pack their trucks. Those who attend primarily for the fun factor stay until the bitter end, when they can bid on boxes full of junk which nobody else wanted. The last time we attended an auction we bought a cardboard box containing 18 clay flower pots, a screwdriver, a plastic coffee cup and saucer, assorted nails, screws, and washers, and a partial roll of duct tape, for a dollar.

But the real reason to attend auctions is to watch the people, enjoy the food, and listen to the auctioneers work the crowd. Country auctions can be a priceless form of Vaudevillian enter-tainment, even if you don't participate in the adrenaline-enhanced bid game.

BODYWORK

B?DYW?RK

Asheville has been a center for healthcare for more than a century. In the old days, folks from around the world came here for the hot mineral springs, the fresh air, and the tuberculosis and mental health treatment centers. Today, Asheville is still recognized for its recuperative and restorative resources.

If you have "issues in your tissues", take heart. In this town, you can't swing a cat by the tail without hitting a massage therapist. And, yes, we do have an animal psychotherapist or two to help the cat get over it.

MASSAGE THERAPISTS / BODYWORKERS

Marilyn Biggers
828.271.0002

She not only has a zillion hours of training in massage therapy and National Certification, she's bilingual (English/Spanish). Marilyn is one of the best bodyworkers we're ever encountered.

Denise Petrey
828.253.0488

Denise is a genius at this stuff and someday she'll hold a doctorate degree in alternative medicine, we predict. If it wasn't for her, the author of this book would still be whining about his pain in the neck.

Barbara Metz
828.254.2850

The author of this book is a rather gimpy wimp, but every time he thinks he's beyond repair, Barbara Metz cures him with her hands. She's powerful medicine, with National Certification.

Nia Orr
828.258.4825

Nia Orr is one of those rare folks who seems to understand that she's been placed on this planet for healing purposes and is getting on with the business of doing it. She's earned a local reputation for strong hands, gentle pricing, and a kindness that simply radiates from her being.

Jennifer Lynn
828.890.2127

Nationally certified, emphasizes deep tissue massage with essential oils, and uses an *Infratonic Chi Energizer* in her healing work. This author considered writing a whole chapter about how gifted she is, but decided to make it a separate book.

CHIROPRACTORS

Dr. Andrew Aguilar

35 Haywood St., suite 209
(Conveniently located
  in the heart of downtown)
828.236.0330

Need an adjustment? Walk-in's were welcomed the last time we checked. Perfectly located to serve those of you visiting Asheville who threw your back out dancing, hauling shopping bags, or just honeymooning.

Dr. David Graham

180 Merrimon Ave.
828.253.5844

Dr. Graham cured the author of this guidebook from all sorts of chronic aches and pains, using a combination of kinesiology, accupuncture, chiropractic adjustment, excercise, and corny jokes.

NATURAL MINERAL BATHS

Hot Springs Spa

315 Bridge St.
Hot Springs, NC
(about an hour from Asheville)
828.622.7676   1.800.462.0933

DROP-IN YOGA CLASSES

Asheville Yoga Center

(at Training Partners gym)
863 Merrimon Ave.
(under Stein Mart)
828.275.6156

The Asheville Yoga Center offers classes for beginner and intermediate yoga students. The focus is on breathing, building of aerobic strength, flexibility and release of tension through the flow of movement. Drop-in classes are offered for about nine bucks each. Instructors Bonnie, Mary Kay, and Stephanie are awesome teachers and made the drop-in sessions we attended fabulous. Please call for class schedules and prices.

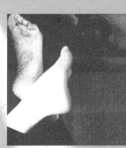

These are the kinds of naturally-heated mineral springs which over a century ago made Asheville an internationally renowned healthcare resort destination. Call to reserve a hot tub filled by natural mineral springs or to book a massage with the therapist on the premises. Tub # 5 offers the best riverfront view and exceptional privacy, so you might ask if it's available.

International Link

87 Patton Ave.

828.255.9104

Mon, Wed, Thu, Fri 12:30pm-3:30pm

Buncombe County is home to native speakers of over 30 different languages. International Link was established as a resource and support center for assisting Western North Carolina's foreign-born population in accessing the community and overcoming barriers to their integration into life in America. It also provides a central place for cross-cultural exchange in an effort to develop greater understanding and appreciation of diverse cultures.

The brain-child of Geri Solomon, an experienced English as a Second Language (ESL) teacher, International Link helps foreign-born residents find jobs, health-care, housing, schools, interpreters, and translators. Their lounge has a small foreign language library and an ESL educational resource library for students and teachers.

If you are interested in eating really well on the cheap while meeting fascinating people from different cultures, don't miss the friendly international vegetarian potluck dinners (Held on the 2nd Saturday of every month at 6:30pm.). No reservations are necessary. The center also offers an International Women's Friendship Circle on the first Thursdays of every month at 12:30pm (children welcome).

ESL educational program and free Spanish Language classes. Call for schedule and details.

> Individual people are like separate foreign cultures. When we experience each other as friends, it's like being a tourist, except you both feel right at home.
>
> — *The Old Timer*

> I went to this art museum one time and everybody was being real quiet and whispering like they do in churches. It just made me think about art in a different way.
>
> —*The Old Timer*

GALLERIES & MUSE-UMS

MARIE HUDSON

Painter Marie Hudson took her first art class when she was in her late forties, after spending years running a series of Asheville gift shops. Nowadays she goes to her River District studio every morning to paint graceful, strong-but-ethereal, often ghostly and unearthly renderings of the female form.

All her hard work is paying off. Marie's solo exhibition at Zone one gallery was a certifiable smash hit. One critic referred to her paintings as "indisputable masterpieces," and called her "the most talented artist in Asheville," which is especially high praise in this art-rich city.

Hudson describes her creative inspiration in this way: "My search is unending, and I am grateful. I do not have time to be old. I only have time to struggle for that one brief, positive moment when the innermost self flows onto the canvas. And when the moment is over, I must start again."

We caught her in between those moments when she puts brush to canvas and asked her to contribute some artistic insight to our guidebook.

What do you think is the best thing about Asheville's art scene?

I think the interest in art has grown so much and some of the galleries have really stuck with it and created a place for artists to thrive.

If you were a tourist in Asheville and got lost, what do you think would be the best area to get lost in?

The downtown area, because there is so much going on. There's something to do on every corner downtown.

What's your favorite street or neighborhood here?

I always love to drive down Kimberly [a wide, tree-lined street in North Asheville]. There's just something neat about it, looking at all the beautiful homes and wondering what's going on in each one. I also like the River District, of course, since my studio's down here. The area is special, naturally, because of all the artists and the studio spaces and I think all of us down here feel a part of what's going on with developing the River District. The French Broad River has become a part of us, and the river is really what the city's going to be centered around in the future, I think. I can just visualize what can happen, with the combination of the old businesses and the new artists.

What makes Asheville home to you, as opposed to just a place to live?

I feel secure here. And even though we're in step with the rest of the world, there's something unique and protected about us. The minute I get out into wide open spaces, I feel really off-kilter. There's a warmth here, too. I feel like the mountains could just reach out and hug me.

Marie Hudson

What do you think is your most admirable quality?

Just about the time I think I have it all together, I go and flub up. But what would seriously be my best quality? Well, I'm loyal, maybe too loyal. Yes, loyalty is a big one for me and so that's what I like most about myself.

If you had to name the single most important event in your lifetime, what would it be?

[Giggles] Getting my driver's license. It gave me freedom. I didn't learn to drive until late in life. See, the city bus drove off and left me this one time and bees were buzzing all around me, chasing me, and I went home that night and said "I want a car." And my husband said "You don't drive." And I said "I don't care. I want a car and I'll learn to drive it." Oh, those bees really got to me.

If you were going to a deserted island for two years, what three things (besides food and water) would you take along?

I'd take pencils or paint or crayons, even. Just some kind of art supplies. And I guess I would need a radio. I like some rhythm going when I paint. And then my mascara, of course. Well, hair curlers, too. Oh, that's four, isn't it? Then the mascara.

What makes a person ugly?

Phony, phony, phony.

What makes a person beautiful?

Sincerity and a real interest in life. And something that's hard to explain that makes you just form a bond with someone. It's intangible.

DOWNTOWN

Asheville Art Museum

at Pack Place
2 South Pack Square
828.253.3227
Tue-Sat 10am-5pm, Sun 1-5pm

The Asheville Art Museum is the only art museum in the region and this city's oldest art space—open in one incarnation or another since it began in a small stone house near the Grove Park Inn in 1948.

Today, the museum is housed in an imposing limestone building smack dab in the middle of downtown's Pack Square. But just because the museum is "established," don't think you'll find "establishment" art on its walls. The AAM's changing exhibitions are as varied as wildly abstract, kinetic sculpture by such contemporary masters as Matthew McCaslin or the collaged "mail art" of the late Ray Johnson. The permanent collection focuses on American art from 1890 to the present, inclusive of the colorful works of Harlem Renaissance master Romare Bearden and Black Mountain College alumni Robert Rauschenberg.

"Women of Iron" featured the downright formidable work of four innovative female blacksmiths. "In the City: Urban Visions 1900-1940," a collection of more than 50 quintessentially American masterpieces on loan from New York City's renowned Whitney Museum of American Art included works by such American masters as Edward Hopper, Reginald Marsh, Franz Kline, and John Sloan.

Colburn Gem & Mineral Museum

at Pack Place
2 South Pack Square
828.254.7162

A great place to view indigenous minerals. The museum exhibits crystals, gemstones, and fascinating minerals from all over the world, but minerals native to these mountains are especially showcased.

The Museum of North Carolina Minerals

Milepost 331,
Blue Ridge Parkway
828.765.2761

This museum is undergoing a grand renovation. There are more than three hundred native minerals on exhibit. It's a wonderful place to browse and the newly-refurbished version promises to be a real gem of a museum.

*Romare Bearden, **Sunset Express**, 1984.*
Collection of the Asheville Art Museum.

Zone one
contemporary gallery
37 Biltmore Ave.
828.258.3088
Mon and Wed-Sat 11am-5pm

Zone one contemporary gallery (yes, only the "Z" is capitalized; that's how the inimitable Connie Bostic, the gallery's co-owner, likes it) is the closest thing to those really cutting-edge little galleries so prevalent in SoHo that you'll find anywhere in Western North Carolina — or in the whole state, for that matter.

Gayle Wurthner in her studio. You may have seen her work in movies; she designs sets for Hollywood. She created a sensation with her chaise lounge show at Zone one contemporary gallery. She may be contacted at her studio (828.281.0555) for appointments to view artwork available for purchase.

Zone one has hosted exhibitions that included: Ceramic works by modern art icon Kenneth Noland, famous for his color-field paintings of the '60s and '70s, many of which now hang in the Museum of Modern Art and the Metropolitan Museum of art. Recent paintings by esteemed German expressionist Heinrich Schilinzky, some of them influenced by his experiences as a prisoner of war during World War II. Mini-retrospectives by such famous Black Mountain College alumni as Fannie Hillsmith (painting), Joseph Fiore (painting), Lore Lindenfeld (textiles) and Susan Weil (mixed-media). Jason Watson's first solo show featured drawings, journal entries, and photographic snapshots and made local art history when it sold out the same day the exhibition opened. Robert Godfrey's compelling "Chicken Alley Wedding" series which employed his unique expressionist style of painting in tribute to his own wedding ceremony. The ethereal paintings of Marie Hudson, a former gift-shop owner who came to art late in life and now creates often ghostly, much-sought-after renderings of the female form.

Robert Godfrey's exhibition at Zone one contemporary gallery

THE RIVER DISTRICT ART STUDIOS

Down by the banks of the French Broad River (in an area called, appropriately enough, the River District), a thriving art scene has developed. Glass blowers, sculptors, metal workers, painters, photographers, woodworkers, actors, dancers, and musicians have converted the industrial and manufacturing zone from an aesthetic wasteland into one of the liveliest, creatively-charged art scenes in this part of the country.

These local artists decided to transform the factory district that runs along the railroad tracks from a sow's ear into a silk purse. They live and work in studios which were once abandoned warehouses in a neglected part of town.

DIRECTIONS TO THE RIVER DISTRICT:

From the Chamber of Commerce parking lot, turn left on Haywood Street and follow it to Patton Avenue. Turn left on Patton Avenue and continue to Pack Square (with the granite oblisque). Turn right and follow Biltmore Avenue to Hilliard Avenue. Turn right on Hilliard and proceed through four lights. At the fifth light, turn left onto Clingman Avenue. The Grey Eagle Music Hall is at 185 Clingman Avenue, and the River District lies just beyond it on the French Broad River.

Twice yearly, in the winter and summer, River District artists band together for a studio stroll, with the Odyssey Gallery as its centerpoint. During the stroll, upwards of fifty artists open their usually closed-to-the-public studios. Call the Odyssey Gallery (828.285.0210) or the Asheville Chamber of Commerce (828.258.6101) for details on this and other River District happenings.

Here are some studios and performance venues to explore while in the River District, to give you a flavor of what the area has to offer.

Corey Harris at the Grey Eagle

The Grey Eagle Tavern Music Hall

185 Clingman Ave.

828.232.5800

Mon-Sat 4pm until (most shows start at 9pm)

Mondays: Contra Dances / Tuesdays: Open Mic Night

Fantastic listening room featuring local, regional, and national acts. This spacious, well-designed music hall attracts some of the best shows of any club in Western North Carolina, because the owners put music first and foremost.

Arlo Guthrie, Beth Wood, Kelly Willis, Doc

Watson, David Wilcox, and scores of other artists perform in this club located at the end of legendary Thunder Road, which was featured in the movie classic of the same name.

The Gnomon
828.255.8648
Call for hours or an appointment

The studio of Christopher Mello is more a greenhouse than an art space. He combines a little of both to create horticultural artwork. He used to create massive cut-flower arrangements for the elaborate rooms at the Biltmore House, before venturing into what he calls "container gardens"...rusty, found-object vessels filled with cacti, succulents, and other hardy plants. He recycles everything from railroad spikes to washing machine parts in the process of designing wonderfully original living works of art (which require very little maintenance and watering).

Great Southern Glassworks
9-A Riverside Drive
828.255.0187
Call for hours or an appointment

This is where fine art is produced at 2,100 degrees Fahrenheit. Vases, cups, bowls, and other decorative and functional glassware are created and sold by the artisans who operate this glass-blowing studio. This is some of the most beautiful and colorfully utilitarian artwork in the entire River District.

Odyssey Gallery
242 Clingman Ave.
828.285.0210
Thu-Sat 1pm-5pm

At the nexus of the whirlwind of artsy activity in the River District is the Odyssey Gallery, which is the only formal gallery in the River District (at least at the time this book went to press).

It's the offshoot of the Odyssey Center for the Ceramic Arts next door, a ceramics school that's home to five resident artists who work and teach there (director Mark Burleson once called Odyssey "a halfway house for artists"). The Odyssey Gallery offers impressive exhibitions in ceramics and also showcases works by painters and mixed-media artists.

The Studio Theater
191 Lyman Street
828.254.6057
Mon-Fri 9am-5pm and during scheduled rehearsals, performances, and meetings

This theater on the French Broad River is an experimental venue for new plays, innovative productions, and any art form served by the rough-and-ready nature of a warehouse setting. It contains the headquarters of Black Swan Theater (David Hopes and Ellen Pfirrmann, directors), and Urthona Gallery (David Hopes, director).

Functional Pottery Ware and Raku by Julie Payne
10 Richard St.
828.236.0178

Julie sells exceptionally well-made pottery ware and raku at very reasonable prices. Beautiful blues and greens are the distinguishing colors of her functional ware, which is in big demand in Asheville.

We first met Julie years ago when she still sold pottery from her front porch in historic Montford. We were immediately drawn to her display of hand-thrown pots, dishes, and goblets. But what caught our eye (and sometimes disrupted traffic on Montford Ave.) was a series of vases sculpted in the image of her own heart-shaped derriere.

Later she moved into a space on Lexington Ave. and set up her potter's wheel in the storefront window. Crowds of people used to gather on the sidewalk to watch her spin wet clay into delicately designed works of functional art. Now her working gallery is in her home, but if you call for an appointment she'll be thrilled to open her doors to you. She's a wonderful story teller (that's her other profession) and no visit to Asheville is complete without a "Julie Payne Encounter." Call for an appointment to visit her home studio and purchase her work.

*Mark Peiser, **Armored Lips**, 1998, cast glass, 16" x 9" x 7.625"*

Penland School of Crafts
Penland Gallery
Penland, NC
828.765.6211

This institution is nationally-renowned for its curriculum, which is dedicated to the preservation, celebration, and creation of arts and crafts. Some of the most talented artists in the country teach at the rigorous Penland School, and this makes its gallery one of the most uniquely rich and diversified. Jewelry, photography, printmaking, fiber arts, blown and cast glass, woodwork, iron work, book arts, ceramics, and other kinds of artistic creations are available for purchase in the school's gallery. Call for hours and info about special events or exhibits.

INTRODUCING
A FEW LOCAL ARTISTS:

The artists listed below work from their studios and are available for commissioned work when time allows. Call for an appointment.

Vadim Bora
828.254.7959

This artist from the Caucuses region of Russia now lives and works in the historic Battery Hill district of Asheville where he maintains a gallery and studio. He offers custom portraits in bronze, oil, ceramic, pastel, or pencil and is well-known for his work which appears in exhibits and private collections throughout the city. He also teaches art classes in his studio. Call for information.

Tami Barry
828.232.1177

Whatever doesn't get expressed by this flamboyant actress while she's on center stage manifests in a practical fashion at her art studio. Tami creates functional, whimsical, and in her own words "dysfunctional" art. She does everything from collages and mosaics to hand painted furniture, floor coverings and glassware. She makes pieces for eclectic interior decoration from recycled furnishings and accessories and acrylic paint. Call her to find out about local gallery exhibits and tours of her own studio space.

Craig Comeau
828.281.4453

Craig is a carpenter by trade who is known for his artistic woodwork creations in Asheville's historic homes. But his passion is comic book drawings. When he lived in Boston he was in high demand by local bands for his eye-catching graphics. His pen and ink drawings characterized by high depth and contrast remind some of early Disney; others compare him to R. Crumb. He's in negotiations with national distributors for his comic book creations, but was still available for custom work the last time we spoke to him.

Katie Crawford
828.255.9170

Katie is well-known for her sketches, paintings, and traditional henna body adornment. She has been commissioned by nationally-known musicians to do their CD cover artwork, by local merchants to paint murals, and by this guidebook to provide pen and ink drawings and custom lettering. She's another artist in increasing demand, but she's still accepting local projects as this book goes to press.

Erin Marie Hunt
828.236.3810

We first met the elegant and reserved Erin at a jazz concert, where she was painting at an easel that stood directly to the right of the stage. At that time in her life she was looking for a pair of elbow-length satin evening gloves to wear while painting.

She incorporates mixed media into her abstract artwork, using paints, inks, and found objects like feathers, crystals, and stones. Her work is on display at some popular restaurants in Asheville, and those fortunate enough will find her creating new paintings at concerts and theatrical performances throughout Western North Carolina.

Nico
828.281.6210

Nico is the consummate romantic artist who creates exquisite line drawings and sketches, when not busy dancing the tango, singing, playing classical violin, restoring 18th Century French Provincial pieces, or scribbling poetic fragments on scraps of paper.

Nico's work appears from time to time in fashionable galleries and boutiques throughout Asheville and is also included in this book. You can find it decorating the pages which describe the Asheville music club scene. The sketches of facades of area nightclubs are typically "Nico."

Accoutrements Etc., Inc.
69 Madison Ave.
828.281.0332

This is the metalwork studio of "two women turning iron into gold" who have won national acclaim for their industrial art metal furniture. Noll Van Voorhis and Lana Garner create tables, chairs, lighting fixtures, and one-of-a-kind accessories from scrap metal. Their creations, which are in demand from designers nationwide, can be seen and purchased at the studio. Another metalwork artist, Cynthia Wynn, also works from this location. Call for hours or an appointment.

The work of Asheville sculptor Jhierry Lewis

© Alice Bain

THEATRE
DANCE
PERFORMANCE
ART

DAVID HOPES

David Hopes was born in Akron Ohio, attended Hiram College, Johns Hopkins, and earned his doctorate degree at Syracuse University. He came to Asheville in 1983 to direct the creative writing program at The University of North Carolina Asheville. He is the founder of Pisgah Players, Black Swan Theater Company, Urthona Gallery, and Urthona Press.

David's a provocative writer and poet, an engaging actor, and has a fabulous singing voice. His recent publication, A Childhood in the Milky Way, was nominated for both the National Book Award and the Pulitzer Prize. He gave the best lecture we've ever heard on the subject of Greek mythology, and is one of the professors at UNCA about which students say "Make sure you sign up for his class."

He also knows directions to all the best pubs in Ireland, which is the kind of knowledge that would convince us to consider him for an honorary Doctorate degree. And that's why we are thinking of collaborating with him on an underground guidebook to that mythological part of the universe.

David (who has played philosopher Karl Marx as well as politician Huey Long in recent productions) once wrote "The power of the artist is the only power I've ever really wanted." We asked him to share some of that power with our readers, and he graciously agreed:

If you could declare a holiday in Asheville, what would it celebrate?
No idiots on the opinion-editorial page of the Asheville Citizen Times today day.

If you were going to live on a deserted island for two years, what three things would you take, besides food and water?
A pen and supply of paper, an extra pair of glasses, and a really resourceful and accommodating friend.

What movie do you wish you had acted in?
I want to be Feste in the movie Twelfth Night. Or maybe what's-his-name in Field of Dreams who gets his lost ones back and everything comes out all right.

What Greek mythological figure would you like to be?
Glaukos, because he was a good man who got to be a god.

What's your favorite book?
<u>The Crock of Gold</u>.

What's your favorite vista in the Asheville area?
Get off the Parkway where it crosses Bent Creek Road the second time, high up, past Sleepy Gap. Turn left, walk about a mile, turn right up a grassy access road. Walk onto a high meadow with the Smokies spread out before you, blue and fantastic, rolling toward the horizon like a herd of dinosaurs.

What do you like most about Asheville?
1) Its potential. 2) The kids that were driven off Pack Square, shame on us!

What's the most important historical event in your lifetime?
The moon landing.

What is one place you would take a first-time visitor to Asheville?
The parking lot of Best Foods in Grace Plaza, to see the most beautiful tree in Asheville, a tremendous old sycamore.

What souvenir would you like to own?
A toy or an ornament dug from the ruins of Troy.

If you could speak to anyone, past or present, who would it be?
My own great grandmother before she came to America.

Whom do you admire?
Jane Goodall, Stephen Jay Gould, Matthew Fox, and Madonna, because they would not be diverted from their vision.

David Hopes
Ghost Rider of Lissadell, *1997*
acrylic on pasteboard, 7.5" x 9.5"

THEATRE
DANCE
PERFORMANCE
ART

Asheville is an exciting place when it comes to the arts, and dance and theater are no exception. To find out where you can see a performance, check the listings in the arts and entertainment sections of our local rags.

Asheville Center of Performing Arts
9 W. Walnut Street
828.258.3377

The Asheville Center of Performing Arts (ACPA) has three dance companies that work in their studio. The City Ballet of Asheville, Asheville Jazz Works, and the Asheville Tap Company led by Nicole Kemcza, Tracey Raper, and Mickey Bass respectively. ACPA Performs two shows a year at Diana Wortham, the shows being a collaborative effort between all three companies. Shows combine tap, jazz, modern, and ballet with performers ranging in age from three to sixty (with sometimes over one hundred performers).

Asheville Community Theater
35 E. Walnut Street
828.254.1320

The Asheville Community Theater (ACT) was organized in June of 1946. One month later, ACT staged the first amateur production of **Dark of the Moon**. ACT's second production, **The Glass Menagerie**, was directed by the young Charlton Heston and his wife Lydia. ACT focuses on popular main stage productions including musicals. ACT's rigorous performance schedule provides year round entertainment for all ages. ACT's Youththeater produces shows for and by local young talent. "ACT I Mystery Theater" performs locally for conventions, workshops, and fundraisers and has a full summer schedule of mystery train ride shows (contact the railway) with the Great Smokey Mountain Railway.

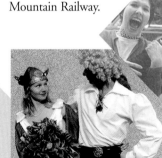

The Studio Theater
191 Lyman Street   828.254.6057
Mon-Fri, 9am-5pm and during scheduled rehearsals, performances and meetings

This theater on the French Broad River is an experimental venue for new plays, innovative productions, and any art event served by the rough-and-ready nature of a warehouse setting. It contains the headquarters of Black Swan Theater (David Hopes and Ellen Pfirrmann, directors), and Urthona Gallery (David Hopes, director).

One hot August night in 1945, thousands of people poured into the streets of downtown Asheville and began dancing with one another, to celebrate the end of World War II.

Asheville Contemporary Dance Theater

20 Commerce Street
828.254.2621

Asheville Contemporary Dance Theater (ACDT) is the oldest active modern dance company in Western North Carolina. Founded in 1979 by Susan Collard, the company currently has six members and six apprentices. ACDT is known for breaking new ground in performance art, frequently including live music, poetry, and puppetry in their shows. ACDT productions have effectively combined sculpture, photography, video, and multi-media art with dance. ACDT is also responsible for bringing French modern dance to the Asheville community through their exchange program with Sylvie Deluz of *Theatre Iseion* from Montpellier, France.

add dance

Together for the past six years, add dance continually captivates audiences with their contemporary performances of pure dance. The company is comprised of nine dancers with backgrounds in classical, modern, and ballet. They have more than thirty company performance pieces in their repertoire. Add dance offers a unique style of classically oriented lyrical modern dance and performs only one season per year, usually during the first or second week in June.

Bittersweet Productions

Bittersweet Productions has been bringing foreign talent to the Asheville area since 1993. Notable events have included *The Bolshoi Ballet* and *Theater Koleso* from the former USSR.

Bittersweet produced a touring production of *The Grapes of Wrath* that traveled to Kiev in 1994.

Black Swan
828.236.9444

Founded in 1995, as an outgrowth of the Pisgah Players (1989), Black Swan focuses on the production of previously unpublished plays. David Hopes, poet and literature professor at UNCA, is the primary motivating force behind Black Swan. Shows produced by Black Swan are typically cutting edge, avant garde works that might not receive show time in more traditional theaters.

Blue Plate Special

Katie Kremer has been the driving force behind the Blue Plate Special since its beginning in 1979. Blue Plate, a professional theater company, specializes in short innovative skits. A typical Blue Plate show involves between ten and fifteen skits throughout the course of an evening. Blue Plate represented NC in the Southeastern Theater Conference in 1998 and won first prize for community theater at the NC Theater Confer-ence in the same year.

The Green Door
on Carolina Lane
49 Broadway   828.258.9206

Carolina Lane used to be the center of Asheville's red light district and was supposedly within the jurisdiction of teenage Thomas Wolfe's newspaper route. According to the allegations of some historians, he routinely visited the alleyway in order to collect payments from prostitutes who were subscribers and they offered him special perks in lieu of cash. Nowadays, the alley is best known not for its red lights but for its green door. Plays, poetry readings, concerts, and other theatrical exhibitions take place at the Green Door, a hole-in-the-wall performance space in the basement of the Broadway Arts building.

JD Project
Founded in 1995 by Dana Davis and Julie Gillum, JD Project is a regional touring repertory modern dance company. With between five and nine dancers in the company, JD Project provides a style of dance that is accessible to a wide range of audiences. Props, spoken text, and visual projection are also used in their choreography.

Lipinsky Auditorium
(UNCA Cultural Events)
828.251.6584

Located on the picturesque campus of UNC-Asheville, this venue offers an exceptional variety of staged performances at incredible ticket prices. Lipinksy Auditorium recently hosted author David Sedaris signing books and reading from unpublished manuscripts. Later in the same season, UNCA screened the award-winning prison documentary *The Farm*.

Call for a schedule of events and prices but allow yourself time before the show to walk around campus where chipmunks, bunny rabbits, songbirds, or flowering trees of every description abound, depending upon the season.

Montford Park Players
828.254.5146
Summer Production Location:
Hazel Robinson Amphitheater
(Located behind the Montford Community Center at 34 Pearson Dr.)

Founded in 1973 by WNC native Hazel Robinson, the Montford Park Players (MPP) bill themselves as North Carolina's oldest existing Shakespeare festival. MPP is a non-profit community theater group organized by a board of volunteers.

Each summer MPP presents two full productions of Shakespeare, and each December, a production of Charles Dickens' *A Christmas Carol*. Since its inception, the primary goal of MPP has been to make high-quality theater accessible to the entire Western North Carolina community. As a result, summer shows are performed free of charge, although they do pass the hat at intermission. Ticket prices for *A Christmas Carol* are set only to cover the cost of renting theater space in the winter.

Southern Appalachian Repertory Theater
Mars Hill, NC   828.689.1239

Southern Appalachian Repertory Theater (SART) began performing in 1975, organized as a bicentennial project to celebrate Madison county's artistic contributions to WNC. Performing at Mars Hill College, SART specializes in producing new shows relevant to the people and culture of the Southern Appalachian region. Staging six shows each summer, this professional theater has premiered over forty original works. Their efforts are well worth the twenty-minute drive to Mars Hill from Asheville (take hwy 19/23 N and follow signs to Mars Hill College).

Fine Arts Theater
36 Biltmore Ave.
828.232.1536 (movie line)
828.232.0257 (office)

This beautifully renovated Art Deco movie house with two screening rooms, a big "critics' lounge" to sit around before or after the show, and a sufficient array of wines, beers, coffee drinks, and traditional movie snacks, is what every theatre ought to be. Specializing in first-run art and independent films, this theater often attracts great movies before the bigger cities get them. A state-of-the-art sound system insures that the technical aspects of the movie-watching experience won't suddenly remind you of how old the theater really is.

The first time this author attended a film in the theater, it was 1966 and he had to first show a fake identification card because he was thirteen years old and it was a XXX cinema that ran films like "Reefer Madness" and "Nympho Aliens". Thanks to the current owners, it has been preserved in its former grandeur but not its former notoriety as a smut house. Fortunately, this author's taste in movies has evolved such that the Fine Arts Theater is still his favorite, 33 years later.

The movie space is also available for private parties. Call for movie times and other details.

SPOKEN WORD PERFORMANCE

Spoken word performance, including poetry reading and story telling, is a long-standing tradition in these mountains.

Glenis Redmond, a former clinical and family counselor, teaches poetry and performance to folks of all ages. She is an inspiring, passionate performer who has earned herself a reputation as one of Asheville's most powerful and engaging poets.

Glenis Redmond

Julie Payne is one of Asheville's favorite young story tellers. She transforms ancient fables and classical tales into contemporary yarns and leaves her audiences laughing, crying, and stomping their feet for encores.

The venerable **Ray Hicks** is an internationally acclaimed story teller from Appalachia who spins "Jack Tales" in the old mountain tradition, transporting listeners to the world of his own earthy imagination with uplifting stories that please hearts of all ages and backgrounds. He has won praise from the National Endowment for the Arts and was profiled in The New Yorker magazine.

Julie Payne

These and many other spoken word artists can be seen and heard throughout the year during special events like **Tell It In The Mountains Storytelling Festival** or the **Poetry Alive! Festival**. Check bookstore bulletin boards, listings in local papers like Mountain Xpress, or the information desk at the Chamber of Commerce for information about scheduled spoken word performance events in the Asheville area.

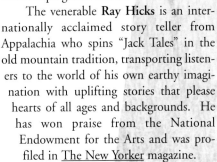

NIGHT LIFE & MUSIC

MUSICAL ASHEVILLE

Ruby Mayfield and Kat Williams in concert.

The local music scene is a mixed-bag which never ceases to mutate, innovate, and amaze. When Bob Dylan played at the Thomas Wolfe Auditorium, Doc Watson (a world famous old-timey music player who lives up the road a piece in Wilkes Barre) was in the audience. When the Blue Rags played at Asheville Pizza & Brewing Co. (formerly Two Moons), Corey Harris (an award-winning Delta blues player) and members of George Clinton's P-Funk band were in attendance. When the Cowboy Junkies played here, a local bass player was in their band. It's just that kind of town. In October of 1999, Elton John set aside his musical fashion extravaganza format for one night and instead put on a rather intimate solo show at the Civic Center. The performance earned him the Key To The City, presented by the Mayor. Three days later, Ani Difranco and her band positively transformed the Thomas Wolfe Auditorium while instigating the most powerful ovation any audience has offered in the entire history of the venue. Her revolutionary encore song "To The Teeth" earned her the key to the hearts of hundreds in attendance. Willie Nelson chose to celebrate his sixty-sixth birthday there, performing with his sister on keyboards to a sellout crowd.

Some of us got a chance to hang out in the back of Be Here Now club talking to international singer-songwriter sensation Jewel Kilcher after she warmed up the audience for a rather bland college circuit band.

Robert Moog, inventor of the Moog Synthesizer (which the Beatles and others used for its surreal sound effects) lives in Asheville and continues to invent exotic electronic musical tools. And don't forget that Dolly Parton's Dollywood Theme Park is right over the mountain from here, in case Elton needed to borrow a wig or some sequins on short notice. Asheville's just that kind of town.

John Phillip Sousa, Jimmie Rogers, Billie Holiday, Elvis Presley, Gene Autry, Sam Cooke, Otis Redding, James Brown, and Bill Monroe are among the stars who have performed in Asheville. And the fabric of the current music scene reflects their diverse influences.

Some of the best music in the world is performed free of charge in Asheville, on back porches, city sidewalks, and around campsites out in the mountains. If you're a player, you'll have no problem finding a jam to join.

PEGGY SEEGER

Peggy Seeger was the inspiration for the song "The First Time Ever I Saw Your Face." Her late husband, Ewan MacColl, wrote the song after seeing Peggy for the first time. (It is of particular local interest that the song was later recorded by Asheville native Roberta Flack. Indeed, the tune has been credited with launching Flack's international musical career.)

Peggy began to play the piano at age seven. By eleven she was transcribing music and was conversant with counterpoint and harmony. Over the next 25 years she learned to play guitar, five-string banjo, autoharp, Appalachian dulcimer, and English concertina. She majored in music at Radcliffe College in Cambridge, MA, where she began singing traditional songs professionally. From there she went to Holland where she studied Russian in the language of Dutch, if you can get your head around that. In 1959 she moved to London with MacColl, who was a British playright, dramatist, and singer / songwriter. After his death in 1989, she returned to live in the USA and eventually settled in Asheville.

Peggy has made seventeen solo records and has lost count of the work she has done with other performers. Probably over 100 recordings, she says. She is considered to be one of North America's finest singers of traditional songs and took a leading role in the British folk music revival, not only as a singer and instrumentalist but as a songwriter and activist. Her recordings are included in the Folkways Collection of the Smithsonian Institute.

Peggy's mother was Ruth Crawford Seeger, one of America's greatest female composers and the first woman to be awarded the Guggenheim Fellowship Award for Music. Peggy's father was Charles Louis Seeger, a pioneer musicologist and the inventor of the melograph, an electronic tool for notating music.

Peggy's half-brother Pete Seeger is considered the father (now grandfather) of the American folk-music revival. He has probably had more influence upon the development of modern folk music than any other single individual.

Her brother Mike is a virtuoso on several dozen instruments. In addition to enjoying a well-established musical career of his own, Mike has contributed significantly to the preservation and perpetuation of old timey music. It was Mike Seeger who persuaded North Carolina native and family acquaintance Elizabeth Cotten to take up performing at the age of sixty. She became a legendary singer / songwriter and influenced musicians like John Fahey, Joan Baez, Joni Mitchell, and Bob Dylan with her idiosyncratic "Cotten-Picking" guitar style.

The Seeger family has been involved in folk music in the USA for about half a century. As a matter of fact, the revival and evolution of American folk music probably owes more to the Seeger family than to any other single source.

Peggy Seeger is mother of three and grandmother of seven. She lives in our Montford neighborhood, where she is an elegant, proactive asset to the community. And, yes, she is an exceptionally attractive woman whose face is easy to behold and remember but hard to forget.

We were blessed with the opportunity to talk to Peggy and ask her a few questions:

What's the most important historical event in your lifetime?
I remember the headlines when Hiroshima was bombed. The headlines were about 4 inches high. I didn't realize the significance of it because I was only 10.

What do you most admire in a person?
Self-awareness.

What three things would you take if you were going to live on a desert island?
A musical instrument, a partner and some sun oil to keep from burning.

What's the strangest thing that ever happened to you at a show?
Most of them have been distressing. Like the night the auto-harp keys flew out. A screw had fallen out and all of the auto harp keys fell out all over the audience. They were all scrambling about in the dark for the screws and springs.

Oh, and the time when the banjo peg kept slipping so I looked in my banjo case and realized my screwdriver wasn't there. I said, "Does anybody have a screwdriver?" and at least ten blokes got up with screwdrivers. One of them was this long (gestures about 2 feet with her hands).

And there was the time in Montreal when Ewan was in the middle of "Lord Randall" and the curtain came down because the union said they would only work until ten pm.

What music are you listening to at the moment?

For pleasure I listen to the old divas like Billie Holiday, Ella Fitzgerald, Patsy Cline, Dolly Parton. Depends what mood I am in.

What's your idea of an ideal way to spend a day in Asheville?

I like sitting in restaurants with friends. I like places that don't have loud music and if there are enough people there you don't need music at all. That way you can eavesdrop on other people's conversations.

Why did you choose to move here?

I wanted a small town where I could get to know people. I wanted the mountains, the traditional music, a front porch swing, and people walking by who you could say hello to.

When you have visitors come to Asheville, where do you take them?

Grove Park Inn. If they are here on a Sunday morning we go for brunch. I take them to the Grove Park Inn after Gold Hill, because Gold Hill has such good coffee. I take them to the wedding cake building, the City Hall. That's one of the main reasons I stayed here. I came up Pack Square, looked up and just fell in love with that building. It's so beautiful. So generally I'll walk them around the town center or I'll drive them up Town Mountain Road.

What's the best compliment you've received lately?

The gardener told me he liked my cup of tea! Even better than that, he made the tea as I showed him. That's a real compliment, if you taught somebody something.

If you could create a holiday in Asheville to celebrate something, what would it be?

Older women friends. There are lots of older women here that I really enjoy the company of.

RAYMOND KELLY

Raymond Kelly, a Vietnam veteran and retired computer systems expert for the federal government, has been drumming professionally since junior high school. He learned to play by ear at age nine. By age thirteen, he was playing for local bands in the predominantly African American nightclubs that used to thrive along Biltmore Avenue. Because he was underage, the clubs had to sneak him in the back door for his gigs. He hid in the shadows at the back of the stage behind his drumset and, during set breaks, he'd wait in the alley, to avoid being spotted by the vice squad. His band *Bermuda* was the headliner mainstage attraction at Asheville's first Bele Chere Festival. Now he's the bandleader for *Information Network*, one of Asheville's most popular dance bands.

What do you admire in a person?
Someone who ain't afraid to tell you how they feel about it. Somebody who doesn't put on airs.

What's the most important historical event of your lifetime?
Well, even though there was Martin Luther King's death I'd have to say it was when President Kennedy got killed and I was in the fourth grade. They let out school. It was sad, but we were just little kids and we were so happy because they dismissed school. That's how I remember it. I'll never forget that.

What's one place you'd take a first-time visitor to Asheville?
Downtown. And then I'd take them up to Mount Mitchell, which I think is one of the most beautiful sites around here.

What do you consider an ideal way to spend the day in Asheville?
You might not want to print that (laughter). I like to sleep late, read the paper, and then hang out with my friends and listen to someone play music, or play it myself.

If you could declare a holiday in Asheville what would it celebrate?
If it's 12 people on the City Council and I see six blacks and six whites, I believe that'll be the best holiday I've ever seen.

What's your favorite meal?
Picnic shoulder ham, potato salad, and collard greens.

Favorite record?
I guess Aretha Franklin's "Respect." My Mom, when I was a little kid, played that constantly.

If you could have any souvenir, what would it be?
I'd like to have a video of the time when I was young and I went out with a friend of mine and another fellow and we got into some devilment. It almost cost one guy his life. Some guys were shooting at us and we thought he got shot. The next day we were crying, wondering how we were going to tell his mother. And he came walking down the street, whistling. He wasn't shot. That was the happiest day of my life.

If you were going to be on a desert island for two years, what three things (besides food and water) would you take?
My drums, my bass player, and then I'd say an Air Force friend of mine. The guy I did military time with. I met him out on the drill. The sergeant had me teach him how to march. We hung around each other just like we knew each other for life. He's my man.

What's the strangest thing you've ever witnessed at a show when you were playing music?
A guy got shot. I was seventeen years old at the time. The guy who ran our band, the bass player, told me to keep playing. I said, "No, there's shooting going on!" He said, "Keep playing, keep playing." We stopped playing until after the ambulance got him out of there. Then we finished the show.

What's your best memory of a music show?
That was in about 1967. We went out to UNCA for a Battle of the Bands competition. We were the only black band. We didn't think we'd get picked. When the judges came out, we had won, over all the white groups. That's when I first said, "Finally, we've been treated fair." It was all white judges. Then we won it the next year. And the next year. Then they told us we couldn't be in it anymore. They wanted to let somebody else have a chance to win.

What makes Asheville home to you?
I've been here since I was three, and it's a good, safe town. Asheville's a laid-back town. I can possibly leave my door unlocked and nobody will come in.

RALPH LEWIS

Ralph Lewis first picked up "a scrappy little mandolin that we had around the house" around age five. He's been playing music for more than sixty five years.

Ralph grew up on a farm in rural Madison County, the youngest of seven brothers in a musical family. His father was a bluegrass picker and his two older brothers, Blanco and Erwin, were successful professional bluegrass musicians by the time Ralph was a tot. When his oldest brother, Blanco, was killed in World War II, the young Ralph headed to Niagara Falls where the *Lewis Brothers Band* (featuring Blanco and Erwin) was based. Ralph stepped into his big brother's shoes and the *Lewis Brothers Band* blazed on. Ralph eventually fronted his own bluegrass band in the Detroit area and did a stint in the Navy before moving back to his beloved Western North Carolina and playing with a series of respected bluegrass groups, including the *Piney Mountain Boys*.

In the mid 1970s, Bill Monroe, the father of bluegrass music (he invented the style of music known as bluegrass and gave it the name), invited Ralph to become one of his legendary *Bluegrass Boys*, a role he fulfilled to the hilt for more than two years. These days, Ralph is happy showcasing his mandolin (and guitar) prowesss with his

sons, Don (fiddle, banjo, guitar, and bass) and Marty (guitar, bass, and pedal-steel guitar). Along with drummer Richard Foulk they are the progressive bluegrass quartet *Sons of Ralph*. And progressive is probably an understatement. They are just as likely to play traditional bluegrass tunes with reggae beats and electric guitars as they are to do a bluegrass rendition of a Jimi Hendrix hit. This distilled little band represents some of the best talent to ever take an Asheville stage.

We caught up with Ralph Lewis at a cookout at his second home in Madison County's "Lewis Holler."

Who do you most admire?

I would have to say that would be my family. But other than that, I'd say my mentor would be Mr. (Bill) Monroe. He was a great musician and he was a real straightforward person; he was a great guy. He didn't get to go to school very much. He had to drop out at an early age, in fourth or fifth grade, and that always really bothered him. He told me that's the one thing that really bothered him, that he couldn't converse or convey himself to people. He had a great complex about that. I told him, I said "If the Queen of England, which we played in front of, thinks you're great, I think you're doing okay."

What do you think is the best thing about Asheville's music scene, right now?

Well, really I think the mix of different styles, different kinds of music is the best thing. I don't think you'd find a city anywhere the size of Asheville or even a lot bigger that would have as many bands and as much live music. Asheville and Western North Carolina have been known for having high quality music since the beginning and it's continued. And Asheville's the hot bed for all that now.

If you had to name the single most important event in your life thus far, what would it be?

Well, getting married would be one of them. And one of the greatest things in my life has been to see both my sons play on the Grand Ole Opry Stage. Marty played with us in the mid-'70s when I was with Bill Monroe, and then I got to see Don play the Opry just this year (1999).

What's your idea of a perfect way to spend the day?

Catching trout fish and eating ramps with branch lettuce, that'd be my perfect day. (Author's note: See our section on Annual Festivals for an explanation of what "ramps" are.)

If you had to pick your favorite meal, what would it be?

Ramp meatloaf.

If you were going to live on a deserted island for two years, what three things (besides food and water) would you take along?

Let's see. I would *not* take golf clubs.

This is a rough one. (laughs) Probably I would take my instrument, my mandolin (Lewis' son Don interjects "He'd take his 'instrument' and a mandolin!"). I'd take my mandolin and also, let's see. A frying pan and two rabbits.

If you could have one question answered, what would it be?

How do you control aging? Or reverse aging? Because, you know, when you get up around where I am, you can look back and see parts dropping off.

You've lived in this area pretty much your whole life. What are the best things about living here?

I guess probably what draws more people than anything to this area are our distinct four seasons. You know what winter, fall, summer and spring really are here, and I think that's one of the strongest points. Plus, the mountains and the people. The mountain people.

What is it that makes Southerners different from other people?

Well, I think we were raised a little slower and learned to get more living in a day or a week, and in the meantime, in kind of doing things slow—walking instead of running—we experience things better and enjoy them more. If you're born running and don't slow down, you don't know you're running. Somebody needs to tell you to slow down a little bit and smell the flowers.

DOWNTOWN NIGHTLIFE & MUSIC VENUES

Asheville Civic Center

87 Haywood Street
828.259.5544
Tickets by phone: 828.251.5505

Elvis Presley, Bob Dylan, Elton John, Ani DiFranco, Tori Amos, Joan Baez, John Prine, Willie Nelson and George Clinton have all performed at the Civic Center. The Thomas Wolfe Auditorium is one of the region's best medium-sized venues for good seats and great acoustics. The larger downstairs venue is big but still has an overall seating capacity limited enough in numbers to retain a critical degree of closeness between the audience and the performers.

Asheville Pizza & Brewing Company

675 Merrimon Ave.
828.254.1281
Daily 10:30am-1pm

Great American style pizza (the author's Mom has a standing account at the place, she likes it so darned much), Thursday night beer specials, pool tables, air hockey, and dollar movies. Free kid's movies every Saturday and Sunday at 11:30am. Great concerts featuring local, regional, and national acts. Call for a concert schedule and for special event info.

The Basement at Almost Blue

Beneath 92 Patton Ave.
(entrance in back alley off Coxe St.)
828.285.0808
Daily 4pm until

Basement nightclubs can be like moldy smoke-filled cellars, but this one reminds us more of an upbeat roadside diner. It's got fresh baby blue and pastel gray paint, an attractive, well-stocked beer and wine bar, and a friendly atmosphere perpetuated by the good-hearted folks who run it. They also own the record store upstairs. They have *great* taste in music, *great* connections to the music community, and a *great* space to party. Plus they have draft beer from $2.50, bottles from $1.50, wine, and light snacks.

Be Here Now

5 Biltmore Avenue
828.258.2071
Call for ticket info and box office hours

For years it was downtown's only major music venue. Be Here Now consistently showcases the top names in music from all genres. Popular songwriter Jewel Kilcher, internationally acclaimed blues diva Rory Block, folk singer Richie Havens, mountain music maestro Doc Watson, blues legends Jimmy Rogers (in one of the very last concerts before his death), the "grandfather of the British blues revival" John Mayall, the inimitable Los Lobos, performance poet Patti Smith, jazz-fusion giant John McLaughlin, dobro master Jerry Douglas, and revolutionary song-

*Don Lewis fiddling around
at Jack of the Wood Pub.*

writer Ani DiFranco have all played this venue.

The club metamorphoses from sit-down listening room to dance club, according to what each night's music dictates. The club generally opens at 4 p.m. to accommodate the grab-a-beer-or-cocktail-after-work crowd.

The New Grey Eagle
185 Clingman Ave.
828.232.5800
*Mon-Sat 4pm until
(most shows start at 9pm)
Mondays: Contra Dances
Tuesdays: Open Mic Night*

Fantastic listening room featuring local, regional, and national acts. This spacious, well-designed music hall attracts some of the best shows of any club in Western North Carolina, because the owners put music first and foremost.

Arlo Guthrie, Kelly Willis, Corey Harris, David Wilcox, and scores of other artists are right at home at the Grey Eagle. You will be too, when you sink into the comfy couch which is right in front of the stage. This club is located at the end of the legendary Thunder Road, which was featured in the movie classic of the same name. Good karma for a great location for fine and dandy entertainment.

Tell 'em we sent ya; we're gonzo about this particular joint and the folks who run it and we love bragging about it.

Jack of the Wood Pub
95 Patton Avenue
828.252.5445
*Mon-Fri 4pm-2am, Sat Noon-2am
Sun 1pm-2am*

Owner Joe Eckert measures the success of this authentic Irish pub by how comfy its patrons feel on any given night. "One guy told me coming here was like staying in his living room, except with really good beer," Eckert notes. Jack of the Wood is indeed the closest you can get to a real Irish pub in Asheville. It's cozy, low-lighted, and, perhaps most importantly, drenched with rich, brewed-on-the-premises Green Man Ales. Try the Wee Heavy, the Nutbrown Ale, the Cream Ale, or the mighty Porter . . . the list varies from day to day.

As for the music to be enjoyed seven nights a week, Jack of the Wood leans heavily on bluegrass, mountain music and raucous Celtic sounds. The Sons of Ralph, one of the most talent-laden bands in town, performs at this pub regularly, to standing-room-only audiences. If you want to experience the flavor of Asheville's musical mix, catch their act; they are one of the most progressive little bluegrass-influenced bands in the United States.

The New French Bar
1 Battery Park Ave.
828.252.3685
Daily 11am-1am (or later)

The NFB (If you want to pass as a local hipster, it's essential that you refer to it by these initials.) offers prime Asheville people-watching space — from upscale shoppers headed toward Wall Street's cobblestone sidewalks and quaint shops to colorful downtown street characters headed we're not sure where. This place rates high amongst local bars on the hip, sexy, and romantic scale.

But if you're in the mood to hide out, never fear: The dimly lit NFB offers cozy tables away from the action, too. As for libations, besides the regular large selection of beers, wines and harder spirits, the NFB's nightly drink specials are fast becoming legendary. And the NFB features a different menu each day — always, true to the bistro's name, prepared with a French flair — offering rich homemade soups, specialty sandwiches, hot plates and signature items like the baked-brie-and-Granny-Smith-apple plate and the warm spinach and artichoke dip served over toasted pita chips. They have the best chocolate mousse in town, at a great price, after-dinner apéritifs, and premium cigars.

If you go clubbing and drink or imbibe other intoxicants, please don't try to operate any heavy machinery afterwards, especially the automotive variety. We wouldn't want you to spend your hard-earned vacation in a local jail or hospital, because the last time we reviewed the music scene in those places it was worse than drab. It just plain sucked.

O. Henry's
59 Haywood St.
828.254.1891
Mon-Fri 1pm until 2am
Sat-Sun Noon until-2am

This members-only club is open seven days a week with two levels, pool tables, a dance floor, weekly live entertainment, and drink specials.

It's the oldest "Gay and Lesbian Friendly" bar in Western North Carolina. We think its owners deserve the Key to the City of Asheville for their pioneering efforts in establishing it as such, long before other establishments followed suit in what has become one of the most Gay and Lesbian friendly towns in America. Better yet, maybe it oughta be added by special provision to the North Carolina Historical Register. That's wishful thinking, but it comes from our pride of knowing that this socially historic little pub is in our own fair city. Call for information about membership and special events.

Stella Blue

31 Patton Avenue
828.236.2424
*Call for hours and schedule
of performances*

Stella Blue is marked by psyche-delic, 3-D art, comfortable barstools, way-cool mood lighting, and a top-flight sound system.

The club most often showcases up-and-coming young bands, like Athens' Albert Hill and Atlanta's Soul Miner's Daughter. It's the Asheville club-of-choice for young slide-guitar virtuoso Derek Trucks (nephew of Allman Brothers drummer Butch Trucks). Hot local bands like hip-hop favorites M.C. Huggs and the Groove Crust pack the club frequently, as do a host of Dead-inspired jam bands like Refried Confusion and the Ominous Seapods. A recent coup was New York City jazz trendsetters the Sex Mob. Internationally known theatrical showman El Vez rocked the house with his Elvis-inspired extravaganza.

Brevard Music Center

Brevard, NC
1.800.648.4523

The Music Center draws some of the most talented music students and teachers as well as internationally-acclaimed performers and guest artists, to its beautifully serene 140 acre cam-pus on the outskirts of Brevard. Over 50 performance events are held during the summer months, including some of the best jazz, blues, and classical music in the region. Call for schedule of events and ticket information.

Tressa's

28 Broadway
828.254.7072
Mon-Fri 4pm-2am, Sat 7pm-2:30pm

This is the hot place in town to see and be seen on any given night. Local and international celebrities frequent the bar, as do all sorts of glamorous people who are from some superior planet in the universe, as far as we can tell. This is a swanky bar with a relaxed New Orleans atti-tude where the folks are friendly and the atmosphere is downright sexy. Great music from jazz and blues to funk and salsa. Not only are the people in the place gorgeous, the room is beautiful too...the owners won a prestigious Griffin Award for their restoration of the building.

"Nothing is so effective in keep-ing one young and full of lust as a dis-criminating palate thoroughly satis-fied at least once a day," reads the cover of Tressa's bar menu. A first-class selection of drinks ranging from the finest single malt whiskeys to Dom Perignon by the bottle and a scrumptious light fare menu. Fine cigars are avail-able as well.

Tressa'a Jazz & Blues Club

Vincent's Ear

68 N. Lexington Ave.
828.259.9119
Mon-Thu Noon-Midnight
Fri-Sat Noon-2am, Sun 3pm-Midnight

This basement cafe (with a cool upstairs lounge) has earned a reputation for bringing some of the most unique music to town, where it's performed in the small brick basement to standing-room-only audiences. This is the premier place in Asheville to find avant garde music at its freshest. Vincent's also has a wonderful outdoor patio with shade trees and chess tables. Great selection of coffee drinks, sandwiches, and desserts (as well as beer and wine) at really reasonable prices.

The Asheville Symphony

Thomas Wolfe Auditorium
(Asheville Civic Center)
87 Haywood St.
828.254.7046

Under the direction of maestro Robert Hart Baker, the Asheville Symphony provides uplifting and outstanding entertainment. World renowned guests performers (like bass-baritone John Cheek and sensational violinist Philip Quint) add to the excitement of each season. Call for ticket and schedule information.

Elvis performed at the Asheville Civic Center in August of 1975, and his father Vernon Presley was in attendance and came onstage for photos. Some say Elvis used a pistol to shoot out the television tube in his hotel room later that night, but last time we channeled his spirit, he said he didn't remember doing any such thing. Elvis was scheduled to play again on August 26, 1977, but his death ten days earlier canceled the show.

There's at least one fellow in Asheville who claims to be Elvis or a version thereof. But you'll find out about that soon enough, if you spend much time on our streets. A lesser-known fact that we are proud to reveal is that one of the contributing writers for this guidebook is related to Elvis as a cousin. Marsha Mae Barber is an award-winning writer and editor who once sang into the same microphone that her cousin Elvis used to record his first record in Memphis. That's the gospel truth and we think it proves that this guidebook was maybe inspired by Elvis all along, as part of his plan.

MUSIC STROLL THROUGH DOWNTOWN

The Basement

Even those of us who get a regular dose of downtown music sometimes have the sweet quandary of indecision regarding which show to catch on a given night. Here's our recommended formula for working through the music scene impasse:

Pick up a free copy of *Mountain Xpress*, the region's most popular alternative newspaper. Check the Club Land listings, Smart Bets page, and feature articles in the Arts and Entertainment section, to get the scoop on what's going on. Then jot down your top choices and go for it. But if you can't decide, walk the downtown club circuit and sample the bands from the sidewalk. Then zero in on the club that gets your mojo working.

Keep in mind that this music stroll is by no means comprehensive. There are a few venues in town offering awesome music, which are not included here. And there are venues out a short distance which are fabulous too. But this stroll will give you a pretty representative overview of the downtown clubs, without wearing the soles off of your shoes. After all, you need those shoes for dancing, which is Asheville's unofficial favorite pastime.

From the Civic Center on Haywood St. (across from the Basilica with its romantic tolling bells), walk into town past Malaprop's Bookstore, which offers in-store concerts from time to time. At the corner of Haywood and College St., turn right past Karmasonics music store. They also have singer/songwriter performances on special occasions.

Follow College St. as it parallels the small city park, and you'll come to Jack of the Wood (95 Patton Ave.) pub. This is a great place to get the flavor of a neighborhood Asheville pub while hearing some of the most talented musicians in America, up close and personal. Also situated near the Coxe Ave. intersection is The Basement. It's a fun and cozy little club which happens to be run by some folks who are kin to members of the *Allman Brothers Band*. It's beneath Almost Blue record shop, with an entrance in the alleyway just a few yards from the Coxe Ave./Patton Ave. intersection.

Head back up the other side of Pritchard Park along Patton Ave. and you'll find Shotzy's, a new club still forging its musical identity. It's in the classic S&W Cafeteria Building with its knockout Art Deco architecture and interior design. (Translation: Even if there is no music playing, it can be an interesting place to stop by long enough to have a drink because it's in one of America's coolest-looking buildings.). Proceed to 31 Patton and the Stella Blue club, which showcases local talent but also brings in regional, national, and even international acts (El Vez brought down the house with his imported theatrics).

Stella Blue

Be Here Now

Continue uphill to Pack Square. The street to the right is named Biltmore Ave., and when it goes to the left it changes names to Broadway. Hang a right to nearby Be Here Now (5 Biltmore Ave.) which is sort of the granddaddy of downtown music venues. Performers like Jewel, John Mayall, Ani Difranco, and Patti Smith have graced its stage. Or turn left and proceed to Tressa's at 28 Broadway. This New Orleans-style bar is known for its sexy, snazzy, swanky-yet-relaxing ambience. This is where Glamour goes to let her hair down and shake it all around. From Tressa's, continue along Broadway to Walnut St. and go left. Turn right at Lexington and go to 68 N. Lexington Ave. where Vincent's Ear is tucked away behind a gothic-gated patio. This is the place to hear the kind of music the other clubs probably can't handle. Until Asheville gets its own truly alternative music club, this place will fill the gaps in that aspect of our cultural void.

To return to Haywood St., backtrack up Lexington Ave. to Walnut St., turn right, and climb the hill. The Civic Center, where you started this musical walkabout, is up the street to the right.

Not far from downtown are two clubs we recommend: Asheville Pizza & Brewing Company at 675 Merrimon (254.1281). and Grey Eagle at 185 Clingman Ave. (232.5800). Their locations don't lend themselves to inclusion in a walking tour of downtown, but they are worth checking out if you are looking for music because they offer some of the best.

Tressa's

The sultry torchsong singer Vendetta Cream.

WALK-INS WELCOME

If you are visiting Asheville and want to go out dancing, but are in need of a lesson, not to worry. Arthur Murray was one of the first to offer dance classes in Asheville, back at the turn of the century. He had a studio at the Battery Park Hotel where he taught all the new moves one could want to keep up with the popular dance scene.

Nowadays, at the other end of the century, several professional dance studios offer classes on a walk-in (and dance your way out) basis. Call for schedules and prices but be sure to clarify if the price quoted is for one person or for a couple. Check local newspapers like <u>Mountain Xpress</u> for listings of others not included here. We listed a few for you to sample:

Asheville Center of Performing Arts
828.258.3377

Visitors are welcome to take ballet, tap, jazz, modern, or acrobatics classes at the Asheville Center of Performing Arts. All of the teachers are enthusiastic, well-trained and qualified professionals.

Broadway Arts Swing Dance
at The Broadway Arts Building
828.258.9206

These are exceptional dances, and are very popular with the locals. The space evokes the feeling of an indoor garden party with a wonderful hardwood floor. Dances are held once a month with a live swing band, except during June and July, and include a free lesson beforehand. Since the building is a gallery full of delicate, expensive stuff, it is not suitable for children under twelve.

Dance Lovers USA
828.658.2242

If you want to spruce up on your couple dancing call Dance Lover's America. They specialize in American ballroom styles, which include cha cha, rumba, swing, shag, tango, and waltz. Call to set up a private lesson.

Fletcher School of Dance and the Asheville Academy
828.252.4761

Take a drop-in dance class at the oldest most respected dance studio in town. Children or adults are invited to drop in and take any of the classes. Classes are offered in ballet, modern, jazz, tap, pointe, composition, dance history, acrobatics, and creative movement for preschoolers. All the classes are fabulous.

MOONSHINE

Over 200 years ago, Congress imposed an excise tax on distilled spirits. But many folks in the mountains ignored the legislation and continued perfecting and selling their homemade liquor.

Nowadays, Asheville-area moonshine is primarily sold to markets in the urban Northeast, including Philadelphia, Baltimore, and Washington, D.C. It sells for around $35 a gallon. But a goodly amount stays in this neck of the woods. If you attend enough Bluegrass festivals, you'll sooner or later encounter it around a campfire.

The liquor is usually distilled from sugar and a blend of grains used to fatten pigs (oats, rye, and corn). But the best quality moonshine is made primarily from corn. During harvest time, apple or peach brandy is the drink of choice, and consumers are willing to pay an extra twenty bucks or more per gallon to get it.

We know a city-dweller who used to make moonshine for personal consumption, in his apartment. He used a portable apartment-size still connected to the kitchen sink. The high-tech copper cooker was given to him by a New Englander who created it from scrap metal.

Our most colorful moonshine story was told to us by a family practice physician who lives near Asheville:

"I work in a rural county medical center. If I get sick and can't see my patients, it's a real hardship for the community because I'm the only doctor for miles. One day I called in sick, during a flu epidemic. Within hours the local deputy sheriff showed up at my doorstep with a jar of clear liquid which he said would cure me. It was moonshine. He delivered it while on duty, in uniform, in a marked patrol car. He said, 'I keep a jar of it in a file cabinet at the office for emergencies'. I drank it, slept all day, and was back at work in the morning, feeling fine."

But moonshine doesn't necessarily cure what ails you. All homemade liquor contains enough alcohol to fuel a drag racer, and alcohol poisoning can be lethal. Some batches contain lead, at levels high enough to kill you.

You'll wish you'd stuck with microbeer when your leaded blood starts setting off metal detectors. And if you're the kind of passenger who likes to smuggle a flask of moonshine onto the plane, you don't need the unwanted attention from airport security. They'll spot you soon enough.

We've observed folks under the influence of moonshine whose behavior was downright peculiar, at best. Barking at the neighbor's dogs, wearing nothing but a bearskin toga to church, and trying to instruct a sofa to play "Foggy Mountain Breakdown" on the banjo are among the warning signs that you've gotten hold of an award-winning batch of corn mash.

Good quality moonshine is similar in taste to agave tequila. It has an unforgettable aroma, like magnolia blossoms soaked in rainwater and then marinated in witch hazel. Most folks drink it "neat", like single malt scotch.

Here's one piece of advice passed along by a seasoned old timer: "Shake the jar real good a time or two, not too vigorously, just enough. If little champagne bubbles rise to the surface of the moonshine, that's an indicator of good liquor. Sip it, don't slam it back like a shooter. And give it time to get into your system or you'll wind up drinking way more than you bargained for. Don't drink anything else with it or you might get sick, and that would be a terrible waste of good moonshine. Don't even think about driving a car or tractor and don't take your electric guitar into the shower with you, no matter how good it sounds at the time."

CONTRA DANCES ♥

New in town and want to meet some people in a hurry? Try contra dancing.

Contra Dancing is an ole timey dance style not unlike Scottish or Irish folk dancing or American square dancing. Folks in these parts are wild about it and are especially enthusiastic when it comes to teaching newcomers the simple steps.

The preferred method of instruction is to grab you off the bench and include you with unabashed gusto. The first time this author tried it he felt like a piece of dough in a game of swing-the-biscuit, but soon he got the hang of it and was reeling and jigging and swirling like a dancin' fool. Someone even claims they heard him yell "Hee-ha-yippy-yippy-yo!" but that hasn't been officially verified.

The cool thing about Contra Dancing is that it's not just a "couple thing," it's a community dance. During one song, everyone gets to dance with everybody else at least a time or two. By the end of an hour, you're on a first name basis with a whole room full of other dancin' fools. Next thing you know, you're fast friends...or maybe even slow-dancing sweethearts.

To find one in progress, you can do what this writer did one night. He took his guitar downtown and began strumming and singing, "Buffalo gals won't you come out tonight and dance by the light of the moon." Sure enough, they came skippin' by in no time at all, shouting, "Hot diggidy!"

More conventional type people (including yourself, most likely) can just check local papers and music halls for announcements of scheduled Contra Dances. They are a regular part of Asheville life, so rest assured that you'll find one pronto, Buckaroo.

> They say that you can test the quality of moonshine by lighting a match under a teaspoonful of it. If it burns with a true-blue flame, straight up, that's a good sign. If it sparks and starts to sputter and hiss, it's dangerous. I guess that might work with people too.
>
> — *The Old Timer*

134

ARCHITECTURE & LITERARY
HISTORY STROLL

EDIBLE PARK

WALL STREET TOUR

DOWNTOWN
EXCURSIONS

ARCHITECTURE & LITERARY HISTORY STROLL

(WITH STOPS ALONG THE WAY AT BOOKSTORES & CAFES)

We are present in the details of our lives; our presence confirms itself and leaves footprints and palm lines in the form of the architecture, literature, and social conversation of our world. This tour is intended to provide you with a sampling of Asheville's architecture, while pausing along the way to reflect on some of its literary history.

F. Scott Fitzgerald, Wilma Dykeman, Pat Conroy, Gail Godwin, Kurt Vonnegut, Charles Olson, Robert Creeley, Aldous Huxley, Patti Smith, Allen Gurganus, Michael Rumaker, Bob Dylan, and favorite homeboy Tom Wolfe have all walked these streets, collecting imagery. We encourage you to do likewise, and to use the journal pages scattered throughout this guidebook to record your poetic impressions.

The following is our cultural strut across Asheville, conveniently fueled by caffeine, bagels, books, and coffeecake *(Note: This writer prefers to begin the excursion a few minutes before the top of the hour, in order to enjoy the sound of the tolling of the bells at the Basilica St. Lawrence.):*

Basilica of St. Lawrence

Leaving the Chamber of Commerce, take a left along Haywood St. until it crosses O. Henry Ave. William Sydney Porter, alias O. Henry, for whom this street is named, is remembered as an author of over 300 popular short stories including *The Gift of the Magi.* Porter lived here after a sequence of events which involved working in a Texas bank where some money went-a-missing, fleeing to Honduras, returning to be with his ailing wife, serving three years in prison, and (from his jail cell) launching a successful career as an author. He came to Asheville late in life, to marry Sara Coleman, his childhood heart throb. They were both North Carolina natives from Greensboro.

Continue to the Basilica Saint Lawrence, one of Spanish (Catalan) architect Rafael Guastavino's most brilliant projects. This grand example of Spanish Baroque Revival style architecture was created without wood or iron; it was built entirely of mortar, brick, stone, and tile. Guastavino was internationally known for his "cohesive tile construction" methods.

He combined Portland cement with tile to create self-supporting domes of tremendous weight. The entire tiled dome of the

Basilica was built without scaffolding. Craftsmen, many of them local African American masons, laid about 18 inches of tile per day. By the next morning, the section they laid the previous day was dry, cured, and had enough structural integrity to support the weight of the workers themselves. They literally stood on their previous day's work to continue adding to the structure, until the last row of tiles closed off

the center of the dome. Hidden inside the Basilica's towers are spiraling staircases. In the traditional Catalan architectural style, they are constructed in such a way that they appear to support themselves, creating a sort of structural and optical illusion.

English sculptor Fred Miles, who came to Asheville to work on the Biltmore Estate, carved the life-size limestone figures above either side

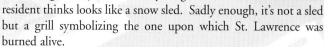

of the entranceway. Because a halo around one figure looked like a baker's cap from below, it was chiseled away a short time after being created. The figure of St. Lawrence, a patron saint and religious martyr, was sculpted holding an object that one young Asheville resident thinks looks like a snow sled. Sadly enough, it's not a sled but a grill symbolizing the one upon which St. Lawrence was burned alive.

The Basilica used to be open 24 hours a day. We went inside one midnight and thought we were experiencing an epiphany because the song "Free Bird" was vibrating inside the vaulted ceiling. Then we realized that there was a *Lynard Skynard* concert next door at the Civic Center and that we were actually listening to the live encore as it hummed through the Basilica's dome. The song has never sounded so good as it did at that exquisite moment. Because of problems with vandalism, the caretakers of the church were compelled to start locking its doors at night. But if you pass by at the stroke of the hour, you can still hear the sound of bells tolling from the twin towers. It has a way of drawing you back to the turn of the century, if you're willing to go.

The architect Guastavino died the year before the church was

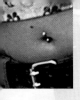

completed (by his son) and is interred in a crypt inside the Basillica. Visit during open hours and give yourself the opportunity to be inspired by the gifts he left behind for us to celebrate.

Now cross the intersection to the side of Haywood St. where the Civic Center is located. **Bob Dylan, who was nominated for a Nobel Prize in Literature by Beat poet Allen Ginsberg**, performed there in 1997. **Ani Difranco** visits this venue regularly, redefining poetic songwriting and spoken word theater with each fresh performance. Continue along Haywood St. to the public library, where readings have been performed by Mountain native and NC poet laureate **Fred Chappell**. Author **Pat Conroy** was spotted browsing the stacks in this library while apparently researching a screenplay about **Thomas Wolfe's** *Look Homeward Angel.*

If you are ready for an intermission, pause at the nearby **Gold Hill Espresso and Fine Teas** which is located at 64 Haywood St.

You will pass a pharmacy at number 57 Haywood St. It's located in the **Castanea Building**, an unusually intricate example of the talent of Asheville's early masons. Notice how the rooflines of this block of Haywood St. are not entirely straight but curve in a long, subtle line against the sky. Nearby is **Malaprop's Bookstore**. A veritable *Who's Who* of literary figures has graced the threshold of this monumental establishment.

Did the caffeine we suggested two paragraphs ago wear off already? Serious java heads can pause again at **Malaprop's Cafe** which is located inside the bookstore at 55 Haywood St., between the **Castenea Building** and **Walnut St.**

Turn at **Walnut St.** and continue down the hill. Take notice of the granite curbs on Walnut St. which look chiseled and rough-cut. These are fine examples of the **hand-carved curbstones** found throughout Asheville. Local masons, almost all of them African American, created these with hand tools at the turn of the century. The hand-carved stones actually extend about 18 inches beneath the surface of the street.

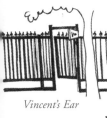

Vincent's Ear

You can cross Lexington Ave. and turn left to get to another great coffee shop. **Vincent's Ear**, which is situated in a basement behind the wrought-iron gated patio at 68 N. Lexington Ave., is also one of the best places in town to find a challenging chess match.

Follow Walnut St. uphill past **Carolina Lane**. Thomas Wolfe used to deliver papers in this lane which was at the very heart of the Red Light District. More recently, historian/playwright **Howard Zinn** and notable others have performed or watched performances

When walking around town, be aware of what's up..literally. The upper floors in the old town center are intricately designed with attention to obscure and delightful details. And the view of mountains in the distance is the proper cure for architectural overload if you have seen one building too many and hanker for visual space.

When walking around town, look up. It's good for your posture, plus the rooflines of some of the buildings are the best feature of Asheville's world-renowned architecture. Check out the subtle curvature of the buildings along Haywood St. near Malaprop's Bookstore or the details in the Self Help Building on Patton Ave. You really need binoculars to appreciate the gargoyles atop the Jackson Building in Pack Square...and the wedding cake crown of the City Building can almost fool you into believing that the government exercises some modicum of good taste.

at Carolina Lane's eclectic Green Door theater. Continue up Walnut St. to Broadway and turn left. This block provides a good sampling of commercial architecture from the 1900s to the 1920s. The stone trim against polychrome brickwork of these two-to-four-story structures is representative of that boomtown building style.

At **80 Broadway** is the Scottish Rite Cathedral and Masonic Temple building, a powerful building with a tall portico and ionic columns. Turn onto Woodfin St., pausing to notice the three-story archway on that side of the Temple. In the grassy area next to the sidewalk is a brick relief model of a mansion that used to be across the street but no longer exists. It was the residence of one of Buncombe County's wealthiest slave owners. There are vintage fallout shelter signs on the back of the Masonic Temple building.

The City Hall Wedding Cake Building

Turn right onto Market St. and continue along to the Thomas Wolfe Memorial. Be prepared to spend some time browsing. The Thomas Wolfe House is behind it. A fire seriously damaged the writer's former home and its contents in 1998, but restoration efforts are underway.

Follow the bricks of Market St. to College St., turn left, and go to the courthouses. These were originally planned as twin Art Deco wedding cake buildings (in the style of the City Building which is the one on the right) but the city and county had a squabble and wound up making separate arrangements. The City Building was designed by Douglas Ellington and is one of the most colorful examples of Art Deco geometry. Georgia pink marble, orange brick, green tile, and a somewhat eccentric feather design combine to make this work a classic. It cleverly reflects the form of

the Blue Ridge mountains while faintly acknowledging American Indian symbolism. The interior treatments of the building are fabulous; take some time to look around inside and ride the snazzy old-timey elevators up and down.

Then go next door to visit the Buncombe County Courthouse. This conservative, neoclassical stud-muffin-of-an-edifice employs granite, marble, plaster, and wood in an attempt to dominate those who venture inside. The two courthouses provide excellent examples of the opposite ends of a circa-1920s architectural perspective and philosophy. Their juxtaposition tells us as much about politics as it does about design theory.

When you leave the courthouses, veer to the left behind the police station to reach historic Eagle St. The YMI Building is at the corner of Eagle and South Market. It was designed by Richard Sharp Smith (George Vanderbilt's supervising architect) and is one of his trademark pebbledash and red brick projects. At 47 Eagle St. is the Mount Zion Missionary Baptist Church. This historic Gothic Revival masterpiece has striking front and side gables, three and four-story towers, and exquisite stained-glass windows.

Returning to Court Plaza, go left into Pack Square. The Jackson Building, a Ronald Greene project at 22 Pack Square, is a svelte creation of 13 stories which was erected on a plot about the size of a parking space. This was North Carolina's first skyscraper and stands on the site where Thomas Wolfe's family once owned a stonecutting shop. The Gothic ornamentation and carefully detailed gargoyles deserve a closer inspection, so binoculars are especially helpful during this phase of the tour.

The rather phallic granite obelisk in the center of Pack Square is another Richard Sharp design. It honors one of Asheville's natives, Civil War governor Zebulon B. Vance. The capstone on top weighs more than a ton. Nearby is Be Here Now nightclub, where poet Patti Smith recently unleashed her onstage magic with a ferocity seldom witnessed in this neck of the woods.

Vance Monument

Follow Pack Square toward the BB & T Building. Locals call it lots of names but often refer to it as the *Big Beige & Tall Building*. It has one notably redeeming and remarkable feature: From the top floors it affords some of the best views available. Perhaps that's because the views from this building are about the only ones in town which aren't overpowered or obscured by the BB&T Building itself.

If you cross College St. at the BB & T Building you will find Beanstreets Cafe located on the corner at 3 Broadway. It is not only a coffee spot, but a melting pot. *Try to say that sentence real fast three times. If you can't, maybe espresso is needed.* The communities of Asheville crisscross here over java, chess, poetry, and biscotti.

Proceed down Patton Ave. (which runs parallel to College St. on the other side of the BB&T Building) and you will arrive at the

spiffy Kress Building with its happy blue lettering. The original work on this tan and cream glazed terra-cotta delight looks good enough to eat. Once upon a time there was a magnificent European-style Grand Opera House across the street from the Kress Building at the present asphalt site. Al Jolson, Sarah Bernhardt, and the famous American band-master (and lesser known comedic opera composer) John Phillip

Sousa, were among the luminaries who performed there.

Sousa would promote his opera house performances by arriving early in town and marching his band up and down the street and around Pack Square. Bernhardt, on the other hand, didn't need to advertise: The

Drhumor Building

French actress was an international superstar and practically the whole town turned out to greet her at the train platform. The gorgeous traveler was accompanied by an entourage of about two dozen people and lugged along a stupendous teakwood coffin. She saw it someplace, decided she couldn't live without it, and always traveled with the fancy white casket just in case she was buried while on the road.

Local and regional acts like the popular African American singing group the Rhododendrons also performed there. But, alas, as singer/songwriter Joni Mitchell once said, "They paved paradise to put up a parking lot."

At 48 Patton Ave. is the Drhumor Building, affectionately referred to by some as the Doctor Humor Building. It's one of the region's finest examples of the Romanesque Revival style. Friezes by Fred Miles, wonderfully arched windows, rounded limestone corners and some downright voluptuous high-relief decorations make

Asheville used to be a town of rounders, rowdies, and ruffy-tuffys. They came into town on horseback, herding livestock or prospecting for gold, with their pistols in their pockets and ready to "tie one on." Check out the old-timey horse-hitching rings made of hand-smithed iron imbedded in Asheville's curbstones. One is on the curb in front of 22 Broadway; another is in the proximity of 39 Biltmore Ave. near the Aston St. intersection.

it one of the city's most striking facades.

The **S & W Cafeteria** building next door is another of Douglas Ellington's **Art Deco** masterpieces. Cream, black, blue, green, and golden-glazed terra-cotta work serve up visual desserts in a classically geometrical formula. Don't miss a chance to step inside of the building, which currently houses a nightclub. The interior has been restored to its original Art Deco cafeteria frump glory, and is one of downtown's most interesting-looking spaces.

Follow Patton Ave. past the triangular Pritchard Park which was featured in Gail Godwin's novel *A Mother and Two Daughters*. Turn right at Coxe Ave. to the **Public Service Building** at 89-93 Patton Ave. This building combines playful **Romanesque and Spanish** features in polychrome terra-cotta. There is an entranceway at street level which leads into the building. Take the elevators or the stairs as a shortcut up to **Wall St.** and the historic **Flat Iron Building**. This structure's flying wedge resembles the bow of an ocean liner

Public Service Building

cutting across the skyline.

Follow Wall St. to the right, toward the sculpture of a big black iron, hang a left past the hotdog stand and park benches, and continue along **Battery Park** going west (away from Haywood St.).

At **18 Battery Park** is the **Old Europe Coffee Bar** which has the best key lime pie this side of Miami. Situated in the ground floor of the historic Flat Iron Building, this cafe/mini-bakery is a marvelous place to increase your caloric intake. They usually have fantastic background music on the CD player. Perhaps you want to dance off that cheesecake before you continue your walking tour of downtown.

Looking west down Patton Ave.

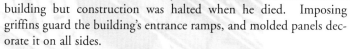

Flat Iron Building

Continue up Battery Park until you see the Grove Arcade building. The Arcade was constructed as America's first indoor shopping mall by E. W. Grove. Mr. Grove leveled a 100-foot high,

tree-and-rock-covered hill in order to build the Arcade. Bear in mind that the same ambitious chap tore down a sprawling, low level, 500-room hotel

Miles Building

in order to erect a 14-story one in its place. He planned the Grove Arcade as a 20-story building but construction was halted when he died. Imposing griffins guard the building's entrance ramps, and molded panels decorate it on all sides.

As this book goes to press, the inside of the Arcade is undergoing a stunning restoration, complete with gargoyles, wrought iron bridges, and ceilings high enough to fly a kite. A huge shopping arena is scheduled to open at the dawn of the new millennium and promises to forever change the rhythm of old Battery Hill, which was once a wooded area primarily noted for its dense squirrel population.

Behind the Grove Arcade is the Battery Park Apartments building, formerly the Battery Park Hotel. Get out your binoculars for this one to enjoy the colorful ornamentation which decorates the front facade.

Then reach for your handkerchief and weep to consider that the Vanderbilt Apartments building (between the Civic Center and the library) once had a very similar facade. It was stripped away after World War II in order to make some structural improvements to the once-adorned exterior. Turn left in front of the Battery

Grove Arcade

Park Apartment to O. Henry Ave. and you will see the Chamber of Commerce (the starting point of this jaunt) on your right.

AMERICA'S FIRST EDIBLE PUBLIC PARK

Asheville's Bountiful City Project
828.236.2299

A pedestrian bridge across South Charlotte St. connects the back of Court Plaza to the historic Stephens-Lee Recreational Center, which is situated on a hillside above the first edible public park in the United States. The park affords a magnificent view of the Asheville City Hall, an Art Deco masterpiece designed by Douglas D. Ellington in 1926.

To the left of City Hall one can see Eagle Street which is distinguished by the prominent Mount Zion Missionary Baptist Church which stands at the bottom of the steep lane.

Asheville's pioneering *edible* park, a self-sustaining permaculture garden, is a veritable Eden-in-progress. The result of a cooperative effort between the *City Seeds* organization and *Asheville Parks and Recreation*, it is the first *Bountiful City Project*.

Local project volunteers include neighborhood children, students from regional colleges and universities, and groups of kids enrolled in special programs for so-called "at-risk" youths.

City Seeds director and visionary landscape designer Jonathan Brown explains, "We are trying to demonstrate how you can grow an amazing amount of food in the city while beautifying abandoned pieces of property."

On only one acre of land, an astonishing variety of edible plants is growing:

Apples (including mountain varieties and "antique" varieties no longer grown commercially) • Blackberries • Blueberries • Cherries • Cranberries • Elderberries • Figs • Grapes • Herbs: every type of culinary herb (legally) available in North America is grown in the park, including catnip. • Jujubes • Kiwis • Mulberries (The Weeping Mulberry is a beautiful tree whose branches lean downward and spread across the ground. When leaves are on the tree it becomes a beautiful gazebo-like canopy.) • Nut Trees (hazelnuts, pecans, walnuts, filberts, and chestnuts) • Peaches (several varieties) • Pears (several varieties) • Persimmons • Raspberries • Strawberries • Swamp Sunflowers • Tulips (edible culinary varieties) • Watercress

By late summer the park is so green and crowded with vegetation that the only way to stroll through it is via a gracefully winding boardwalk. Because chemicals used to preserve wood can potentially contaminate the ground water or food in the edible park, the boardwalk is made from untreated Cyprus. There is a natural amphitheater with *burm* and *swale* benches which are

Photograph courtesy of City Seed, Inc.

144

made of earth cut into the hillside. Springy, resilient culinary herbs are planted in them, creating living, edible, fast-drying seat cushions.

Other non-edible park benches are made from recycled soda bottles. There is also a comfy sofa constructed entirely from broom straw. Thorny raspberries and blackberries provide a natural fence at the perimeter of the park.

Because the park is heavily mulched it retains water naturally. In fact, it required auxiliary watering, or extra irrigation, for only three days during the drought of 1998 (a drought so severe that the city had to purchase water from other municipalities in order to maintain a critical supply).

This is precisely the kind of self-sufficient project that taxpayers and city governments love. The park was intentionally designed to become self-sustaining by the year 2002. That means it won't need weeding or irrigation...it will take care of itself as a properly balanced ecosystem. Shading from trees will help control the growth of weeds and falling leaves will provide annual mulch. A healthy variety of growth will entice wildlife and beneficial insects. Even if there is a flood, the overflow will drain down the hill, nourishing an exotic cranberry bog.

From time to time, artistic visitors create shrines and altars inside the park from twigs, stones, and plants. One gentleman visits the park each morning to pray beneath the branches of a Paw-Paw tree where he has created a crucifix from fallen twigs.

On opposite sides of a fifteen-foot section of the boardwalk, like-species trees have been planted. As they grow up and over the walkway they can be grafted together to create a shady fruit-bearing tunnel. Further along the boardwalk is a grape and kiwi fruit arbor. The compatible vines will eventually intertwine to form a rather romantic archway beneath which lovers may feed one another the ripe and juicy organic treats, without having to weigh their produce or pay a cashier.

Many of the plants in the park will have fruit on them eight months out of the year, free for the picking. The Bountiful City Project encourages visitors to frequent the park and have a pickin'-'n-grinnin' good time eating the fruits of a local labor of love (and love of the land).

To get to the Edible Park, walk down the stairs that are between the City Building and the County Court House downtown. At the end of the stairs, turn right and follow the sidewalk until you see a pedestrian walkway which crosses over Charlotte St. (a major street you'll notice behind the city parking lots.) When you get to the other end of the pedestrian walkway (which is a cyclone-fence enclosed covered bridge) follow the sidewalk a few paces and you will see the entrance to the park on your right. (It's situated below the parking lot of the historical Stephens-Lee Recreation Center.)

145

WALL STREET TOUR

In the 1920s, Wall Street's architects named the shopping area "Greenwich Village." The rather ambitious title didn't stick, and later it was renamed "Wall Street."

But no, it's not named for its more famous namesake in NYC but for the retaining wall built behind the small one-block street of shops. The attractive store fronts, old street lights and exotic ginko trees add to this curving street's appeal. Now it's one of Asheville's most popular shopping venues and an easy place to spend an entire afternoon dilly-dallying about.

Walking onto Wall St. from Battery Park Ave. note the buildings on either side of you. On your right is the **Flat Iron Building** (1926), an eight-story tan brick office building with ornamented limestone facing. Look up high to see the molded copper parapet. On your left is the **Miles Building** (1925), a spectacular pentagonal building with white glazed terracotta cornices and Baroque Classical style trim.

As you walk down Wall St. take time to visit My Native Ireland and A Far Away Place, whose back entrances are found on the right side of the lane. **My Native Ireland** features high-quality Irish crafts and clothing hand-picked by a discerning native Celt, AnnMarie McConnell (*12 Battery Park Ave. 828.281.1110*). A Far Away Place offers an eclectic and intriguing mix of drums, didgeridoos, flutes, pan pipes, world music CDs, clothing, artwork, bedspreads, rugs, stationery, jewelry, masks and antique artifacts such as 17th century Mexican stone columns. "River," the store's owner, has made many trips to exotic locales to bring this fascinating collection to his home town (*11 Wall St. 828.252.1891*).

What makes Asheville home to you, as opposed to just a place to live? "Twenty-one years ago when I drove through this area, it was the first time I felt connected to a place, to a people—the first time I'd felt at home anywhere. I fell in love and that was that. I can't put it into words. I can only tell you Asheville is the right size, the right make-up, the right visual experience. I wake up every day and look out the window and thank God I'm here."
(Asheville Mayor Leni Sitnick)

146

Upstairs at 12 1/2 Wall St. Suite H is **Studio Chavarria** (*828.236.9191*), the hair / makeup / color stylist studio of Guadalupe Chavarria. If you are lucky enough to get an appointment with him, you'll be invited into his elegant, antique-furnished studio for personalized attention from one of Asheville's most sought-after hair designers. New York and LA supermodels have stopped to see him en route to photo shoots just to get their locks spruced-up in his luxurious space which is more reminiscent of Rodeo Drive than urban Appalachia.

Further along Wall Street is **Natural Selections**, a nature shop and art gallery with an emphasis on the Southern Appalachians. Natural Selections stocks a formidable collection of science, astronomy and birding equipment. Naturalists or naturalist-wannabes will appreciate the good range of natural history books, hiking guides and flora / fauna identification guides. Kids will love treasures such as the realistic sticky slug toy. John Frost is the friendly and well-informed owner of this environmentally-conscious store. (*10 Wall St., 828.252.4336*).

Next door is **Paul Taylor Custom Sandals**, selling comfortable custom-made designs at reasonable prices. Worried about paying the price difference for custom work? The window display visually demonstrates the answer to the question "How long do they last?" It has several pairs of Paul's leather sandals of various vintages, showing the degree of wear and tear. Evidently these hand-crafted sandals keep on truckin' for 25 years or more. A decidedly wise long-term investment (*828.251.0057*).

Walk a little further along the left side of Wall Street to get to **Fired Up**, a creative lounge where you can paint unfinished ceramic pottery with your own design. Budding artists of all ages are welcome. The friendly staff will fire your masterpiece and you can pick it up about a week later or have it shipped to your home. The comfortable, attractive lounge is decorated with luxurious arm chairs and photos of finished ceramic pieces for inspiration. Fired Up caters to private parties such as birthdays and bridal showers at a reasonable rate, providing a creative alternative to the traditional booze-up (*26 Wall St. 828.253.8181*). The **Bazaar** is a gift

shop next to Fired Up which sells an interesting range of local art work, cards and T-shirts of Asheville, including one in the style of Van Gogh's "Starry Night" (*28 Wall St. 828.253.8850*).

If your creative urge is still unsatisfied, head across the street to Beads and Beyond, which sells all the supplies you need to create your own jewelry. Beads range from fresh water pearls to ceramic pterodactyls. A collection of antique and rare beads, Native American craft materials, and books about jewelry making and other crafts make this an interesting one-stop craft center (*35 Wall St. 828.254.7927*).

Slip back across the street to the High Country Hemporium, which, as its name suggests, sells everything you could think of that is made of hemp. It also sells teas, coffees, soaps, smoking paraphernalia, books, herbs, and build-your-own organic gift baskets. Hemp advocate and owner of the Hemporium, Maria Birchfield, likes to stock local products and helps organize annual trips (no pun intended) to Amsterdam for the Cannabis Cup every Thanksgiving. The Hemporium also houses the office of massage therapist Nia Orr, who offers excellent bodywork at very reasonable prices (*call 828.258.4823 for a massage appointment*).

In 1939 a Buncombe County resident entered the Guinness Book of World Records. "Big Boy" earned the international distinction of being the largest hog on record, at a whopping 1904 pounds. "Big Boy" was nearly six feet high at the shoulder. Several eyewitnesses compared him in size and shape to a Volkswagen automobile. The couple who raised him told reporters, "Yeah, he's a big 'un. That's why we call him 'Big Boy'."

Learn some interesting facts about "the world's most versatile fiber" from texts available for sale at the Hemporium. Did you know, for example, that there are more than 25,000 known uses for hemp? Some of these uses include fabric, paper, beauty products, animal feed and bedding, building materials, as well as less obvious industrial and technical products. In fact, almost any product that can be made from wood, cotton or petroleum (including plastics) can be made from hemp. Additionally, hemp is a highly productive crop that requires far fewer growing acres than trees to provide a similar yield. It is also a quickly renewable crop that is highly pest-resistant and improves the quality of soil. If you ever had any doubts about the common sense of legalizing hemp-growing, one visit to the Hemporium will have you slapping "Legalize Now!" stickers to your bumper. As one poster declares: "Hemp is NOT a gateway fabric. It's durable, it's natural, it's illegal (to grow in the USA). You could smoke all the hemp hats in this room and never get high!"....Just in case you wanted to try that at home, kids (*30 Wall St. 828.236.0068*).

Another attractive store on Wall Street is Future Visions, selling contemporary home furnishings and gifts such as picture frames, stationary, clocks, candles, and lights (*37 Wall St. 828.254.3477*).

Check out Wall Street's Public Service Building, a tall red-brick office building said to be one of the most attractive 1920s skyscrapers in North Carolina. Built in 1929, the building's majestic Romanesque style and glazed terracotta ornamentation make an interesting backdrop to the modern stores below.

If all the shopping has tired you out, try eating at any one of Wall Street's excellent restaurants, which include the following:

Laughing Seed Cafe
40 Wall St. 828.252.3445
Mon-Thurs 11:30am-9pm
Fri-Sat 11:30am-10pm
Sun 10am-9pm
Serving excellent vegetarian and vegan cuisine, wines, beers, home-made bread, smoothies and scrumptious desserts, this is a long-time Asheville favorite. Non-smoking.

The Market Place Restaurant and Wine Bar
20 Wall St. 828.252.4162
Mon-Sat Wine bar 5pm-9:30 or 10
Restaurant 6pm-9:30pm (last seating)
A pricier option for lunch or dinner, this stylish joint offers mostly meat and fish dishes with some veggie options. Great wine selection and a wonderfully restful ambience conducive to romantic conversation. It can be a great place to get away from the social claustrophobia often associated with living in a small town like Asheville, where everyone you know seems to show up everywhere you go.

Possum Trot Grill
8 Wall St. 828.253.0062
Tue-Sat Lunch 11:30am-2pm
Dinner 5:30pm-8pm or 9ish, depending on how busy they are.
A non-smoking establishment with a Cajun / Southern theme whose classically trained chef is from Switzerland. This restaurant epitomizes America's eclectic culinary mix. Most entrees contain meat or fish, but several veggie options are offered. Don't forego the delicious appetizers, (especially the "roasted sweet onion and goat cheese bouche") in your haste to tuck into that tempting Creole Gumbo.

If your interests lean more towards spiritual nourishment, visit Jubilee! Celebration Center / Church, next door to the Laughing Seed Cafe. This spiritual community center hosts visits by musicians, a writing group, and a men's gathering, as well as three non-denominational Sunday morning services at 8:30, 9:45 and 11:15 am. (*46 Wall St. 828.252.5335*).

And if you want to wear off some of that Wall Street restaurant fare, stop by Climbmax, an indoor / outdoor climbing center. The facade of the store is an actual climbing wall facing Wall Street. It has redefined the experience of people-watching and turned it into an exciting spectator sport. Patrons of the restaurant across the street have been known to place bets on how high the climbers will get before falling (the loser pays for dessert).

The experienced staff can instruct you in safe bouldering and rock climbing techniques. Equipment can be rented at the center, and private parties are popular, especially with kids. There is no age limit, lower or upper, for enjoying Climbmax's services. The center also offers half or full-day guided climbing excursions for all ability levels to local climbing havens such as Looking Glass Rock or the ominously-named Rumbling Bald. Individual or group excursions available (*828.252.9996*).

Herds of livestock used to move through the streets of Asheville en route to market. Pritchard Park used to be the location of a major annual hog auction. Hundreds of pigs would be corraled into the park which became a public pig wallow. What a sight that must have been, and what a scent.

THE WRAP
(OF 11 BLOCKS OF ASHEVILLE'S HISTORICAL ARCHITECTURE SLATED FOR BULLDOZING)

In the year 1980 much of Asheville's most unique old architecture was nearly bulldozed because of a short-sighted urban development scheme. It would have been a loss not only locally, but nationally, in terms of the destruction of historical property.

A developer proposed to build an indoor shopping mall encompassing eleven blocks of downtown's historical district. To some it seemed like a progressive idea. Other cities around the country, especially those in cold climates, were erecting  indoor shopping plazas to ensure year-round commercial activity without interference from Mother Nature. Asheville's city officials were sold on the idea too, and proceeded with plans to permit the demolition.

The development would have  destroyed an area enclosed by approximately two miles of sidewalk. It would have disrupted the rhythm of life in the heart of the city while creating a monolith shopping mall of monstrous proportions. The city's historical character and personality would have been smothered in the rubble of the old town. The potential aesthetic ramifications were inconceivable.

The project proposed to raze such landmarks as our Art Deco masterpiece, The Kress Building. The T. S. Morrison Store, a general mercantile store in business since 1891, was slated for destruction. Finkelstein's Pawn Shop on Broadway (circa 1903) and the whole of lower Lexington Avenue (all the way from College Street to the 240 overpass behind the Civic Center) would have been demolished, on both sides of the street. Walnut Street and its hand-carved granite curbstones, from Haywood Street all the way to Broadway, would have been laid to waste by wrecking balls and bulldozers. Some buildings that had just been painstakingly restored by a local architect were going to be leveled. Carolina Lane, where Thomas Wolfe used to deliver newspapers as a boy, would have likely become the location of an indoor mall's food court.

Thanks to a spontaneous grass roots effort organized by a handful of conscientious residents, the controversial project was halted in the eleventh hour.

As part of the effort, artist Dana Irwin produced a colorful poster to inspire citizens, artist Jean Penland made badges with the slogan "Asheville—Love it don't level it.," and film maker Al Ramirez made a documentary about how the project would displace people who lived downtown. University art major Peggy Gardner decided to raise public awareness by creating a living work of art involving two hundred humans holding up about three thousand yards of cloth.

She acquired a city permit allowing her to "wrap" the area in question with a piece of "ribbon". Then she stayed up all night tying together 4 X 5 foot large placards of cloth donated by the Slosman Corporation, a local rayon recycling plant. On a Saturday afternoon, two hundred volunteers posted along the route held up the cloth to form a perimeter of people and a cordon of colorful fabric.

The demonstration (which was described by Gardner as "not a protest but an educational event.") lasted only ten minutes. But the publicity generated by the "Visual entertainment to honor the artist Javacheff Vladinirov Christo" (who became famous by wrapping monuments in Italy with cloth) gave Ashevilleans a graphic wake-up call. It allowed citizens to visually conceptualize the scope of the proposed destruction.

An ensuing firestorm of protest forced city officials to reconsider and cancel the project and saved eleven blocks of antique architecture from destruction.

(Author's note: Special thanks to Danielle, Dana, and Peggy for their help in researching this story.)

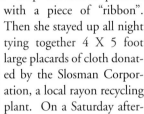

LITERARY DESTINATIONS

Situated on historic Haywood Street next to Walnut St.:
Malaprop's Bookstore & Cafe
55 Haywood St.
828.254.6734
1.800.441.9829
Mon-Thurs 9am-9pm, Fri-Sat 9am-11pm, Sun 9am-6pm

Close to the Chamber of Commerce at the starting and ending points of this excursion:
The Reader's Corner
31 Montford Ave.
828.285.8805
Mon-Fri 11am-7pm, Sat 10am-6pm, Sun 1-6pm

Close to Walnut St. between Haywood and Broadway, on historic lower Lexington Ave:
Downtown Books and News
87 N. Lexington Ave.
828.253.8654
Mon-Sun 8am-6pm
Summer only Fri-Sat 8am-8pm

Across from the Grove Arcade and near the Flat Iron Building:
Captain's Bookshelf
31 Page Ave.
828.253.6631
Tues-Sat 10am-6pm

HISTORIC MONTFORD TOUR

BILTMORE VILLAGE EXCURSIONS

CHURCHES & CEMETERIES

SCENIC DRIVE

NATURE WALKS

EXCUR-SIONS NEAR DOWNTOWN

THE HISTORIC MONTFORD NEIGHBORHOOD

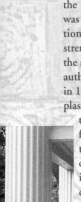

Montford neighborhood stretches over approximately 300 acres, from the outskirts of downtown to the French Broad River.

Near the downtown entrance to Montford, Cherokee Indians played a stick ball game at the turn of the century and Montford residents were treated to a rare and exciting glimpse of American Indian recreational culture. More than a thousand Ashevilleans turned out to watch the lacrosse-like competition, which was played using sticks with nets attached. Much ceremony and tradition surround stick ball matches, which remain an important and festive community event for the Cherokee.

The origin of the neighborhood's name is unknown, although is may be a contraction of the words *Mountain Ford*. The French Broad River runs in this vicinity, and there may have been a river crossing here at one time. But most folks accept the theory that the neighborhood derived its name from the Montfort family. Samuel Ashe, for whom Asheville was named, had a son who married the daughter of Colonel Joseph Montfort. It is likely that the neighborhood was named Montfort or Montford when she moved here to live near her in-laws.

Montford's Historical Horse Hair Houses

Prior to the advent of asbestos in the mid-1920s, hog or horse hair was mixed with building construction plaster. It added to the strength and structural integrity of the sloppy mud-like material. The author's home in Montford, built in 1927, was made with horse hair plaster. An environmental consultant in the Piedmont once found the entire tail of a pig in the plaster of a turn-of-the-century dwelling, while he was inspecting for possible asbestos contamination.

More houses of architectural and historical distinction can be found here than in any other neighborhood in Asheville, thanks to preservation and restoration efforts in Montford. About 650 original structures remain from the boom days of 1890-1930, when Montford was advertised as a place to "live in the country without leaving the city." The architects who designed the houses here made extensive use of shingles, pebbledash, stucco, stone, brickwork, and Victorian woodwork ornamentation. They blended architectural types and incorporated a diversity of influences to create a fresh, cosmopolitan style of design which is characteristic of Montford. Their work has passed the test of time both structurally and aesthetically. The following tour of

Montford can be made on foot or by car, and is intended to give you an overview of some of the neighborhood's most interesting historical sites.

From the Chamber of Commerce parking lot, turn right onto Haywood St. and then take an immediate right across the Montford Ave. bridge to enter the historic neighborhood.

Do keep in mind that these buildings are on private property and are private residences and private places of business. Appreciate the structures from a respectful distance, and get appropriate permission before venturing onto or photographing private property. If somebody throws a water balloon at you from an upstairs window or invites you in for a glass of sherry and some long-winded Southern anecdotes because you've invaded their personal space, don't say we didn't warn you.

A WALKING, CYCLING OR DRIVING TOUR OF HISTORIC HOMES IN MONTFORD

This excursion begins on Montford Ave., which Thomas Wolfe called "the most fashionable street in town," and returns to the Chamber of Commerce. We listed a few of the most interesting homes in the neighborhood, but our list is by no means comprehensive. Along the way, be sure to notice those in-between the ones we highlighted.

89 Montford Ave.

This house, which features irregular massing and a corner tower, was probably built in 1890. Some call it Steamboat Gothic and others say it's a variation on the Queen Anne style of architecture, with lots of interesting surface ornamentation.

One youngster we spoke to said "It looks sort of like a gingerbread house with the scales of a dragon on the roof." It's lovely, no matter how you choose to describe it.

288 Montford Ave.
(The Black Walnut Bed & Breakfast Inn)

This circa 1899 Richard Sharp Smith (supervising architect for Biltmore House) design artfully mixes features of Shingle, Queen Anne, and Colonial Revival styles. The current owners restored the home in 1992. The gigantic and stately old trees on the property are one of its most pleasing features.

155

Turn left onto Waneta Street and go up the hill to Pearson Drive to continue this tour.

In the 1800's, gravel was removed from the vicinity of Montford and Cumberland Avenues between Bearden and Blake in order to improve streets in downtown Asheville, which were notorious for bogging down wagons in their mud and muck.

152 Pearson Drive

This house's symmetrical facade and formal character make it stand out as one of the most unusual residential designs in Montford. The Colonial Revival architecture resembles that used for banks, courthouses, and other formal structures of the period (circa 1920).

Fan shaped glass over the doorways, "awnings" made of stone and plaster over the windows, and stylish Corinthian pilasters (faux columns of shallow relief) add to the classic lines of this dignified-looking brick house.

167 Pearson Drive

This house displays typical Queen Anne features and a stunning polygonal corner which extends three stories from the porch to the roof. Multiple gables of varied design add to the unique beauty of this interesting home.

Nighttime Montford Strolling

We recommend that you tour the neighborhood in daylight as well as in the early evening, to fully appreciate the beauty of the old houses. Their clever and artistic architects designed them to appear elegant under all circumstances, but the transformation of their features from daylight to night is dramatic and charming.

Not only do we preserve old houses here, we maintain what one resident calls "a romantic level of street lighting." Romances can use a little mystery to spice them up, granted. But that doesn't really apply to sidewalks, which serve us better when all their secrets are out in the open where we can avoid stubbing a toe on them.

Sometimes a tiny flashlight is a good thing to carry on a darkened street, especially if you're not familiar with the neighborhood or don't have the greatest night vision. We wouldn't want you to trip on a loose antique brick or walk into a guidewire holding up a telephone pole (which this writer managed to do in broad daylight because he's such a daydreaming romantic).

Of course, another option is to go to a hunting supply store and get some of those night-vision goggles popularized by the Persian Gulf War and now used to track ferocious deer. But we suspect that might detract from your hot pursuit of the elusive Cupid (or his pursuit of you). He lives in amorous ambience, which is his natural habitat. It's threatened with extinction unless we strive to preserve and protect it (So recycle love, y'all).

No matter how you prepare for it, an evening stroll in Montford can be a lovely and lovey-dovey experience. Old houses (like old flames) take on a completely different aura when bathed in moonlight beneath a dome of stardust.

214 Pearson Drive

This formal Colonial Revival house was built for the daughter of one of turn-of-the-century Asheville's most ambitious and important developers, Colonel Frank Coxe, who built the original Battery Park Hotel.

235 Pearson Drive
(The Wright Inn)

Multiple gables, a gazebo, a conical roof, and Doric porch posts are but a few of the notable features of this circa 1900 house. It is one of the neighborhood's most celebrated ornamental structures and a textbook example of Queen Anne style architecture.

It was once nicknamed "Faded Glory" by adoring residents, but has been skillfully restored to its original "Wow, look at that place!" glory.

Turn right onto Watauga Street and go downhill toward Montford Ave. to continue the tour.

346 Montford Ave.

Designed by William H. Lord, this Colonial Revival style mansion has an entrance portico with ionic columns and three prominent dormers. It is a powerful structure set behind a large, elegant front yard extending along Watauga St. to Montford Ave.

Turn left onto Montford to continue the tour. Take a right onto Panola Street, and another right onto Montford Park Place, which is a steep lane alongside Montford Park. Turn right at Cumberland Avenue.

333 Cumberland Ave.

The building's name (The Frances) is above the doorway in exquisite Art Nouveau font. The fellow who built the apartment building in 1926 named it after his wife. Isn't that sweet?

Skintled (jutting, irregular) brickwork and untooled mortar joints are juxtaposed against a symmetrical form in a most unusual way, to create an amazing look. Stucco and cast concrete were also incorporated into the facade. This is one of Montford's most unique-looking buildings.

The Montford Park Players

This is a theatrical troupe which performs in Montford. Please refer to our section on Theater and Dance for more information.

Follow Cumberland Ave. to the intersection of Soco St. Look to your left and you will see the next house on this tour. *(Note: This is a somewhat challenging intersection for traffic because visibility of Cumberland from Soco is limited, so drive carefully.)*

249 Cumberland Ave.

This circa 1908 residence is most likely the creation of architect Richard Sharp Smith. Its pebbledash exterior, which was lovingly restored, is a great example of that type of facade. The paired polygonal towers which anchor each end of the house are separated by a central gable entrance which is set beneath a shallow roofline.

209 Cumberland Ave.

This circa 1901 Richard Sharp Smith design features one of his trademark peaked gambrel roofs, stuccoed walls, and heavy porch post brackets. One of its most endearing features is the line of hemlocks which shelter the house from the street.

The architect called this grand home a "cottage." But we figure that was because he had just finished working on the Biltmore House, which has *four acres* of floor space or almost 175,000 square feet. You could just about fit every house on Cumberland Avenue inside the Biltmore.

170 Cumberland Ave.

This house was built by a musician who invented a kind of breakfast cereal, oddly enough...since most of the musicians we know don't even wake up in time for breakfast.

He was from the cold state of Michigan, and this structure resembles a northern design, with its dramatic rooflines and a wide surface area of wooden shingles. Its gambrel roof has some of the most sweeping lines of any house in Montford.

Since you're probably just dying to know, the cereal was called *Biltmore Wheat Hearts*.

The Edible Park Project Comes to Montford

An edible park (a self-sustaining permaculture garden of edible plants and fruit trees) project is being planned for Montford. It will be located on the western hillside of the Montford Park Complex, adjacent to the community building. One day soon there will be an edible forest at that location, with the best views of the mountains in town. Groundbreaking is scheduled for late 1999. For information call City Seeds at 828.236.2299. And read our section on downtown excursions for information about the first Edible Park Project, which is already in full swing.

Riverside Cemetery

Riverside Cemetery is located on the west side of Montford, off of Pearson Drive. We dedicated a large section of this guidebook to writing about it, and encourage our readers to refer to that self-guided excursion (see Cemeteries and Churches section) and then visit it while in the Montford neighborhood.

Riverside Cemetery

118 Cumberland Ave.

The conical stone tower and jutting porches of this house, which is situated on a corner lot, display the natural beauty and power of Asheville stonework. It is another example of the Queen Anne style. It was built in 1897 and has beautiful interior woodwork.

111 Cumberland Ave.

"The Colonial" apartment building with its massive columns and porches is mentioned in Thomas Wolfe's novel Look Homeward, Angel.

Now it has the added historical distinction of being included in the book of another guy named Thomas, The Underground Asheville Guidebook. The guidebook was hatched in the back room of apartment number one at the dawn of the new millenium.

Keep in mind that Thomas Wolfe's novel was originally banned in Asheville and only time will tell what will become of the book you're holding in your hands right now. Meanwhile, the author has moved into an undisclosed safe-house in historical *Underground Montford*.

To return to the Chamber of Commerce, follow Cumberland until it deadends at Cherry Street. Turn right onto Cherry and go to the stop sign. Prepare to get into the far left lane as you approach the traffic light at the Montford Avenue Bridge. Turn left onto Montford, left again on the other side of the bridge at Haywood Street, and take an immediate left into the C of C parking lot.

Recommended Reading

For more information about historic Montford, we recommend the inexpensive and informative book entitled *Historic Montford*, published by The Preservation Society of Asheville & Buncombe Co., which is available at area libraries, bookstores, and the Preservation Society's office at 13 Biltmore Ave. (828.254.2343).

The Montford Resource Center

235 Montford Ave. (828.255.4946)

The Montford Resource Center, a neighborhood information center staffed by volunteers, is located in the center of the neighborhood. A publication, called *A Guide To The Historic Montford Neighborhood* which provides a walking tour of historic houses in Montford, is available there, at the Chamber of Commerce, and at various local retail outlets.

Note: At the time of this printing, the Center's hours are somewhat irregular because the center is entirely staffed by volunteers.

CHURCHES & CEMETERIES

Some of the Asheville area's significant churches and cemeteries are listed in this section to provide you with a sampling of what the region has to offer.

Exploring Asheville's churches and cemeteries can constitute its own distinctly different journey into history, art, architecture, and nature. The eccentric diversity of Asheville's people, the rich flavor of its colorful history, and the style and grace of its enduring character come together in a powerful way in its churches and cemeteries.

We recommend that you save as much time as possible for this aspect of your sightseeing. Not only are there numerous sites to visit, but there are countless stories waiting to be told. Once you get involved, you will want to hear each one, in its own illuminating (yet mysterious) voice.

Riverside Cemetery

Established in 1885, the 87-acre Riverside Cemetery is considered a favorite spot in Asheville by many locals. If you like cemeteries, Riverside is fascinating. It was not only the final resting place of world-renowned luminaries, but historians have also found evidence of a large Cherokee hunting encampment near the north-east corner of Riverside.

If you are not crazy about history, Riverside still has a lot to offer. The towering 250-year-old oaks are some of the tallest and loveliest in Asheville, and the network of roads offers a great place to bike or walk. We don't recommend walking there in a snowstorm or thunderstorm, however. Falling limbs can dramatically decrease your life expectancy. The cemetery loses 2-4 trees a year to lightning, as it sits on the highest hill in the area and has an abundance of metal, both above and below ground. One tree was hit by lightning and exploded, scattering splinters as far away as 200 feet.

Riverside's tombstone designs range from intricate Celtic knotwork and angels fashioned from Italian marble, to the Hebrew-inscripted stones in the Beth Ha-Tephila Cemetery (this is a section of the cemetery leased to the Asheville synagogue in 1891). Make a point of examining the ornate family mausoleums, (such as the Terry Mausoleum) with their detailed bronze doors and stained glass. The angel at the Buchanan family gravesite was carved by Fred Miles from limestone left over from construction of the Biltmore Estate. Miles also crafted the intricate stone carvings on the Drhumor Building on Patton Avenue in downtown Asheville (Now, is that Dr. Humor or Drew-More?).

Begin your visit by taking the right-hand road and then the left fork towards the small brick building. Cemetery manager David Olson can provide you with a map / walking guide of the cemetery, help you with genealogical research, and regale you with fascinating tales collected during his more than sixteen year tenure at Riverside. History buffs can purchase the excellent video about the cemetery, entitled "Journey Beyond the Gates," which was produced in 1997 by local high school students.

Visitors come to Riverside from all parts of the U.S. and abroad to find out more about relatives, and to peruse the cemetery records. Searches can be complicated by the fact that many Depression-era graves are unmarked. Poverty forced families to forego the placement of tombstones. Riverside contains remains of people who were once buried in earlier cemeteries. Their remains were moved when Riverside opened. Additionally, many burial records for the African American section of the cemetery were lost forever in a fire. Probe bars have been used to locate graves where markers are nonexistent. A computer database of all grave sites is currently being established to facilitate genealogical searches.

Many German visitors come to research relatives interred in Riverside. Several thousand civilian sailors were incarcerated in the town of Hot Springs during World War I. When a typhoid epidemic raged through Western N.C., eighteen sailors were transferred to a hospital in Asheville, died, and were laid to rest in Riverside. The most remarkable story relating to the German graves is that of one Gerda Kostynski, who discovered in 1933 that her long-lost son, Richard Paul Schlauss, was buried in Riverside. For fourteen years, his mother grieved his death without knowing his fate or his body's whereabouts. By an amazing coincidence, a German magazine published a photograph of Riverside Cemetery that just happened to have Schlauss's cross in the foreground. After some research, his mother sent a letter addressed "To the American Legion, Asheville, Nordamerika." The Legion's response confirmed that it was, indeed, her son's grave.

The much-lauded 20th century writer Thomas Wolfe, arguably the most famous person buried in Riverside, was born and raised in Asheville. His home on Spruce Street is currently being reno-

vated after a devastating fire in 1998. Wolfe's <u>Look Homeward, Angel</u> and short story "Child By Tiger" recount turn-of-the-century events in Asheville that have allowed us glimpses into the lives of many Asheville residents now buried in Riverside. For example, "Child By Tiger" tells of a shooting incident in 1906 by drunken Will Harris, whose victims **James Bailey** (a police officer) and **Ben Addison** (an African American business owner) are interred in Riverside. Addison's grave in the once-segregated section is inscribed: "Killed by a Desperado."

Riverside is also the final resting place of another talented literary figure: **O. Henry**, born William Sydney Porter. Before writing his most famous story, "Gift of the Magi," O. Henry had several articles published while detained in an Ohio prison for embezzling funds from a bank.

One of the oldest engraved tombstones in Western North Carolina is that of **John Lyon**, an acclaimed English botanist whose grave was moved three times until he found his final resting place in Riverside.

Also of note are the graves of Isaac Dickson, George Masa and Caryl Florio. **Isaac Dickson** played a pivotal role in establishing and developing an educational system for Asheville's African-American population. **George Masa** (born Masahara Lisuka) was a Japanese photographer and avid hiker who laid out and measured the Appalachian Trail and the Great Smoky Mountains National Park. **Caryl Florio** (born William John Robjohn) was an internationally known late-19th century composer. George Vanderbilt was so taken with Florio's talents as a musician, actor and composer that he commissioned Florio to be choirmaster and organist of All Soul's Church in Biltmore Village in 1896.

Civil War buffs can make a day of it by visiting some sixty sites outlined in a special map available from the Riverside Cemetery office. Some of the most notable Civil War-era graves are as follows:

A signpost leads you to the grave of **Zebulon Baird Vance**, two-term North Carolina governor, U.S. Senator and member of the N.C. and U.S. House of Representatives. While Vance opposed secession, he nonetheless served as a colonel of the NC 26th Regiment during the Civil War. The granite obelisk in Pack Square is a monument to Vance, and his home in Weaverville is open to the public.

Another grave immortalizes the author/illustrator of the Civil War, **Allen Christian Redwood**. Redwood, a Confederate veteran, depicted battle scenes and inspired dewy-eyed Southern pride with

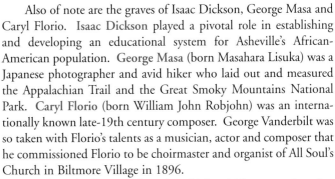

Directions to Riverside Cemetery

Located in the Montford area, you can walk to Riverside Cemetery from the Chamber of Commerce, but there is vehicular access to the cemetery if you'd rather drive. Take a right out of the Chamber of Commerce parking lot onto Haywood St., then an immediate right onto Montford Ave. Take a left onto W. Chestnut St. where there is a sign for the cemetery. Take a right onto Pearson Dr. and look for the white cemetery sign.

his images of the common soldier he named "Johnny Reb." Colonel Stephen Lee, (yes, kin to Robert E.) a Confederate, lost half of his eight sons to the Southern cause. Lee's well-trained company, the "Silver Grays," helped to prevent the burning of Asheville in 1865. They defended the town from 1,100 Union soldiers with a paltry crew of only 300. Lee lived through the war and gave tracts of his land at Chunn's Cove to his former slaves.

Another noteworthy protector of Asheville was one-armed General James Green Martin, who gathered Confederate forces at Swannanoa Gap and once again foiled Unionist intentions to burn our fair town.

South Asheville Cemetery

Some folks refer to it as the "Slave Cemetery" because so many African American slaves are buried there. Indeed, it was the primary burial ground for African Americans for nearly a century, from the 1840s until it was closed in the 1940s. Nobody knows how many people were laid to rest there. Oral history regarding the graveyard is incomplete and inconclusive and written records, generally kept by family members of the deceased inside family Bibles, are scarce. But estimates indicate that as many as 5,000 people were interred in this small, historic cemetery.

Originally, William McDowell and his wife Sarah Lucinda Smith owned the land where the cemetery is located. McDowell also owned the historic Smith-McDowell house, which is now a museum on the campus of Asheville's A-B Tech community college. And he owned forty-four slaves, making him one of the largest slave owners in the region. McDowell provided the land for the cemetery, and one of his slaves, George Avery, became the caretaker.

African Americans could be buried in the city-owned Riverside Cemetery, but their graves would be placed on a back lot, near the road, in a marginalized section of the predominantly white burial ground. So most were buried in Southside Cemetery, which was named The South Asheville Colored Cemetery. Because most of the

163

deceased had little money, few headstones were erected. Often a rock or a planted tree was the only marker and bodies were buried in makeshift pine boxes. In many instances, loved ones were laid to rest in long handwoven wicker baskets.

George Avery was freed from slavery after the Civil War and continued to maintain the property as a gravedigger and caretaker until his death at age ninety-six. He was buried in Southside Cemetery in 1944. Ironically, and sadly, the cemetery became neglected and overgrown with weeds and brush in his absence, since it no longer had a caretaker.

George Gibson, President of the South Asheville Cemetery Association, is the foremost authority on the old graveyard. He has worked tirelessly over the years to restore the cemetery. But without sustained support, the site suffers from perennial neglect. Recently, a restoration committee headed by Gibson and Eula Shaw (a local school teacher) has made significant progress toward cleaning up the cemetery and getting it placed on the National Register of Historic Places.

Because many of the gravestones are sunken into the ground or lost among the trees, the best way to discover the cemetery is to wander and explore. There are mysteries here that will never be recovered. Perhaps the only way to really appreciate this sacred place is to offer a moment of silence in honor of those whose gravesites have been lost.

Directions
to the South Asheville Cemetery

Leaving the Chamber of Commerce parking lot, turn left onto Haywood St. and follow it as it curves past the Civic Center into downtown. Turn left when Haywood St. deadends at Patton Ave. (in front of the S&W Cafeteria Building) and continue along Patton until it deadends at Pack Square, in front of the tall granite obelisk.

Turn right onto Broadway and drive south down Broadway, until you pass the hospital and Broadway becomes Biltmore Avenue. Turn left onto Caledonia Road, go up the hill, and merge right onto Forest Hill Drive. Turn left on Kenilworth Road, left onto Wyoming Road, and take the immediate right onto Dalton Street. Follow the signs to the St. John A Baptist Church. Park in front of the church and take the dirt road/path into the woods.

Mount Zion Missionary Baptist Church
47 Eagle St.

This Gothic Revival church dominates the lower end of historic Eagle St. It was built in 1919, in one of early America's most vibrant African American commercial districts.

Anthropologists have described the Eagle St. section of town as "Perhaps one of the two or three most important examples of African American urban vitality in the nation", due to its unique character and place in history.

The church, with its numerous stained glass windows, large front and side gables, and tall towers, is magnificent.

First Baptist Church
At the corner of Oak and Woodfin St.

The architect Douglas Ellington first made his mark on Asheville in 1927 with this Italian Renaissance / Art Deco creation. Ellington liked to design buildings by drawing upon inspiration from their natural surroundings. The patina of the copper dome blends with the green colors of Asheville's mountains, while the base of this edifice resembles the red and orange hues of earth. Gorgeous pink marble was used in the walls.

Basilica of St. Lawrence
97 Haywood St.

This is one of the most important examples of church architecture in North Carolina, if not the entire Southeastern United States.

Rafael Guastavino, a Spanish (Catalan) architect of international renown, created this masterpiece and is interred in a crypt at the church. He died during the last phase of construction which was completed by his son. The massive tile dome was built without scaffolding, using a special technique which Guastavino called "cohesive bonding construction."

Please refer to the section of this guidebook which offers a tour of downtown architecture and literary history, for a more comprehensive description of the Basilica. Visit at the top of the hour and you can hear the sound of church bells tolling, which is a splendid experience.

Central Methodist Church
27 Church St.

This stone structure, with its massive corner tower and matching smaller tower, was built between 1902 and 1905 in a mixed Gothic Revival / Romanesque Revival style. The builder, J. M. Westall, was author Thomas Wolfe's uncle.

First Presbyterian Church
Northeast corner of Church St.
at Aston St.

Although expansion and remodeling have changed the original size and design of this church, it remains a striking edifice. Established in 1884, it is one of Asheville's oldest churches.

Trinity Episcopal Church
Southeast corner of Church St.
at Aston St.

A powerful example of Gothic Revival style, this church was designed by Bertram Goodhue, who was an important contributor to the so-called Arts and Crafts movement. Erected in 1912, the church combines red brick with granite trim and features a corner tower and belfry.

St. Matthias Episcopal Church
1 Dundee St.

This church was built for the earliest African American Episcopal congregation in Western North Carolina, which was comprised of freed slaves. It is a beautiful example of Gothic style architecture, made from brick, and the inside is decorated with detailed woodwork. It was established between 1894 and 1896 by Bishop J. B. Cheshire.

Hopkins Chapel A. M. E. Zion Church
321 College St.

This grand Gothic Revival church was designed by Richard Sharp Smith who was the supervising architect for the Biltmore House. It has unusual brickwork which fans out in a sort of buttress fashion, and a tall corner tower. There is a restoration effort underway. The master brickmason on this project was James V. Miller, an African American builder who is one of the most important masons / builders in the history of Asheville.

All Souls Episcopal Cathedral
Biltmore Village District

This incredible masterpiece of designer Richard Morris Hunt was built for George Vanderbilt, the proprietor of Biltmore Estate. Red tile, pebbledash, and brick buttresses combine in sweeping, dramatic lines around a cone-shaped roof and a large tower. Exquisite woodwork, beautiful stained glass, and extraordinary angles and perspectives make this a brilliant building to behold.

All Souls
Episcopal Cathedral

BILTMORE VILLAGE EXCURSIONS

American Indian Site

The Cherokee are called *Aniyunwiya, The Real People*. The naturally abundant confluence of the French Broad and Swannanoa Rivers provided an ideal site for a thriving Cherokee community, trading post, or seasonal hunting ground encampment. Cherokee never used teepees, which were designed for use in the western plains. At sites like this they lived in wattle-and-daub houses with thatched roofs. When polished, the clay floors shined like a mirror. The houses were set upon stilts for air circulation, to discourage insects and animals from entering, and in case the rivers flooded. The actual confluence of the rivers is visible from the Amboy Road bridge. There is a city park nearby.

Directions to the confluence of rivers:

As you leave downtown via Biltmore Road there is a stoplight at the bottom of the hill just before you enter Biltmore Village. Turn right onto Meadow Road (if you cross the railroad tracks on Biltmore Ave. you have gone too far). Remain on Meadow Road which will take you over a bridge and across the railroad tracks. Just past the railroad roundhouse on your right, at the first stoplight after the bridge, turn left onto Amboy Road and cross the Amboy Road bridge. This affords the best view of the convergence of the Swannanoa and French Broad Rivers. After crossing the French Broad River bridge, take an immediate right onto Riverview. The city park entrance is on your immediate right.

Biltmore Estate and Winery
828.255.1700
1.800.543.2961

Many of the 250 rooms in Biltmore House (America's largest privately owned home on an 8,000 acre estate) are open to the public. If you plan to tour the estate, we suggest setting aside at least half a day, if not more, to complete the experience. Be sure to rent one of the audio headset devices that talks to you informatively as you walk around the house. They are comfortable to use and are well worth the rental fee.

Hours and admission prices are subject to change on a seasonal basis, so call ahead for details, information on package deals and discounts, and special events. The ticket office is open from 9 a.m. to 5 p.m. We recommend calling ahead to find out if there is a waiting time for tours. Sometimes the lines can be long, especially during peak tourist seasons, but if you plan your visit carefully you might minimize any potential inconvenience. Above all, wear comfortable walking shoes and begin your excursion well-rested and ready for some major stroll action.

Biltmore Village Walking Tour

In 1887, George Vanderbilt, Asheville's most famous tourist, was captivated by Asheville. So captivated, in fact, that he chose it as the site of the largest private home in the world, his Biltmore House. It is said that the name Biltmore was derived from the name of his ancestral home of Bildt, Holland, combined with the word moor — an English term meaning "rolling hills."

On the site of present-day Biltmore Village was the small village of Best and an industrial area known as Asheville Junction.

George Vanderbilt bought up this piece of land and relocated its inhabitants to build an idyllic village modeled on an English country design. Vanderbilt envisioned the village as a fitting entrance to his mansion, Biltmore House.

Construction began in 1889, with workers filling in the flood-prone tract of land with earth. The existing brickworks served as a source of building materials for the village, whose first buildings were the church, the estate office, the plaza, and a new station. Next came some 30 dwellings for the professionals and artisans that were to service Vanderbilt's sprawling fiefdom. Luxurious for the time, the family cottages were built with indoor plumbing, furnaces and a fireplace in almost every room. The attention to architectural detail in the Biltmore House was mirrored in the artisan's cottages. For example, all wash basins were made from the same pricey rose marble as the mansion itself. Renting at $25 a month, these princely dwellings were hardly comparable to the company towns of the time, and were accessible only to Vanderbilt's most esteemed and well-paid staff.

Vanderbilt essentially recreated the physical and social design of an old feudal estate, where inhabitants depended on the health and whims of the lord of the manor. However, Vanderbilt was clearly a thoughtful person. He and his wife cared for their dependents rather well, unlike many entrepreneurs and barons of his time.

In 1905, Mrs. Vanderbilt helped estate workers establish cottage industries to promote mountain crafts such as weaving and woodworking. Individual craftspeople filled private orders for crafts which they made in their own homes. Their products bore the name "Biltmore Industries" and carried an insignia of a scroll emblazoned with the word "Forward!"

Unfortunately, several years after George Vanderbilt's death in 1914, his widow was forced to sell Biltmore Village to a Charlotte developer. Despite her attempts to protect the town's integrity by strict deed restrictions, these were neglected by new owners, and the "ideal village" began to disintegrate. Renewed interest in the late 1950s and early 1960s led to the first wave of renovation of what had become a run-down relic. It is only since the mid 1980s that conservation efforts have been concerted. Unfortunately, the village has not entirely survived the encroaching commercialism of late 20th century America. Inevitably, gas stations and fast-food joints have sprung up near the biggest tourist attraction of the area (Biltmore House), and 4-laners now bisect the village.

Once a thriving "model village" with its own stores, markets and workers, Biltmore Village is now mostly a strolling ground for tourists ready to shop (or find a convenient place to rest their bunions) after a long traipse through the Biltmore House. At one time, Biltmore law enforcers had to ready jails for the drunk and disorderly "country people" who came to town with their moonshine jugs. Nowadays the biggest obstacles to law and order in Biltmore Village seem to involve expired parking meters. It's a relatively tame district with a conspicuous lack of moonshine.

The present-day village, dramatically altered in appearance, offers shoppers the chance to purchase that indispensable must-have item such as an inflatable cupid or a rotating Saint Nicholas figurine manufactured in China. This is in vivid contrast to Biltmore Village's utilitarian past, when craft and function were wedded by necessity. However, high-falutin' tourist traps aside, there are interesting stores and eateries worth visiting in the modernized Village.

On the way to Biltmore Village you will pass a gas station and fast-food restaurant. Although it is hard to imagine, in a gentler age, this was a grassy plaza where Village residents played sports and relaxed under a covered pavilion. *Start your tour by turning left onto Lodge Street (part of Sweeten Creek Road) from Biltmore Ave., then turning right onto Kitchen Place and (hopefully) parking in one of the free spaces there.* Cross the street to check out the newer Biltmore Oteen Bank building, built between 1925-30. The building, whose architect is unknown, is an impressive 2-story Georgian Revival structure with Doric pilasters. Take a moment to look at the small pebbledash house beside the Hot Shot, which is now an old-fashioned shoe repair shop. This was the original Biltmore-Oteen Bank Building which was moved and turned sideways to accommodate the newer bank.

For a totally different dining experience, head next door for a plate of white soul food at the Hot Shot Cafe, a local favorite, especially at 2am, after a hard night on the town. Prepare to be welcomed by the smell of fresh-made biscuits, collards and bacon grease most times of the day or night at the Hot Shot. If you are a large man, chances are you will be greeted by the delightful staff as "tiny" or "honey", as they tirelessly refill that bottomless cup.

For some unusual N.C. glass artwork, check out the Vitrium

Gallerie next door. Don't miss the exquisite, yet affordable, glass and silver jewelry of Ruthie and Mike Cohen. Next to the old Oteen Bank is the Biltmore Depot (now a restaurant), which looks directly onto the train tracks. The inside of the restaurant has been "modernized" so many times that it bears little architectural resemblance to the original design, but the original exterior has changed little since the Vanderbilts disembarked in 1895 for the grand opening of Biltmore Estate. Designed by Richard Morris Hunt, (who also designed the Biltmore mansion), the depot remained in use as a passenger station until 1972, when passenger service was discontinued. Don't miss the wacky parking signs posted on the right side of the building that read "Jeff Gordon fans and Import Bike Parking This Way" (with sign pointing onto the railroad tracks). The other reads: "Harley Parking Only. All Others Will Be Laughed At." Talking of interesting sign-posting, don't miss the nearby Biltmore Barber Shop that advises us: "We need your head in business." Just to the right of this shop is a green-roofed building (now vacant) which was once the Biltmore Village post office.

Continuing your walking tour, re-cross Lodge Street and take a right on Kitchen Place until you reach the McGeachy Building on your right. Built in the mid 1920s, after Biltmore Village was sold off from the Biltmore Estate, architect Ronald Green's design harmonizes with existing structures with its simple ornamentation and decorative brick patterns. The McGeachy Building now houses the Early Music Store. Enjoy a leisurely time listening to Celtic, Native American and miscellaneous folk music before buying CDs. If you are musically inclined, try out their collection of dulcimers, drums, harps, autoharps, penny whistles, recorders and Indian flutes. Owner Cathy Toler claims she was thrown out of the Glee Club as a child because she sang off tune, and opened a music store with a partner out of "sweet revenge."

As you leave the Early Music Store, look across the street to the building housed by Talbot's. This was the site of the original plaza, the "commercial district" that served the villagers in Vanderbilt's time. It was turned into a recreation center in the 1940s. You can still see the ornamental bowling pins on the spire of the building.

Next door, in the same building, is the Biltmore Village Historic Museum (hours Mon-Sat 1:00-4:30), which features interesting photographs, newspaper articles, old postcards and other artifacts of the Village from the good old days. Next door is Bellagio, a classy, albeit pricey women's clothing store with silk designs to swoon for. Bellagio is part of the New Morning Gallery, whose entrance can be found just around the corner (to your right) on Boston Way. The New Morning Gallery is a well-established venue that sells exquisite local and not-so-

local crafts and artwork to discerning shoppers. The Gallery has the best selection of functional pottery in town, and perhaps in all of North Carolina. We know folks who got married just so they could set up a bridal registry at New Morning Gallery. That's how good the merchandise looks.

All Souls Episcopal Cathedral

Double back along Boston Way after your visit to New Morning Gallery and notice the ornate lampposts that look like they belong more in Prague than Western North Carolina. Take a right onto Kitchen Place and walk to **All Souls Episcopal Church** (now Cathedral of All Souls). Walk around the church until the sidewalk disappears, to fully appreciate its architectural features.

Built in 1896, and also designed by the prolific Richard Morris Hunt, All Souls was once the focal point of Biltmore Village. George Vanderbilt deeded the church to the Episcopal Diocese in 1891, but continued to support it financially after that time. The church extended its realm to provide a school and hospital (for Village residents), both of which were considered progressive for their time. The school fostered self-expression in its students, allowing them to publish a twice-annual unedited newspaper, until the school closed in 1905.

The Romanesque architecture of the church blends Gothic pointed arches and buttresses with the circular-topped windows more reminiscent of the Normans. The church's interior, shaped like a Greek cross, is surprisingly simple. However, the stained-glass windows (designed by Maitland Armstrong) are of richly colored opalescent American glass, rather than the customary painted antique glass. This opalescent glass was first produced in the U.S. in the 1880s by John La Farge, who wanted to revive the manufacturing methods of pre-Gothic Europe.

Leave the church by taking a right onto Angle Street, then a right onto Swan St, and follow it to its end, stopping at **Blue Goldsmiths**. This attractive store features highly original and wearable jewelry creations by two talented local designers. Cut through the small alleyway to the right of the store (check out the beautiful stained-glass to your right) and find yourself on All Souls Crescent.

On your left is **2 on Crescent**, another upscale store filled with women's clothing in soft, natural fabrics that will have you digging for your checkbook once more. They feature Birkenstocks®, Bluefish® handpainted cotton and linen designs, and the work of local artist Lisa Mandle, who hand-makes and embroiders her wearable creations, using antique buttons. Don't miss the especially Ashevillean affirmations on the labels sewn into the outfits, such as "My life is a picture of my mind," and "I believe in fun."

Turn right on All Souls Crescent, admiring the cottages designed by Richard Sharp Smith. Smith was Richard Hunt's protegé who supervised most of the Biltmore Estate's construction, and who also designed the YMI building in downtown Asheville. While each two-story cottage was different, Smith unified the buildings by including common architectural features such as half-timbering, pebbledash walls, and dormers. Smith's traditional English design was superimposed on a French fan-shaped layout to produce one of America's first planned communities.

If all this rampant consumerism has tired you out, stop by Hathaway's Village Cafe and Market (2 Boston Way), a friendly family-run coffee shop/cafe that brews a great cup of coffee and fresh bakes tempting pastries. Across the street on All Soul's Crescent is Once Upon a Time, selling toys, educational gifts and clothing for children.

Return to your car on Kitchen Place by doubling back on Boston Way.

It is worth visiting the Gardener's Cottage and Fireside Antiques and Interiors at 32 All Souls Crescent. However, walking from All Souls Church across Hwy 25 is tantamount to suicide, so I recommend driving this part. Get there by going down Kitchen Place, then taking a right onto Angle St, crossing Hwy 25 very carefully. The stores are directly in front of you. Gardener's Cottage is a landscaping, floral design and interior design studio that smells really good and makes you want to go straight home and re-pot that struggling *aspidistra* that your Aunt Ethel gave you last Christmas.

Fireside Antiques and Interiors is owned by Robert Griffin, a local architect who has been instrumental in preserving what is left of Biltmore Village's historical dwellings. His up-market antique store is comprised of two of Smith's cottages. Griffin, an architect by trade, actually moved all three cottages on the row from the other side of All Souls Crescent to save them from demolition in 1985. Griffin has described the area's encroaching modern buildings as "red flannel patches on the brocade tapestry that is Biltmore Village."

And before brocade tapestry was traded at this confluence of magical waters, the indigenous *Carolina Parakeet* flew through the virgin forest. *The colorful, tropical-looking parakeet vanished around the same time that the ceremonial fires of the Cherokee were extinguished from this vicinity.*

A DRIVE ALONG
TOWN MOUNTAIN ROAD
TO THE BLUE RIDGE PARKWAY

Town Mountain Road is a winding, switchback road which has stunning scenic views and narrow lanes which will challenge your defensive driving skills. Be careful not to space out on this journey because even some veteran mountain drivers find that it demands special focus, even when road and weather conditions are excellent. This route ascends quickly to the Blue Ridge Parkway, without the prerequisite bummer of Interstate traffic.

From the Chamber of Commerce, take I-240 east to the Charlotte St. exit going south. Turn left at College St., go to the Town Mountain Road intersection, and hang a left.

On your immediate right you will see the Hopkins Chapel Mount Zion, a Gothic Revival church designed by Richard Sharp Smith and executed by James. V. Miller, who rose from slave parentage to become one of the most celebrated builders and brickmasons in Asheville's history. Notice the quasi-flying buttresses which arc out from the sides of the building. This is one of the most unusual examples of Asheville church architecture. A restoration effort is underway.

Follow the somewhat treacherous Town Mountain Road a few miles, until you come to a rather discreet sign for Mt. Olive Church. The church, with its small but historic cemetery, is about three-tenths of a

The Etiquette of Mountain Driving:

When driving on the Parkway, please observe speed limits and, by all means, use the designated areas to pull over and let faster motorists pass. It's a safe way to drive, it's common courtesy, and it won't deprive you of reaching your destination in a timely fashion. Plus, you don't have to worry about some angry motorist shooting the back end of your new camper with a paint gun — or spitting chewing tobacco at your Cadillac when they finally get a chance to overtake you.

Incidentally, there is no need to ride your brakes all the way from Georgia to Vermont. The constant flash of red taillights promotes road rage in others. It's a psychological color thing (That's why police cars have soothing blue mood lights on top and farmers don't wear red overalls when they go out to feed the bull). Plus, that kind of driving wears out your brakes in a hurry. And brakes are really cool things to have when you're going down a mountain with three tons of luggage in your trunk and a pulpwood truck comes at you sideways in the wrong lane.

Try for an overall slower speed, and try to brake and reduce speed before entering curves, rather than during a panic attack in the middle of a hairpin turn. While you're at it, pretty-please-with-cherries-on-top don't straddle the white line in a 50-foot motor coach that's as wide as the Gulf of Mexico.

Recent studies show that drivers who observe these simple rules of horse sense lead more peaceful, guilt-free lives and often survive to tell about it.

Parkway Closures:
A golden opportunity for some forms of recreation

Sometimes sections of the Blue Ridge Parkway are closed because of weather conditions, budget-foolishness on Capitol Hill, or fallen trees and rocks which obstruct the roadway.

But even if the Parkway is closed to automotive traffic, walking, snowskiing, or bicycling may still be permitted. Such limited closures can be a special treat because you don't have to compete with cars, trucks, and motorhomes. During such closures, those who are permitted to use the Parkway have the whole thing to themselves and it's an exceptional opportunity. We know mountain bikers and cross-country skiers who pray incessantly for Parkway closures.

For Blue Ridge Parkway information and announcements call 828.298.0398.

mile down a gravel and dirt road which leads off to the right.

Continue up Town Mountain Rd. until you come to the entrance to the Blue Ridge Parkway. On a clear day, the vistas along Town Mountain Rd. are outstanding. They get even better once it intersects with the Parkway.

Traveling north on the Parkway about half a mile you come to Tanbark Ridge Overlook, elevation 3,175 ft., near mile marker 377. At mile marker 370 is Beetree Gap, elevation 4,900 ft. Traveling ten miles to milemarker 360, you arrive at Glassmine Falls scenic overlook. At elevation 5,677 ft. Glassmine Falls is the highest point north of the immediate Asheville area. At the base of the falls is what remains of the Abernathy Mine, a source for mica. The transparent mineral was commonly called isinglass or simply glass. For this reason, mica mines were sometimes referred to as glass mines.

If you choose to head south on the Parkway, then five miles from the Town Mountain Rd. intersection you come to the Folk Art Center at mile marker 382. This combination folk art gallery/store/resource center deserves an hour's worth of browsing time. Ask the park rangers here for books, maps, or recommendations of other sites to visit while on the Parkway.

Mid-September:

Experience a sky full of flutter-byes. South past the Folk Art Center is mile marker 415.6, at Tunnel Gap. Each year, in mid-September, many thousands of Monarch butterflies pass through Tunnel Gap en route to Central Mexico from the eastern United States and Canada. Their autumn migration covers approximately 1,800 miles.

We first learned of the Monarch migration from a fellow we met while hiking in the Shining Rock Wilderness Area. We were all admiring a passing butterfly when the gentleman began to describe the experience of waking up at his campsite during a recent migration and "Walking into a veritable fog of fluttering butterfly wings." He told us how to get there, adding, "They swarmed around me like a fogbank of color." In exchange for the information about the Migration, we shared (and showcased) two or three of our freshest banjo player jokes. The jokes worked like laughing gas on a ticklish hyena.

Folk Art Center and Allanstand Craft Shop

Milepost 382
Blue Ridge Parkway
828.298.7928
Daily 9am-5pm Jan-Mar.
Daily 9am-6pm April-Dec.

The Allanstand was the first craft shop in the nation, established in 1895 by Frances Goodrich. Once located in downtown Asheville, the Allenstand is now part of the Folk Art Center on the Parkway. Here you can still find superlative examples of crafts in a variety of media, including pottery, wood, glass, fiber, metal and jewelry.

Craftspeople represented at the Folk Art Center are all members of the Southern Highlands Craft Guild, an educational non-profit organization comprising some 700 craftspeople from the mountain counties in nine Southeastern states. The Guild's purpose is to offer a network and market for local craftspeople, in order to help preserve mountain crafts. However, this does not imply that all the work presented is traditional. The center blends traditional work such as quilting masterpieces with more contemporary pieces such as fabulous raku pottery.

The Folk Art Center hosts art and craft exhibitions in a spacious upstairs gallery and has a bookstore with titles of interest to hikers and naturalists. Staff at the Blue Ridge Parkway information area (located within the center) will help you navigate your ridge-top road trip.

Be prepared to spend at least half an hour at the Folk Art Center and lots more time if you are a shop-'til-you-drop-aholic. Seasoned shoppers may get a hankering to feel the texture of every chenille wrap and try on an inordinate number of handmade earrings. But to avoid marital discord, anti-shoppers are advised to go hiking while the shoppers satisfy their acquisitive urges.

NATURE WALKS
IN ASHEVILLE

If you are interested in getting a little fresh air and exercise, but don't fancy driving far, try these short walks within Asheville city limits.

Botanical Gardens
W.T. Weaver Boulevard

The Botanical Garden's mission statement declares that it is a "non-profit organization dedicated to the collection and display of native plants for the education and enjoyment of the public."

Started in the 1960s by garden ladies and their ever-useful bake sales, the garden is still funded by charitable donations and maintained with the help of UNCA, the City of Asheville and volunteers. The gardens will be on the proposed "Green Route," which will bring long-awaited cycle paths to the city. However, no bicycles or pets are allowed in the garden itself. What makes the gardens unique is the fact that they exclusively grow plant and tree species native to North Carolina. Visiting the gardens is a great way to brush up on your tree identification skills, as most are labeled with their Latin and common names. Delight in the Loblolly Pines, and impress your friends with your intimate knowledge of trees such as the Viburnum Prunifolium ("Black Haw" for the uninitiated).

The sensory garden is a work in progress that may appeal to blind visitors. Look out for special events such as plant sales, slide shows, talks, and informational walks. The gardens have a short but informative walking trail with benches. A great place for a picnic.

The visitor center is open 9:30-4:00, the gardens are open during daylight hours.

Directions from the Chamber of Commerce:

Turn right out of the Chamber of Commerce and take a right at the light onto Montford Avenue. Pass the Reader's Corner Bookstore on your right, (stopping off to pick up a second hand book to read at the lake, if you wish). Take a right onto Chestnut St., and follow this until you get to Broadway and a 5-way intersection. Take a left onto Broadway, then a right at the W.T. Weaver Blvd. traffic light. Get into the left lane, as the Gardens are a short distance away on the left.

Western North Carolina Nature Center
75 Gashes Creek Road
828.298.5600

The environmental educational center is a world of nature unto itself, brimming with exhibits about plants, animals, and everything from weather conditions in the mountains to archeology. Want to see a beehive in action, a real live otter, wolf, peacock, coon, or wildcat? Step into the nature center. There is even a walkway that rises through the tops of tall trees, like a continuous treehouse.

Beaver Lake

Merrimon Ave.

This is a popular spot for North Asheville residents to walk and fish on the weekends or after work. Dogs and kids abound at this scenic spot, as do ducks and the occasional heron. Unfortunately, you can't walk all the way around the lake, so combine this walk with a stroll on the boardwalk built as a nature trail. This area has its own parking lot and is located at the end of the lake which is nearest downtown. Go past the concrete abstract sculpture on a short stretch of sidewalk to reach this trail. Don't forget to take some bread to feed the ducks.

Beaver Lake

Directions from the Chamber of Commerce:

There are several ways to get there, but this one is a little more scenic than taking Merrimon Avenue the whole way: Follow the directions to the Botanical Gardens but pass it and continue on W.T. Weaver Blvd. until the road deadends. Then take a left onto Merrimon Ave. Follow Merrimon until you have gone past the large Ingle's grocery store on your right at an intersection surrounded by small shopping centers. You will come to a part of the road where Merrimon becomes lined with impressive sycamore trees (This always reminds me of a French avenue).

At the end of the tree-lined section, turn left into the parking area off Glen Falls Rd. From here, go around the left side of the lake. If the lot is full, backtrack along Merrimon and park on a widened area on the second section of Midland Dr., to your left.

North Carolina Arboretum and Bent Creek

A visit to these two adjacent sites can be combined. The Arboretum and Bent Creek are popular with locals as a get-away near the city. They offer the best mountain biking and hiking that you can get to in the Asheville area without having to drive a long distance.

The Arboretum comprises 424 acres leased from the Forest Service by the University of North Carolina in 1988 for the purpose of educational programs, research, conservation and the display of plants native to the Southern Appalachian Region. The Arboretum offers educational programs in landscape design, horticulture, plant propagation and gardening, as well as guided garden tours.

Arboretum staff are quick to point out that the three-year-old garden is still in its beginning stages. More elaborate projects are planned for the future, including a demonstration greenhouse and a conservatory. The more natural trails are far from sparse, however, and the Arboretum's subtle tree identification markers enhance one's enjoyment of the area. Call 828.665.2492 to ask for latest information about the Arboretum's educational programs and tours, or just show up and wander around on your own.

They provide an excellent free map of the whole Arboretum property to help you navigate the gardens and trails.

Hours of Operation

Visitor's Center: Mon-Sat 8:00am-5:00pm
2nd and 4th Sundays 1:30-4:30pm
Property access (including access gates):
daily 8:00 am-4:00 p.m.
Greenhouse Hours: Mon-Fri 8:00 am-4:00 p.m.
Guided Garden Tours: Tue-Sat 11:00 am, Sun 2:00 p.m.

Bent Creek Experimental Forest consists of some 2000 acres bought by the Forest Service in 1925. Prior to that time, the area had been heavily logged, and the Forest Service wished to study the rehabilitation of this stretch of Southern Appalachian Forest. The system of trails is documented in the Pisgah National Forest Area map.

Nearby Lake Powhatan Recreation Area, administered by Pisgah National Forest and the Cradle of Forestry, has a swimming / fishing lake, (with a disabled access fishing pier) trails, camping and picnic areas. The campsite is open from April 1st to the last day in October and costs $14/night for tents, $20/RV with hook-up. The campsite has hot showers and most of its 96 sites are secluded and shaded. Many newcomers stay here while apartment-seeking.

Directions to Arboretum, Bent Creek, and Lake Powhatan from Chamber of Commerce

Take I-240W to I-26E to exit 2. Take a left at the end of the exit ramp onto 191S., go past all the mall and strip shopping center stuff and look for the brown sign pointing you to the Arboretum and Lake Powhatan. Take a right here and go 1 mi. until you get to the Arboretum entrance on your left. Go a little further to Hardtimes trail head on your left where you can park for free to get to Lake Powhatan and for hiking or biking on Bent Creek trails. Continue on this road until it deadends into Lake Powhatan Recreation Area if you wish to camp or park close to the lake.

A lifeguard is present at the swimming lake only during warmer months, but you can swim there any time. The water is a little murky, but kids seem to love it. If you want to park near the lake, you pay $3 for parking, but most folks park at no cost at the Hardtimes Trailhead (on the left a little ways before the entrance) and walk to the lake that way. Call Lake Powhatan at 828.862.5960 for information about camping.

Suggested walks in the Arboretum / Bent Creek

Longer walks:

1. Park in the Arboretum parking lot and pick up a map of the area from one of the white mailboxes. Take the sandy-gravel road around the right side of Visitor's Center and continue downhill, taking a right at the first trail intersection onto Bent Creek Trail. Follow the signs to Lake Powhatan as the trail winds prettily alongside the creek. You will come to a fork in the road, with Rocky Cove Rd. going off to your left, and Bent Creek Trail continuing to your right. Stay on this trail, going through the Arboretum boundary gate until you reach Lake Powhatan. You can walk around the lake by taking the small trail off to your left shortly after the fishing pier. Then return the way you came. This makes about a 5 mi. trip.

2. Take the Habitat Hike which passes through several ecological communities including a stream bottom, laurel and rhododendron thickets, hemlocks and various hardwoods. The trail is 3.7 mi. and has interpretive signs along the way. To get to the trail head, park in the Lake Powhatan parking area (or just outside it if you wish to avoid paying $3). Be aware that many of the Bent Creek trails are closed to mountain bikes during the summer months (from about April 15 to October).

Here are some hints for following the trail where the signposting is a little unclear: After seeing the old homestead remains, take a right onto Explorer Trail (with its yellow blaze mark). Later, take a left to go uphill through a dense rhododendron thicket on this trail. At the end of Explorer Trail, you will intersect with an unmarked gravel road. Take a right here, go over the concrete bridge and past the campsites, taking another right onto a bigger gravel road. Go about 50 yards and take an unmarked trail going uphill to the left. At the time of this writing the trail is marked by two white stripes spray-painted on two trees. This is Lower Sidehill Trail and has an orange blaze marker. Follow this to the Habitat Hike's conclusion. You will end up back on the paved road at Lake Powhatan camping area.

Directions

From the campground toll-booth, go straight down the paved road until you cross a bridge. Look out for the beaver dam to your right as you cross the creek. Directly on your right after the bridge you will see the trail head and the first interpretive sign. The Habitat Hike is fairly well marked with brown arrow signs, and is made up of several different pre-existing trails, including Pine Tree Loop, Explorer Trail, and Lower Sidehill Trail.

Trail Features:

Bent Creek valley was inhabited by American Indian tribes throughout the 1800s and later settled by more than 100 European families until it was acquired by George Vanderbilt's estate. You can see the remnants of a settler's homestead on the Habitat Hike. The trail also helps you identify previously inhabited areas by looking for unusual, non-native plant species such as yucca that homesteaders planted around the house.

Look out for the fabric acorn-catching nets on Lower Sidehill trail. They are used to collect acorns to be weighed as part of an experiment to determine how forest management practices affect "mast" production. Mast refers to the edible nuts and berries that provide the main source of food for forest wildlife. The interpretive signs tell you everything you ever wanted to know about acorns, and more. You will also learn how to estimate the age of a white pine (its all in the "whorls", apparently), and the difference between mesic (moist) and xeric (dry) soil sites.

Shorter walk:

Park at the Hard Times trailhead and take the trail downhill, taking a right at the first intersection and going around Lake Powhatan, returning the way you came. This is about a 2 mi. loop.

Walk to the historic Grove Park Inn from downtown Asheville

Distance from the Chamber of Commerce: 4.4 mi.
Distance from Charlotte St.: 3 mi.

This seems like an unlikely trek, but is actually quite lovely. While there is no official sidewalk on Sunset Dr., the traffic is light. The walk takes you through some of Asheville's prettiest residential areas, and the heavily forested roads put one in mind of a country stroll rather than an urban jaunt. In the leafless seasons, there is a superb view of Asheville's modest skyline and the surrounding hills. There is also the potential for an ice-cold gin and tonic at the conclusion of your walk, because the Grove Park Inn serves beverages.

Depending on just how many G & Ts you quaff, you can get back on foot, by taxi (for a few dollars) or by the tourist trolley for about $6.

If you decide to walk back, you can either back track or go down Macon Avenue until you get to Charlotte St. again. From there you would take a left onto Charlotte.

Directions from the Chamber of Commerce

(*If you want to park a little closer to lessen your walk, try parking somewhere around the Charlotte Street area.*) Take a right out of the C of C parking lot, then another right onto Montford Ave. After a few blocks you will take a right onto Chestnut Street and follow it all the way across Broadway, across Merrimon and across Charlotte St. This part of the walk is 1.4 miles. Stay on Chestnut until you come to Furman Ave. and go left. Take a right onto Baird, then a left onto Sunset Dr.

If you are getting tired, get off Sunset Dr. when you see a house with a natural wood fence on your right. On your left, (at 1.6 miles after the junction of Charlotte St. and Chestnut), a grassy path goes down to Macon Ave, where you take a right to get to the Grove Park Inn.

But if you still have energy, keep walking on Sunset Dr. until you see Old Toll Road. Take a left onto Old Toll, then take a right onto a natural trail across from 604 Old Toll Rd (at 2.6 miles). This natural trail goes downhill until you get to the Grove Park Inn grounds.

AMERICAN INDIAN

AFRICAN AMERICAN

MISCELLANEOUS SITES

SPECIAL INTERESTS TOURS

MARIJO MOORE
CHEROKEE AUTHOR-POET
JOURNALIST-ARTIST

© Ellenburg

What do you admire most in a person?
Honesty and open mindedness.

What's the most important historical event in your lifetime?
The Vietnam war ending.

What's the best compliment someone has given you recently?
At a recent lecture I gave, I was told that my words are powerful and full of truth.

What's your favorite quotation?
"Some days you get the bear. Some days the bear gets you. And some days, you can't even find the woods."
(From Moore's book <u>Tree Quotes</u>.)

What magazines do you read on a regular basis?
<u>Native Artists</u> magazine.

Who is your favorite writer?
Rainer Maria Rilke.

What's your idea of an ideal way to spend the day? The night?
My ideal way of spending the day would be to have someone dear read poetry to me under a great hemlock with the crows cawing in the background. The night? Having someone dear read poetry to me in front of a roaring fire.

What is the one place you would be sure to take a first-time visitor to Asheville?
Malaprop's Bookstore.

If you could declare a holiday in Asheville, what would it celebrate?
American Indian youth.

What is the one place you would take a first-time visitor to Cherokee?
Museum of the Cherokee Indian.

What's your favorite place in the region?
Anywhere ancestral spirits are speaking and that is everywhere in these old mountains.

What's your favorite place to go walking?
In the mountains behind my house.

What's the most unusual thing you have ever encountered in the woods?
I am always finding pieces of wood that are shaped like animals or birds. And I am always finding crow feathers.

What makes this area home to you, as opposed to just a place to live?
These old mountains are the homeland of my Cherokee ancestors. Their spirits still linger here, inspiring my writings.

What meal would you love to have prepared for you? By whom?
Lobster Newberg by any good cook.

If you were going to live on a desert island for two years what three things (besides food and water) would you take?
A collection of the writings of Rainer Maria Rilke, the book <u>God Is Red</u> by Vine Deloria, Jr., and lots of blank paper and pens.

If you could meet someone you haven't met who would it be and what would you like to ask them?
I'd like to meet Robbie Robertson and convince him to incorporate some of my writings into his next recording.

What question would you most like to have asked of you and how would you answer it?
I am often asked to define spirituality and I always answer, "Spirituality is paying attention."

183

AMERICAN INDIAN
CULTURAL AND HISTORICAL
EXCURSIONS

The original homeland of the Cherokees encompassed an area from the Ohio River south to what is now Atlanta, Georgia, across Virginia, North Carolina, South Carolina, Tennessee, Kentucky and Alabama. Today, Cherokees live in various states, as well as in Europe and other countries. Qualla Boundary, located about sixty miles west of Asheville, consists of 5600 acres and is home to the Eastern Band of Cherokees.

Bo Taylor, archivist at the Museum of the Cherokee Indian, states that the Cherokee are called *Aniyunwiya* which means "Real People" in their tribal language.

Thousands of distinct American Indian languages have been silenced forever due to pandemics of smallpox and other diseases brought by European contact, acculturation, and total annihilation. However, some still exist and various tribes are doing their best to revitalize their languages.

"Time is of the essence," according to Tom Belt, language instructor at Cherokee Elementary School on Qualla Boundary. He explains that linguists studying Native languages estimate there are maybe 50 years left before all Native languages are completely gone, if they continue to dissipate at the rate they have over the past 100 years. So Belt is extremely enthusiastic about the preschool's current language immersion program. Preschool children are being taught the Cherokee language and will continue in this program until they graduate from high school.

Many scientists cling to the theory that the Western Hemisphere was populated by immigrants who crossed the Bering Strait but many American Indians believe as firmly that the Indian originated on this continent. Some say we have always been in these mountains. My elder aunt says we came from the stars. Regardless, there is definitely a strong creative power within the Cherokees that cannot be destroyed. The power of ancestral blood in which history and hope continually renew themselves, and the beauty it expresses, knows no limitations.

When you visit Qualla Boundary, please try to ignore the tourist trap of stereotyping and do not ask, "Where are the Indians?" Chances are you'll be asking a Cherokee. Traditionally, Cherokees did not wear headdresses or live in teepees.

For those who have Cherokee blood, welcome to the ancestral homeland. For those who don't, welcome also.

MariJo Moore with her Uncle Joe, the sad-eyed wooden Indian of the highlands.

Oconaluftee Indian Village

Visit Oconaluftee Indian Village and you'll find yourself in the shadows of age-old mountains and giant evergreens - in a place where time has crawled inside itself and become an authentic recreated Cherokee village of 225 years ago.

Here you can witness Cherokee men making dugout canoes with fire and axe and carving ceremonial masks from blocks of wood. Cherokee women will be stringing beads, making baskets from strips of river cane, and practicing the ancient art of finger-weaving. The seven-sided *Ana ska yi* (Council House) provides insight into ancient tribal government.

If you are curious about handmade clay pottery, you may stop and watch as a beautiful woman kneads coarse mixed sand and clay in a hand-carved wooden dough bowl with quiet determination—as if she is preparing biscuits for her family. After kneading this mixture to the consistency of putty, she will work it into the shape of a small shallow *dewa li'* (bowl), then shape the outside by beating it quickly with a *gastoti* (small wooden paddle) that is dipped in water now and again. This piece will be allowed to dry for three days before it is propped on its side around a hot fire burning in a hearth of flat river stones sunk level with the earth. The result will be a stunning work of art proudly accentuating the fact that this ancient American Indian tradition can and does live on.

The Museum of the Cherokee Indian

Very rarely does one have the opportunity to use all senses when visiting a museum. Most are cold, somewhat sterile, and at best, boring. Not so in The Museum of the Cherokee Indian in Cherokee, North Carolina. A $3.5 million renovation has brought the history of the Cherokee people to life. Especially touching is an exhibit showing soldiers removing a family

185

from their cabin. Rebecca Neugin, a Georgia Cherokee woman who lived during this time, tells her heartbreaking story as chilling cries muffled with gunfire are heard in the background. Just around the corner, a list of spoken names of those who died on the Trail of Tears float from a wall depicting a beautifully done, albeit sad, mural of the agony of The Removal.

There are many, many emotions experienced while taking this journey. Some scenes will remain in the mind to haunt, some as a reminder that Cherokee people have overcome various obstacles and are determined to educate others about themselves.

Along toward the end of the journey, from a seemingly empty wall, a computerized video suddenly appears. A story belt, which is a symbol of Cherokee tradition, was once consumed by flames, and yet it survived and is still intact today. The Cherokee woman speaks to the hearts of all who will listen as she says, "And just as the belt survived, so do our stories and so does our land, and so do we, the Cherokee, the *Tsa la gi*."

View of the Lost City of *Unta 'kiyasti' yi*

Go to Blue Ridge Parkway Milepost 380 on a clear day and you can actually see the lost city of *Unta 'kiyasti' yi* in its present form and manifestation as Asheville, North Carolina.

Unta 'kiyasti' yi is the Cherokee word for the Asheville area meaning "Where they race." American Indian foot races were held in the land which is now known as Asheville because it is flat and conducive to running. Foot races were an important event; not only were they festive occasions for sporting competition, but also they were vital to communication. The winners of the foot races served their villages as messengers throughout the year. They were depended upon to convey messages on foot, between the geographically distanced communities scattered throughout this region.

Looking Glass Rock

Located at milepost 417 on the Parkway, Looking Glass Rock was so named because of how light reflects from its surface after a rainfall. Cherokees associate it with the legend of *Tsul 'kalu'*, the slant-eyed mountain-dwelling giant. The opulently shiny rock is one of the naturally sacred locations where American Indians visit for inspiration and to share oral history regarding the legends associated with the rock.

Confluence of the Swannanoa and French Broad Rivers

It is believed that the present site of *Biltmore Village*, at the confluence of the Swannanoa and French Broad Rivers, was once a thriving Cherokee settlement. American Indians chose sites with relatively level land located alongside a good source of water for their villages, and this location was ideal. The forests here were lush and the wildlife abundant, so it is likely that this location was either a permanent village or a seasonal hunting camp and trading post.

Directions to the confluence of the Swannanoa and French Broad Rivers

From the Chamber of Commerce parking lot, turn left onto Haywood St. Continue on Haywood St.(which meanders toward the right in front of the Civic Center, and proceed through downtown to the intersection with Patton Ave. Turn left on Patton Ave. and continue to the intersection of Biltmore Ave (the Vance Monument will be directly in front of you). Turn right on Biltmore Ave. and continue for about 20 blocks, passing the hospitals and heading downhill into Biltmore Village.

At the stoplight at the bottom of the hill just before Biltmore Village, turn right onto Meadow Road (if you cross the railroad tracks on Biltmore Ave. you have gone too far). Remain on Meadow Road which will take you over a bridge and across the railroad tracks. Just past the railroad roundhouse on your right, at the first stoplight after the bridge, turn left onto Amboy Road and cross the Amboy Road bridge. This affords the best view of the convergence of the Swannanoa and French Broad Rivers. After crossing the French Broad River bridge, take an immediate right onto Riverview. The river park entrance is on your immediate right.

Shining Rock Mountain and Graveyard Fields Overlook

At milepost 419 on the Parkway is this legendary dwelling place of invisible spirits who still reside there within the winds encircling the mountain. The Cherokee call it *Datsu 'nalasgun' yi* which translates as *Where Their Tracks Are This Way*. At the base of the rock are markings thought to be the tracks of the legendary giant *Tsul 'kalu'*. Listen carefully at Shining Rock; it is believed that there are valuable lessons to be learned from the natural sounds of the site. (The gray trunks of spruce trees and randomly scattered stumps give the pastures at this site the appearance of a graveyard, and that is the only reason for the origin of the name Graveyard Fields.)

Duniskwa 'lgun' yi (also known as Chimney Tops)

Great Smoky Mountains National Park (On the western side off highway 441)

The breathtaking site of this double-peaked rock reminded early settlers of the stone chimneys of their mountain cabins. But to American Indians it looked more like deer antlers. The name *Duniskwa 'lgun' yi* is Cherokee for *The Gap of the Forked Antler*. The name implies that the antlers are still attached to the deer that lies in the mountain below.

The views from the top are awesome, and the potential for an inspirational, spiritually uplifting experience can more than compensate for the physical sacrifice required to get there. American

The Cherokee used to refer to Asheville as *Kasdu'yi*, which literally means Ashes Place.

Indians consider this one of the most sacred, beautiful, and spiritually connected sites in the entire region. Many still go there to read the spiritual signs presented by the natural vista.

Leaving Cherokee, take highway 441 across the park to the Tennessee side, as if traveling to Gatlinburg, TN. The well-marked trailhead for Chimney Tops is approximately eight miles from Newfound Gap. The hike to the summit of Chimney Tops and back is a strenuous four-mile round-trip which takes most hikers about three hours to complete.

Petroglyphs Carved Into Judaculla Rock

This well-marked but not-so-well understood and mysteriously explained site is just off NC Hwy. 107 between Cashiers and Cullowhee, NC.

There have been many explanations and speculations as to the origin of the petroglyphs carved into Judaculla Rock, which is also called *Tsul 'kalu'*. The Cherokee explain the marks as being made by the slant-eyed giant *Tsul 'kalu'* as he jumped from his mountaintop home down onto the rock. He did this whenever he went to get water from a nearby creek to water his fields.

Judaculla Rock is located 3.5 miles south from Cullowhee, NC, via State Road 107, then three miles east on Caney Fork Road (SR 1737). It sits under an open-sided shed in pasture land.

Spirits On The River Restaurant

Owners Flip and Ann Bell operate the region's best-kept secret. This hideaway on Swannanoa River Road is housed in a relatively nondescript building and is easy to miss, even if you're looking for it. But those who discover it keep coming back, and word-of-mouth keeps spreading the secret far and wide.

Feeling lost?
Take a deep breath and learn from the traditional teachings of the Cherokee People: Cherokee tradition explains that there are seven directions—North, South, East, West, Above, Below, and You In The Center.

A maze of Indian artifacts, books, jewelry and carvings greet visitors as they head through the rustic main dining room to the riverside deck, which is decorated with flaming torches atop river cane poles. On a clear night the moon shines across the flowing water, where the sound of the river accompanies the restaurant's Native American music. Sometimes there are live performances of traditional American Indian music, drumming, and dance.

The menu is unique and exotic: Buffalo, rattlesnake, gator, trout, quail, and pheasant. And *Spirits* offers an excellent selection of vegetarian items. Whatever featured entree you choose, try the Sacred Seven Salad and raspberry vinaigrette dressing, and pure wild rice or a twice-baked potato. For dessert sample the authentic Indian frybread with smooth-flowing honey or ice cream on top.

Cherokee Visitors Information
1.800.438.1601

Offices of the Eastern Band of the Cherokee Nation
1.800.357.2771

Council House and Tribal Chief
Eastern Band of the Cherokee Nation
P.O. Box 455
Cherokee, NC 28719

We asked a Cherokee Shaman to comment on the excavation of Indian burial grounds by archeologists in Western North Carolina:

"I hope the ground opens up and swallows them all. You wouldn't let them go into a Baptist Church cemetery and start digging up graves, would you?"

We asked an American Indian for advice we could share with visitors about avoiding the tourist traps surrounding Indian reservations:

"Well, one time I saw tourists offering wads of cash to a Navajo Indian who was standing in his front yard trying to clean out his fish tank. They wanted to buy the discarded aquamarine fish tank gravel from him for fifteen dollars a handful because they assumed it was actually turquoise." (laughter) "I would suggest to tourists that it's wise to avoid that kind of thing."

IN THESE MOUNTAINS

As dreams begin to dance themselves awake
after a day of full flushing rains in these mountains
the bronze hands of women reach from beneath the earth
their bones glowing like neon fishes in cave waters.

Droplets pelt the underfur of delicate wild flowers
steam rises to kiss moistened lips of falling leaves
while I wander around inside the past
watching, waiting, hearing the bronze women calling my name.

Memories unfold from around these glorious ancestral mountains
positioning themselves into low hanging fog
touching the soft breasts of those who pay attention
as the rains fall down into running waters
stopping only when instructed so by the Thunder Beings.

Sweet tobacco smells rise from the white water falling
and I taste the aroma as it floats into my being.
This is when the memories come close enough to smell
but not close enough to touch just close enough to taste
but never close enough to touch.

And sometimes late in the afternoon
after it rains all day in these mountains
if I know in just which direction to tilt my head
and if I listen intently through the raindrops

I can hear gentle, sleepy, rhythmic sounds of small rounded
pebbles clicking inside tortoise-shell rattles
strapped to the ankles of the bronze women
as they dance the Green Corn Dance reminding me

I am never alone in these mountains.

©1995 *MariJo Moore*

*MariJo Moore is a Cherokee author/poet/journalist/artist. Her published
works include **Spirit Voices of Bones**, **Crow Quotes**, and **Tree Quotes**,
all of which are available at Malaprops Bookstore. For more information,
send a SASE to rENEGADE pLANETS pUBLISHING, PO Box 2493,
Candler, NC 28715*

The Arrival of Europeans in Cherokee Territory

Up to 95 percent of the American Indian population in this region was vanquished because of contact with Europeans, according to scholarly estimates. A great percentage of Cherokees died before ever contacting a white person, because smallpox and other European epidemics arrived with the Europeans but preceded them into American Indian territory. In some instances, death would begin within days of the arrival of European ships, and would travel via merchandise traded between the Europeans and American Indians.

Or in other cases, American Indian traders contacted white traders and then returned to their homes and villages, where they, along with their families and communities, were wiped out by the invisible diseases unwittingly imported from contact with Europeans.

The first Europeans to step foot on Cherokee land were the 600 members of De Soto's search party. They arrived well-armed and eager to find the gold which they believed was plentiful in these mountains. They tortured and murdered many Cherokees who could not point to the location of these nonexistent, imaginary gold mines.

Virginia was the first of the thirteen original colonies upon which this country was founded. Some visitors from that state stopped at Cherokee recently for breakfast and their waitress, a full-blooded Cherokee woman, asked them:
"So, where are you fellas from?"
"We're from Virginia, ma'am."
"Well, welcome to America!"
she said with a grin.

AFRICAN AMERICAN HISTORICAL TOUR

African Americans were among the first settlers in this region. In the 17th Century they began arriving as porters and teamsters for American Indian traders. The first white settler, Samuel Davidson, brought African American slaves to work his farmland when he moved here in 1784. Others arrived later as homesteaders, many as laborers, and most as slaves.

The contributions made by African Americans to the creation, establishment, growth, and survival of the city of Asheville are phenomenal, quintessential, beautiful, and....in many respects...tragically unrecognized or systematically minimized. This guided excursion through downtown is intended to provoke an understanding and appreciation of African American Asheville's profound history, by giving you a glimpse into its far-ranging, high-reaching, and glorious panorama.

Beginning from the **Chamber of Commerce***, turn right and walk through the Chamber of Commerce parking lot to the* **Montford Avenue overpass** *which crosses over Interstate 240.* Look east, off into the distance, and you will notice that the Interstate cuts through a range of mountains on the eastern side of town. Parallel to I-240, and a few degrees south, another major city artery cuts through the Beaucatcher Tunnel, which was carved from Beaucatcher Mountain. The original highways and tunnels of Asheville were built by an almost exclusively African American labor pool.

In the 1830s, the great Buncombe tollroad was constructed. In the 1880s, a railroad was built. At the turn of the century George Vanderbilt's Biltmore Estate was created and a burgeoning real estate market, tourist industry, and overall boomtown fever erupted. African Americans came to Asheville in three distinct waves of migration which were intrinsically tied to the town's need for labor. The city grew in relationship to the influx of African Americans because their presence was, in fact, one of the most necessary factors in its development.

Look across the bridge into the Montford neighborhood, where African American craftsmen helped to construct our most celebrated historical houses. On the western side of Montford is a community park complex with a baseball field and amphitheater.

You can't actually see it from the Montford Ave. bridge, but it's about half a mile away, through the trees to the left of Montford Ave. In the early 1900s the park site was occupied by the small but close-knit neighborhood of **Stumptown**, one of Asheville's largest African American communities.

St. Lawrence Basilica

Now return to the entrance to the Chamber of Commerce and head east along Haywood St., to the **St. Lawrence Basilica.** Spanish architect Rafael Guastavino designed this famous church which is constructed entirely of stone, mortar, brick, and tile. He hired local African American masons, many of whom had contributed their craftsmanship to Biltmore House, to do most of the highly skilled work. Continue past the Civic Center, (where **George Clinton** and **P-Funk** performed in 1998 to a hip-shaking crowd of funkaholics), until you come to the Castenea building at 57 Haywood St. The building, constructed in 1921 of locally produced orange-brown brick, is a vivid example of the expertise displayed by Asheville's early masons. African Americans not only laid the bricks showcased in this kind of construction, but in most cases they were the ones who actually created the bricks themselves. And, yes, indeed, the clay from which the bricks were made was dug out of the ground by the hard labor of African Americans.

One of the most remarkable examples of African American craftsmanship in Asheville happens to be one of the most common sights in the city. And yet, it goes almost entirely unrecognized. *Walk down Haywood St. to* **Walnut St.** *and turn left.* Continue down this long steep lane but pay close attention to the granite curbs which line the sidewalk. You will notice that most of them have a hammered appearance, and that the surface of the granite is chipped and beveled in an attractive pattern. These curbstones, which extend below street level (and beyond the view of the naked eye) were handmade by African American stone masons. Throughout the city, these marvelous examples of fine craftsmanship and excruciating labor can be found, humbly lining the streets of Asheville.

Follow Walnut St. to **Lexington Ave.** *and turn right, continuing uphill to the intersection.* Lexington Ave. is one of the most popular and busiest streets in town, famous for its commercial activity generated by the dozens of shops which line both sides of the avenue. But few shoppers realize that the very first storefront enterprise opened on Lexington Ave. was African American owned and operated.

The Newlands:
Lexington Avenue's Entrepreneurial Pioneers

The first business on Lexington Ave. was opened in the 1870s by an African American couple, Mr. and Mrs. Isom Newland. They converted an abandoned livery stable (near the Patton Avenue intersection) into a successful bakery.

Imagine the change in air quality that occurred when the stench of horse manure was replaced by the aroma of fresh-baked bread and apple pie. They served breads, pies, cakes, and an assortment of other scrumptious goodies to walk-in customers, restaurants, and private homes throughout the city. The best hotels, restaurants, and guest houses bought baked goods from the Newlands.

There are several natural springs running beneath the city. The most significant ones run along Pritchard Park on Patton Ave and then curve downhill along Lexington Ave. They used to seep up into the streets so much that the entrances to buildings along Lexington Ave. were designed a full flight of stairs higher than street level, to avoid problems with flooding. Later, dirt was moved from Pack Square and Montford to fill in the gullies and raise the streets out of the mud.

Back then it was necessary to climb a flight of stairs in order to enter the first floor of the bakery, because the dip in the road was so pronounced. The original street level was about eight feet below the present surface. Logs and large stones were laid across the country road to prevent wagons from getting bogged down in the mud. These were discovered decades later by workers excavating Patton Ave., while remodeling the basement of the Kress Building.

Eventually, the Board of Aldermen elected to have dirt dragged from Pack Square to raise the level of the street to the level of the first floor of the building. Other businesses were soon added across the street from the Newland's bakery. These included the T.S. Morrison Store, which is Asheville's longest-running, and therefore, oldest remaining store.

Follow Lexington to Patton Ave. and turn left into **Pack Square.** In the days of Asheville's trolley cars, Pack Square was filled with passengers arriving and departing from all over the city. A streetcar ride cost six cents, and African Americans were the last to board and had to sit or stand in the back of the car. Beneath Pack Square are public restroom facilities which were filled in with dirt in the 1970s. They were in operation during the era of Jim Crow laws in the apartheid South, and included racially segregated toilets, washrooms, and water fountains. The racially segregated Paramount movie theater stood where Pack Place Center is today. African Americans were permitted in the theater, but had to enter through a back door and sit only in the segregated balcony.

Fred P. Martin, Sr.

African American business pioneer Fred P. Martin, Sr. operated a tailor shop on the eastern side of Pack Square from 1914-1916. He had a fine reputation and earned the respect of customers who came from far and wide to take advantage of his expertise. Asheville's best-dressed gents bought their duds from Mr. Martin.

James. V. Miller

Continue across the Square to the Police Station, which was built by African American master brickmason James. V. Miller, whose parents were slaves. He moved to Asheville in 1881 and became one of the city's most prolific builders. He founded Miller Construction Company and his own successful brickyard for making brick from local clay.

From 1910-1930, Miller was considered one of Asheville's most skilled and efficient contractors. Many of the bricks used to create some of downtown's most impressive architecture were made at his brickyard in Buncombe County.

Born in 1891, Miller depended upon his wife, Violet Agnus Jackson, to teach him how to read and write. He was also a generous teacher who shared the knowledge of his craft throughout the African American community. His dedication to the younger generations was so strong that even though he was bedridden for the last five years of his life, he continued to patiently instruct his apprentices. Miller Street in Asheville is named after him.

Benjamin James Jackson

Continue into Court Plaza, which is the grassy park in front of the two courthouses. In 1897, Benjamin James Jackson became the first African American to operate a business in the bustling and prosperous Asheville city market which was located in the previous courthouse which once stood nearby.

Jackson's stall was considered one of the best in the entire marketplace. He grew and then sold fruits and vegetables to customers from all over the city. The ritzy Battery Park Hotel and Grove Park Inn were among his customers. The reputations of their posh dining rooms and renowned chefs directly depended upon Jackson's reliable, outstanding little produce business. Thomas Wolfe described Jackson's produce stand in <u>Look Homeward, Angel</u>. *Continue to the City Building,* the Art-Deco masterpiece which houses our City Hall.

Newton Shephard

Newton Shephard was a street sweeper but he became the first African American to hold public office in Asheville. In 1880 he was elected to the Board of Aldermen where he served his constituency remarkably well, a notable achievement for an elected official in any era.

Isaac Dickson

Isaac Dickson was born into slavery but became a leading civic, church, and business leader in Asheville. He constructed one of the first suburban-style communities in Asheville, designing and building twenty houses in what became known as Dickson Town. He operated a coalyard, a transportation company for both African Americans and white travelers, founded the St. Matthius Episcopal Church, and was the first African American to serve on the Buncombe County Board of Education. He passed away in 1918.

Elvia Thelma McRae Caldwell

Born in 1912, Elvia Thelma McRae Caldwell was the South's first African American to be chosen as an Executive Director of the YWCA. She served on local, state, and national levels, in several capacities.

The Grove St. branch of the YWCA opened in 1924, but was for whites only. It had a separate budget, membership, classes, committees, and a different wage scale than did the branch for African Americans. The branches merged into the new building on South French Broad in 1971. Caldwell became the executive director of both in 1965.

When the Grove St. branch closed its doors in 1970, controversy erupted throughout the community. Many whites withdrew their memberships because of the merger. But under the careful guidance of Caldwell, the interracial merger of the two facilities became an eventual success. It served as a model for the whole nation, and in 1977, Caldwell was appointed to the United States Commission for Civil Rights.

YWCA Building

Reuben J. Daily

Daily was the first African American to serve on the Asheville City Council. He was an attorney and an active participant in the Civil Rights Movement. He single-handedly integrated many facilities in Asheville. He and his family members would often visit local restaurants and other public places for the sole purpose of breaking through racial barriers for the first time.

Orlene Graves Simmons and Joe Anderson

Orlene Graves Simmons, the current director of the YMI center on Eagle St., was one of the first African American women in the South to break through the racial barriers of an all-white college. She was the first African American to attend Mars Hill College in neighboring Madison County. Her great-grandfather, Joe Anderson, is buried on the same campus. His tombstone is inscribed: "In memory of Joe, a slave who was taken by the contractor of the first building of this College as a pledge for the debt due them."

YMI Cultural Center

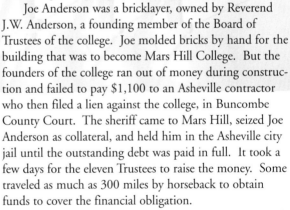

Joe Anderson was a bricklayer, owned by Reverend J.W. Anderson, a founding member of the Board of Trustees of the college. Joe molded bricks by hand for the building that was to become Mars Hill College. But the founders of the college ran out of money during construction and failed to pay $1,100 to an Asheville contractor who then filed a lien against the college, in Buncombe County Court. The sheriff came to Mars Hill, seized Joe Anderson as collateral, and held him in the Asheville city jail until the outstanding debt was paid in full. It took a few days for the eleven Trustees to raise the money. Some traveled as much as 300 miles by horseback to obtain funds to cover the financial obligation.

In 1932 officials had Joe Anderson's remains moved from a private cemetery to the campus in order to honor him for his personal sacrifices to the college. There a granite marker was erected in his memory, near the south entrance to the campus.

Dr. Martin Luther King

In April of 1968, more than 1,000 peaceful and silent mourners marched through the streets of downtown and convened at City County Plaza, to pay tribute to Dr. King, following his assassination. A permanent memorial to him is installed near the Plaza, at the YMI Cultural Center on historic Eagle St.

© City Seeds, Inc.

Volunteers create America's first edible park.

Bountiful City Project
Stephen's Lee Recreation Center

Walk between the two courthouses, down the stairs, and turn right. Continue until you come to the pedestrian overpass (a cyclone-fenced bridge) which crosses above Charlotte St. At the end of the walkway is the Bountiful City Project, an edible park created by an alliance between the city of Asheville and City Seeds, a non-profit organization. Much of the energy that went into developing this project, which is the first of its kind in North America, came from volunteers in the local African American community. Many of them were neighborhood children who helped with the planting. See our section about downtown excursions for a comprehensive description of the Edible Park.

Above the park and to the far right stands a large brick gymnasium building, the Stephen's Lee Recreation Center. This structure is the last remnant of the historical **Stephen's Lee High School** which used to be located here. For many years the school (which was nicknamed by students *The Castle On The Hill*) was the only public high school that Asheville's African American students could attend. Students from all over Buncombe County attended Stephen's Lee.

From the Recreation Center parking lot or the Edible Park, look back across Charlotte St. To the left of the courthouses is a large church dominating the end of a short street, on a steep hill which runs perpendicular to Charlotte St. That's where this tour continues, so *make your way to Eagle St., which is off Market St., just behind the police station.*

Historic Eagle Street

At the corner of Market St. and Eagle St. is the **YMI building**. Constructed between 1891 and 1892 as a community center for African Americans, it was named the Young Men's Institute.

YMI Cultural Center
39 South Market St. at Eagle St.
828.252.4614

The YMI Cultural Center is the most enduring African American socio-cultural institution in Western North Carolina. The three-story building has 7,500 sq. ft. of museum space with permanent and changing exhibits by African American artists. Programs are offered in cultural arts and in community, educational, and economic development.

The YMI was founded by George Vanderbilt in gratitude to the African Americans of Asheville for the quality of craftsmanship they displayed in creating his mansion. It was designed by Richard Sharpe Smith, the supervising architect for Biltmore Estate. It housed a kindergarten, gymnasium, and bathing facilities and offered its facilities to be used by churches, public schools, and civic organizations within the African American community.

In 1977 the YMI building was condemned because it had fallen into a state of disrepair and neglect. African American civic leaders arranged the purchase and renovation of the property, and their efforts resulted in the YMI being placed on the Register of National Historic Places.

Fenton H. Harris Sr.

Mr. Harris owned and operated one of the only African American owned drug stores in Asheville. It was called the YMI Drug Store and was located in the YMI building. The store had an African American pharmacist on duty at all times and was immensely popular with young African Americans who came after school to socialize and enjoy delicious ice cream sodas.

The first combination barber shop and shoe repair business had its start in the YMI building, too. It later relocated to 24 Eagle St.

Dominating the end of the lane is the Mount Zion Missionary Baptist Church. This historic Gothic Revival masterpiece has striking front and side gables, three and four story towers, and powerfully beautiful stained glass windows.

Mount Zion Missionary Baptist Church

The grand Eagle Hotel once stood on the site which is now occupied by the Pack Place parking garage *(at the corner of Eagle St. and Biltmore Ave.).* An archeological team was hired by the city to excavate the area before the parking garage was constructed. Evidence they uncovered indicates that from the mid to the late 1800s Eagle Street was one of the most prosperous African American commercial districts in the entire United States. Eagle Street's restaurants, night clubs, carriage factory, blacksmith shop, leather tannery, funeral parlor, and various other enterprises contributed to the vibrant social and economic scene.

The Biltmore Avenue Music Scene

In recent years, African American performers like George Clinton and P-Funk, Percy Sledge, and Roberta Flack have graced the stages of Asheville's music venues. Flack, herself a native of the

Asheville area, rose to international fame in 1972 when she recorded the hit song ***The First Time Ever I Saw Your Face***. The song was written by Ewan MacColl when he was inspired by meeting Peggy Seeger, who now lives in Asheville.

Willie Stargell, the famous African American outfielder, hit twenty-two home runs in one season (1961) for the Asheville Tourists Baseball Club.

Prior to the mid 1970s, downtown was home to one of the hottest African American music scenes in the nation. Asheville was in the middle of the so-called "*Chitlin* Circuit" (a string of juke joints where African American acts could get consistent bookings and enthusiastic crowds) and attracted both regional and national acts. Sam Cooke, James Brown, Aretha Franklin, Otis Redding, Chubby Checker, Chuck Berry, Bo Diddley, B.B. King, Sam & Dave, Willie Dixon, and other famous performers visited Asheville to play venues like the Orange Peel (which was located near the intersection of Biltmore Ave. and Hilliard Ave).

The Kitty Cat Club and the Brown Derby, located on two floors of the same building at 60 Biltmore Ave., were packed on weekends. And comedians like "Moms" Mabley (who was from Asheville) and "Pigmeat" Markum could be seen in small clubs like those which proliferated along Eagle St.

The *Commodores* played here when they were just starting out with Lionel Richie as a sideman. The band's bus broke down here and they purchased a touring bus from a local African American band to continue their journey. *Kool and the Gang* played here when they were just starting out. *The Platters* and *The Drifters* had a loyal following here, as did Jerry Butler.

Asheville diva Kat Williams

In recent years, African American musical greats such as Buddy Miles, R.L. Burnside, and Richie Havens have performed at Be Here Now on Biltmore Ave. The late Jimmy Rogers, who was in the original *Muddy Waters Blues Band*, performed one of his last shows there in 1997, just a few weeks before his death. This writer was fortunate enough to share a drink of 18 year old whiskey with him during the intermission of that phenomenal concert.

© Totsie Marine

Follow Biltmore Avenue back across Pack Square. Turn left on Patton Ave. Continue to the **Kress Building at 21 Patton Ave.** At the old Kress Store, African Americans were served at a lunch counter in the back while whites were served at a counter up front. African Americans were routinely kept waiting, sometimes for an entire lunch hour, until all white customers were served. In department stores throughout downtown Asheville, it was standard policy to serve African Americans customers last, no matter what they were buying or how long they had to stand in line and wait.

Poet Glenis Redmond

The Legendary Dobbs House

One place they never had to wait behind whites was at the Dobbs House **on Beaucatcher Mountain**, above the Beaucatcher Tunnel in east Asheville. This private home was operated until the late 1970s by an African American couple as a kind of bootleg restaurant. Although it was never officially opened as a restaurant, on weekends the Dobbs House served up the most popular breakfast food in all of western North Carolina. The folks who ran it would not open their doors to the public until about 10pm (when almost all the other restaurants in town had closed for the night) and they served breakfast until dawn.

They operated on Friday and Saturday nights only, when their entire two-story residence was converted into a crowded, festive meeting place for hungry folks from all over Buncombe County. Cars would line the street near the house for a hundred yards or more as stylishly attired club-hoppers arrived. They jammed into every nook and cranny of the house where eggs and bacon, grits and greens, and homemade biscuits and gravy were served up at bargain prices, with soulful enthusiasm.

To continue the tour, follow Patton Ave. to the intersection of Church St. where the **Drhumor Building** (48 Patton Ave.) is yet another stunning example of architecture which African American bricklayers and stone masons helped to create. *Turn right at the Haywood St. intersection and follow Haywood St. to Battery Park Ave.* The Miles Building, another showcase of African American masonry, is on the corner. Follow the avenue west along the Flat Iron Building, where Asheville's first African American owned radio station (WBMU) broadcast during the 1970s and 1980s.

Turn right on Page Ave. The Grove Arcade is on the left side of the street, and beyond it looms the Battery Park Apartments, a 14 floor brick building which was originally the Battery Park Hotel. The brickwork on this building is one of Asheville's most prominent testimonies to the skill and artistry of turn-of-the-century African American craftsmen. The details in the front facade are marvelous.

Did you know that some sections of the water mains beneath Asheville's city streets are made entirely of wood? In olden times, hardwoods like locust or chestnut were hollowed out for water lines. Some are still in use today.

Walk past the front of the building to North French Broad Ave., turn right, and return to the Chamber of Commerce. Once again, go to the Montford Ave. bridge. Face the Montford neighborhood with your back to the Chamber of Commerce, and look toward the mountains which are just to the left of Montford on the horizon.

Once upon a time, a courageous African American man mounted a horse out there in the distance, about eight miles from the bridge where you are standing. Riding fast and hard, he risked his life to deliver an urgent message. If his message had not arrived, the town of Asheville would probably have been destroyed, along with its glorious and beautiful buildings and its sense of peaceful community. And the life blood of many of Asheville's citizens would have surely flowed through the streets in a dark and tragic hour.

Asheville's Anonymous African American Hero

At the close of the Civil War, about 48 hours before General Robert E. Lee signed surrender papers at Appomattox, Union troops marched toward Asheville with the intention of plundering and destroying the entire city. They outnumbered the Asheville militia four to one, were much better armed and equipped, and had enough supplies to sustain them for weeks.

About eight miles west of the city, they came upon the homestead of Mrs. H. E. Sondley and stopped long enough to steal her horses. An African American man was at her home at the time, and he managed to slip, undetected, into the woods where his horse was hidden. He galloped through the forest, avoiding Union scouts, and arrived at the western edge of town ahead of the advancing column of some 1200 marauders.

Thanks to his warning the somewhat ragtag Asheville military guard avoided a disasterous surprise attack and had just enough time to prepare an ambush. The local militia, which was comprised of Confederate soldiers, elderly men, and boys as young as twelve years old, offered such courageous and fierce resistance during the ensuing five hour Battle of Asheville that the Union troops were soundly defeated. They hightailed it back into Tennessee, leaving the city of Asheville relatively unscathed.

Miraculously, there were no deaths and few injuries on either side. To date, the identity of the African American hero who sped into town to save Asheville remains shrouded in obscurity, mystery, and historical speculation.

Rabbit's Motel & Restaurant
110 McDowell St.
828.253.9552

Opens around 5pm most evenings

Rabbit's is the premier authentic soul food kitchen of Asheville. Established more than half a century ago, the cozy little restaurant still serves up original-recipe BBQ, pigs feet, pork chops, catfish, greens, potato salad, and other southern soul dishes. The beer is inexpensive and ice cold, and the last time we were there you could still order Thunderbird by the glass for a buck or two. The folks who run Rabbit's are some of the nicest people you could ever meet, and everything they cook tastes as good or better than homemade.

MISCELLANEOUS SITES
OF INTEREST IN THE ASHEVILLE AREA

Carl Sandburg Home
National Historic Site
1928 Little River Road
Flat Rock, NC
828.693.4178

About 30 miles from Asheville is the farm and home of Pulitzer Prize-winning author and poet Carl Sandburg. The 245 acre farm has multiple barns, out-buildings, pastures, trails, streams, and ponds, as well as flower gardens, vegetable gardens, an orchard, and the Sandburg's award winning Chikaming goat herd. The 22 room house where the poet lived and worked is also open for visitation.

The Sandburg home is a great place to spend a quiet afternoon learning about part of our national heritage. The park is open from 9am to 5pm except Christmas day. There is no entrance fee but an interpretive tour is available for a small charge. Call for directions and special event information.

Vance Birthplace
911 Reems Creek Rd.
Weaverville, NC
828.645.6706

Twenty minutes from Asheville stands the birthplace of one of North Carolinas most charismatic political leaders of the 19th century; Zebulon Baird Vance. This State Historic Site is the pioneer homestead of Vance, who was a Civil War officer, governor of North Carolina, and U.S. senator. Visitors to the site can view a reconstruction (between original chimneys) of his two story log house and multiple outbuildings on the property, including a corn crib, springhouse, smokehouse, and loom house.

The grounds are outfitted with traditional equipment and decoration from the period between 1795 and 1840. Throughout the year, demonstrations of pioneer life can be observed at the park. There is no entrance fee. Call for directions and hours.

Where Elvis Presley Had a Helipad and Chalet

One of the people we interviewed for this guidebook works in a hairdressing place and stays really well-informed.

We chose to keep our source anonymous but we will tell you that she has the strange habit of lapsing out of a mountain dialect and into a posh British one, whenever she gets put on hold on the telephone. Anyway, here's what she said, right before she launched into some unprintable local gossip in her sexiest English accent:

"I don't know nuthin' about Elvis shooting out a TV set in a motel room on Tunnel Road but I know for sure he had a place up on the side of the mountain and the only way you could get to it was in a helicopter. My aunt told me and she oughta know. She said it was near Black Mountain and that Elvis would go there to get away from it all."

We asked if her aunt had ever visited the hideaway and she said "It's possible, knowing my aunt and how much she loves Elvis. But I can't say for sure. So, am I gonna be in your book or what?"

We tried to get directions but like the woman said, you can only get there by helicopter, and we don't have helicopter money in our research budget.

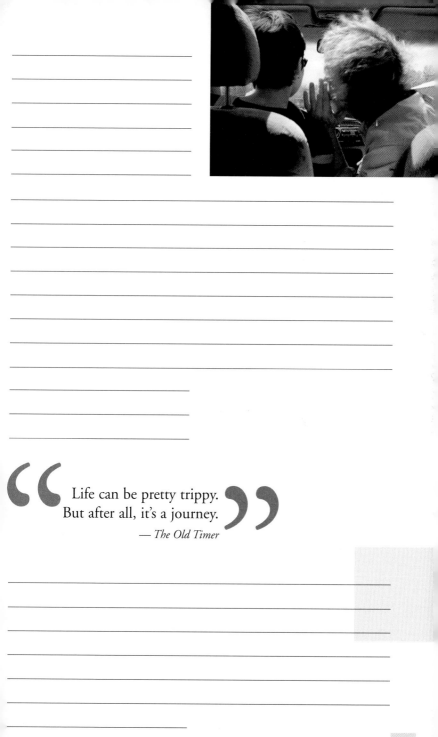

> Life can be pretty trippy.
> But after all, it's a journey.
> — *The Old Timer*

> Celebrate whoever it is you are and whoever it is you want to be.
>
> — *The Old Timer*

GAY & LESBIAN COMMUNITIES OF ASHEVILLE

GAY SHEVILLE

ASHEVILLE'S GLBT COMMUNITIES

Gays and Lesbians deserve much of the credit for the preservation, redevelopment, and continued vitality of this attractive little town. The contributions of Gay and Lesbian individuals and organizations are woven into our town's history, culture, economy, politics, and social life. Thanks in large part to Gays and Lesbians, Asheville celebrates Herself more than ever before, and is a more complete and diverse community.

Downtown Asheville was a "dead" scene until just a few years ago, according to many longtime residents. There were basic signs of life, but Asheville's city center had the pulsebeat of a hibernating bear. Many blocks in the heart of downtown had sleeping streets with abandoned storefronts and empty sidewalks with grass growing through the cracks. The participation of the Gay and Lesbian community inspired Asheville to become a vibrant downtown-focused city.

Entrepreneurial pioneers from the Gay and Lesbian community risked their energy, money, and other personal resources to revitalize Asheville. Beginning in the 1980s with vision, financial investment, and hard-working determination, they helped jumpstart the economy of downtown which led the way to a phenomenal recovery. Now Asheville is experiencing a heyday renaissance in the rejuvenated heart of town. It was Gay and Lesbian business people who helped to pave the way for that renewed celebration of the city which was once dubbed the *Paris of the South*.

Today Asheville has the first or second largest Lesbian population in the country, depending upon whose census you accept. Realistic estimates indicate that more than 40,000 Lesbians live and work in and around the greater Asheville area.

Whether you consider yourself "Straight," "Gay," or "Omnisexual" (One of our friends always writes "Omni" on surveys which ask for one's sexual identity, which we think is kinda cute.), Asheville can be a great place to live, work, and express your community spirit.

Gay and Lesbian Community Resources

Many, if not most, of Asheville's enterprises are owned or operated by Gays and Lesbians or are "Gay and Lesbian friendly" establishments. This book is chock full of such listings.

To find out more specific information about the Gay and Lesbian community and its resources, we recommend that our readers pick up a copy of the publication entitled <u>Community Connections</u>. It's a non-profit newspaper available at newsstands and bookstores throughout the city or by subscription. Check the section called *Community Resources* or the *Community Calendar* page to get an overview of what's happening in Western North Carolina. There are dozens of active organizations listed there, created around everything from potluck suppers or financial workshops to kayaking and ballroom dancing.

GLBT Guidebooks:

The last time we checked, local book dealers including *Malaprop's Bookstore* and *Rainbow's End* (which are listed in the Bookstore and Shopping sections of this guidebook) offered excellent selections of guidebooks which are specifically tailored to the needs of Gays and Lesbians. The guidebooks we perused included information pertaining to Asheville and the whole of Western North Carolina. Check the *Gay and Lesbian* as well as the *Travel and Tourism* sections of area bookstores.

Community Connections
828.251.2449

Established in 1987, this is Western North Carolina's only non-profit Gay/Lesbian/Bisexual/Transgendered newspaper. It's goal is to give voice and visibility to the concerns of GLBT persons living in this area. The monthly paper hosts a series of columns including ones on gardening, spirituality, psychology, parents of GLBT children, transgendered persons, humor, art and artists, and local news of concern to GLBT persons. In 1999 it had a circulation of 7000. <u>Community Connections</u> is available free of charge at numerous shops, bookstores, restaurants, and other venues in Asheville, or by subscription.

LISA MORPHEW

Lisa is a writer and the managing editor of <u>Community Connections</u> newspaper. For a decade or so, she was a professional musician who traveled extensively playing guitar. She's also a talented photographer. But we met her by becoming next-door neighbors, which is one of those old timey relationship traditions most folks around here still honor.

She's one of the most creative carpenters around, and has a genius for restoring and remodeling old homes. Last time we talked, she was on a learning curve about the nearly-extinct art of applying pebbledash. It wouldn't surprise me if, by the next time I see her, she's become the most sought-after pebbledasher in her historic neighborhood of Montford. She's got talent at pretty much everything she sets her mind to doing.

Lisa was in Vietnam in the late 1960s, trying to do her part to assist the victims of war and promote peace. She returned a few years ago, on a healing quest, and is about to publish a book documenting her experiences.

She's created a non-profit foundation which provides financial assistance to combat victims and the 800,000 persons who became childhood orphans as a direct consequence of the war. Many of the donors to the charity are American veterans of the war, so it benefits both the donors and the recipients in a reciprocal healing process.

We asked Lisa to be part of our book by telling us a little bit about herself, and she did:

What quality do you most admire in a person?

I am drawn to people who remain kind in the face of aggression, disappointment, joy, privilege, etc. Because a truly kind person seems to have all the other qualities I admire: Humor, heart, and understanding. A kind person seems to acknowledge how hard it is for people to change and how hard it is to truly love one another in the face of differences.

What do you consider the most important historical event of your lifetime?

The Vietnam War was pivotal in forming my sense of justice and responsibility. I watched women and children burning to death on television during my dinner. At once I was glad they were not me and horrified that they seemed to be such pawns in a lousy game. I became a photographer/witness as a way to deal with my confusion and pain. I recently went to Vietnam to find a project in which I could give something back to the women I had been so moved by. I chose to do a book on the severely wounded women soldiers of the Vietnamese War, from both the North and South, as a way to include their experience in the historic register—as a way to heal.

210

If you were going to live on a deserted island for two years, what three things (besides food and water) would you take with you?

A hat, a lover, and a box of paints.

What makes Asheville home to you, as opposed to just a place to live?

I feel humble here amidst the mountains and that was enough to call me to build a home here.

What's your favorite place to take first-time visitors to Asheville?

Malaprop's Bookstore, as most of my friends love books as much as I do.

What's your favorite place to take a walk? Your favorite scenic vista?

I walk to meditate so any landscape delights me, centers me. I like the idea of going deeper into a small part of a landscape...to focus on spiders or ferns, sometimes birds, the worlds hidden within the easily visible landscape.

Do you have a favorite author?

I love the landscape and sensuality in the work of poet Mark Doty.

Are there any particular magazines or newspapers that you read on a regular basis?

I read *Oxford American*, *The Nation*, *Harper's*, *Poets and Writers*, *Art Papers*, and *Double Take*.

What's your idea of an ideal way to spend the day in Asheville?

I love roaming the bookstores like The Readers Corner, Downtown Books and News, Captain's, Lin Digs, and Malaprop's.

What person, past or present, would you like to meet and what would you talk about?

Eleanor Roosevelt. I would begin with faith and move to grace, trusting that within those two inquiries are the fates of all other discussions.

Have you received a special compliment lately? What was it?

I have been complimented for changing my stance in the world. I had lived a great part of my life over-guarded and critical which left me isolated. I did some hard work to begin to listen better, to give others more room to feel included in conversations, to open to my own vulnerability.

What's the most unusual thing you have ever encountered while walking in the woods?

The hood of a '51 Studebaker with a map painted on it.

If you could declare a holiday in Asheville, what would it celebrate?

Opposite Day, where you become for a day a person you believe to be your opposite. It could be fun if not a little instructive.

211

KEITH BRAMLETT

Keith Bramlett is a professor of sociology at the University of North Carolina at Asheville.

We've all read, seen on television, or heard on the radio those types of interviews or conversations where someone is asked to name the teacher who had the greatest impact on them in their whole school career.

Well, here comes one more *name-that-educator* scenario, "just like deja-vu all over again" as Yogi Berra used to say.

I thought of a *dozen ways from Sunday* to write this intro about my professor and friend whom I've always referred to as simply *Bramlett*, but I just kept coming back to these simple facts:

I'm almost half a century old, in what is arguably the most interesting century in history. In about 1958 I began going to school and I am still attending classes regularly. I've had so many gifted teachers in so many different schools that I can't even recollect them all.

But if I were asked "Which school teacher taught you the most?" Keith Bramlett is undoubtedly the one I would name. Not a day goes by that I don't use what I learned in his classes to live my life. He taught me some powerful lessons in how to educate myself, how to think, and how to express what I think.

And I know more people than you can shake a piece of chalk at who say the same thing about the man.

I'm honored that he agreed to share his thoughts for this guidebook. Here's the Q & A:

What quality do you most admire in a person?
There are two: humility and integrity.

How do you think one can cultivate those qualities?
Only with great difficulty, constant perseverance, and a well-developed internal locus of control which undermines the need to manage impressions and meet everyone's expectations.

What do you consider the most historical event of your lifetime?
The Vietnam War. While I was not directly affected in any personal way, the war lead to the development of my political and social conscious as I watched a generation fight for change and social justice.

If you were going to live on a deserted island for two years, what three things would you take with you?
A knife, a good cooking pot, and depending on my mood at departure, either a violin or the collected poems of Audre Lorde.

What makes Asheville home to you, as opposed to just a place to live?
The mountains which I need, the seasons which I cherish, the sunsets in winter which are extraordinary, and occasionally, the people.

Where would you take a first-time vistor to Asheville, to show them a scenic vista?
My home.

Do you have a favorite artist?
I love art and there are many artists whose work offers provocation and refuge—but overall, it would probably have to be Pablo Picasso.

Do you have a favorite movie?
Hundreds! But generally, the most recent one seen.

Of those you have read recently, which book is your favorite?
Plays Well with Others by Allan Gurganus.

What person, past or present, would you like to meet and what would you like to talk with them about?
My maternal grandfather. We would talk about family.

If you were asked to contribute something of yours to a time capsule, what would you give?
John Kennedy Toole's A Confederacy of Dunces.

What's the most unusual thing you have ever encountered in the woods or countryside?
An operative whiskey still.

What question do you wish students would ask?
How can I challenge the pretense of a "homogeneity of experience" in this culture that doesn't actually exist?

What question do you wish teachers would ask themselves and their students?
What is that piece of the oppressor that is deeply planted within yourself?

If you could declare a holiday in Asheville, what would it celebrate?
Blue skies.

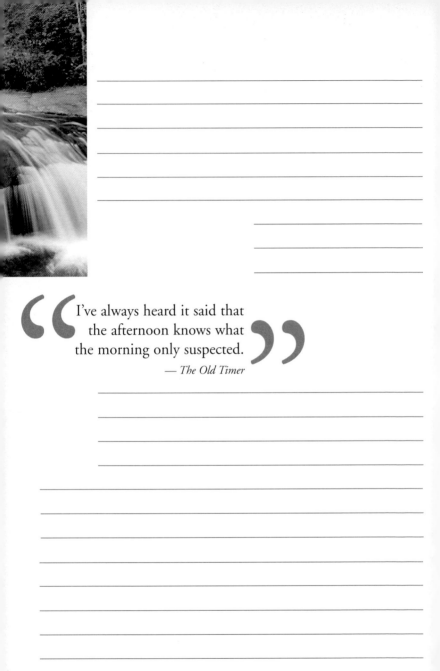

> I've always heard it said that
> the afternoon knows what
> the morning only suspected.
> — *The Old Timer*

HALF
FULL DAY
OVERNIGHT
HIKING
DESTINATIONS

JOHN CAPPS

John Capps is a surveyor for the National Forest Service and has been hiking these mountains professionally for more than 30 years. Raised in a log cabin in nearby Madison County, he attended Berea College in Kentucky where he earned a degree in agriculture before studying agricultural economics at the University of Kentucky. He is the proud father of two grown sons, Kevin and Jesse.

Unlike most of us who can't calculate a restaurant tip without removing our shoes and counting on our toes, John easily does old-fashioned arithmetic in his head. By using the right tools, he can look at one of the planets in the solar

Behind John in this picture is a century old cabin. It was built in Madison County by the family of John Capps.

system and then scribble a few mathematical equations to locate a dime on the floor of a jungle.

An expert woodsman, he once learned how to build a flintlock rifle from blacksmithed iron. Just as comfortable in the kitchen as he is in the forest, John knows how to identify most any tree by looking at its bark, how to construct a log cabin, and how to garden and "put up vegetables" (the art of canning). He has a reputation for cooking some of the finest chicken and dumplings and cornbread in Western North Carolina. And he can make a gourmet feast on an open fire.

He recalls how his parents made homemade hominey (It's a larger-than-life version of grits.) by soaking kernals of corn in water mixed with ashes from the fireplace. The ashes had enough acidity in them to duplicate the chemical reaction of poisonous lye (which is usually used in the recipe), although they added a gray color to the normally yellow or white hominey.

John reads dozens of books per year on every imaginable subject and has a personal library that could put the inventory of most book stores to shame. And he bears a striking resemblance to both Walt Whitman and the 1960s comic book philosopher / folk hero Mr. Natural. But most people think he looks like Santa Claus, and every year photographers try to hire him to be Santa for the season. His friends swear that he not only looks like Father Christmas but that he has a heart as big as Saint Nick's too.

We asked John to contribute some of his insight to our book, and he did.

What do you admire in a person?
Empathy.

What do you consider the most important historical event of your lifetime?
The development of the atomic bomb.

If you were going to live on a deserted island for two years, what three things (besides food and water) would you take?
My hat, boots, and a daypack.

What is one place you would be sure to take a first-time visitor to Asheville?
The Blue Ridge Parkway.

What person, past or present, would you like to speak with and what would you ask him or her?
My grandfather on either side of the family. I would ask, "Would you tell me what you know about your family?"

What souvenir or piece of memorabilia would you like to have that you don't have?
My father's first 22 caliber rifle.

What's the most unusual thing you've ever seen in the woods?
A peacock.

What is one lesson you've learned from spending so much time in the woods?
The hills may get steeper every year, but the joy of reaching the top gets sweeter.

Do you have a favorite hiking spot?
The next one.

The Great Smoky Mountains National Park

America's favorite National Park is a short drive from Asheville and is a wilderness world unto itself. This national treasure is a not-to-be-missed destination, highly recommended.

The Great Smoky Mountains National Park is the most visited National Park in the USA. Straddling the mountains at the border of North Carolina and Tennessee and bordering the Cherokee Indian Reservation, the park covers over half a million acres of protected land. The park contains over a hundred species of native trees, some hardwood trees that are more than four hundred years old, and more than 1,500 varieties of wild flowers. Eight hundred miles of hiking on more than fifty officially marked trails await visitors to the park. in the Nantahala National Forest and the Pisgah National Forest

For more information contact the Visitors Centers:

Oconoluftee Visitor Center
828.497.1900
(Near Cherokee, NC)

Sugarland Visitor Center
423.436.1200
(Near Gatlinburg, TN)

Big East Fork Trail
Shining Rock Wilderness Area

Map reference: USGS-FS MAP: Shining Rock. OR:
Pisgah Ranger District Map #780, location E-4, USFS #357.
Difficulty level: moderate to strenuous, mostly flat terrain,
some uphill / downhill walking.
Miles (round trip): Your choice; 7.2 miles if full trail walked.
Joins up with Grassy Cove trail for a longer walk.
Driving time from Asheville: about 1 hr 15 min.

Trail description

Beautiful all year round, this trail mostly follows the East Fork of
the Pigeon River. Scenic waterfalls, flumes, clear copper-green pools
(great for swimming / fishing) and lush forest make this an unparal-
leled place of beauty. Look out for wildflowers and a wide variety of
fungi in May and June.

There are numerous wild, river-side camping places along the
way but no camp fires are allowed. Sticking to the path can
be confusing in places as walkers have forged new trails. Try
to look out for the improvised environmental markers that
other hikers have laid to help with directions—e.g. tree
branches or rocks laid across a trailhead means, "Don't go
this way."

At 0.5 miles, the trail forks left, and leaves the river. It's
worth taking the short dead-end trail to the right, as it leads
to a lovely green pool and small cascade. Backtrack a little and continue uphill on the trail. At about 1.2
miles, don't miss the small sandy beach and
tranquil six-ft. deep pool fed by a pretty
waterfall. A great place to laze around or
camp. At 1.3 miles, the trail again leaves
the river, to rejoin it at 1.8 miles. At about
2 miles, where the right bank of the river
rises more steeply, you will hear the sound
of a waterfall. Scramble down the bank to
admire the brightly colored rocks and a
surging channel of white water that makes
for an exhilarating swim. If you want an
overnight trip, this trail links up with
Grassy Cove Trail, which leads to the Art
Loeb trail and Ivestor Gap trail.

Directions from Chamber of Commerce, Asheville

*From about April through late
November (when the Parkway is open):*
Take 240 W to I-26E and get off at
exit 2. At the end of the exit, go left
onto 191S and follow signs for the
Parkway. Go south on the Parkway,
then take a left turn onto US-276-N.
Turn right towards Waynesville at the
stopsign. Follow the winding 276-N
for 2.8 miles to an unmarked parking
area on the left. This is where the trail
begins. Alternatively, go 2.9 miles to
the Big East Fork parking area on the
left, and backtrack uphill on 276 to
the trailhead.

Big East Fork Trail in Winter Months

(when Blue Ridge Parkway is generally closed):

This route presents an interesting slice of rural Appalachia. Along the way on 276-S you will see the charming Mt. Olive Baptist Church with its improbable steeples (on your left). A little further on, crane to your right to see a rusty old mill. On entering Cruso, (whose welcome sign reads: "9 miles of friendly people, and one old crab"), don't miss the ultimate symbol of rural living: a satellite dish forest! On your left, see seven closely clustered dishes point up to space, shortly before the peaceful Blue Ridge Motorcycle campground. Also, keep your eyes peeled for an assortment of rustic barns and run-down cabins with interesting porch clutter.

Directions for the winter months

Take 240W to I-40W and get off at exit 27, towards Waynesville. You are now on U.S.19/23/74. The first Waynesville exit (exit 102) will lead you to US-276-S towards Brevard. This road winds its way through downtown Waynesville and is well sign-posted. Follow this road for 8.1 miles and pass the junction with Hwy 215. The Big East Fork parking area is 11.8 miles from this junction, on your right. Go about 0.1 mile further and pull off to your right at an unmarked parking area that can hold about six cars. This is where the trail begins. If there is no parking there, backtrack and park at the Big East Fork parking area and walk up 276 until you reach the trail head.

Hiking and Safety

The last time we went hiking, we encountered someone on the trail who needed immediate medical attention and was in danger of slipping into a coma due to a concussion caused by a simple fall. Fortunately, we had a cellular telephone and blankets with us and there was a fantastic rescue squad team nearby which we contacted by calling 911.

But accidents happen. Familiarize yourself with safety procedures before hiking. Call a Park Ranger Station before setting out, for free information on how to make yourself safer in the woods. Here are some basic safety tips:

1. Take warm clothes and one of those high-tech emergency blankets in case you get caught in the woods when temperatures drop.
2. Carry a good flashlight, matches, a compass, an emergency first aid kit, a knife, a whistle, and up-to-date maps. Take a cellular phone if you have one.
3. Respect waterfalls. Every year people are killed or seriously injured due to falling from the tops of area waterfalls.
4. Please don't hike into the woods by yourself; take along a companion and share the journey.

Looking Glass Rock
Pisgah National Forest

Map reference: USGS-FS MAP: Shining Rock. OR:
Pisgah Ranger District Map # 780, location F-5, USFS #114.
Follow yellow blaze.
Difficulty level: strenuous. Steady uphill walk with switchbacks.
Elevation change: 1,369 feet.
Miles (round trip): 6.2.
Driving time from Asheville: about 1 hour.

Trail description

This frequently used trail can be tiring, but worth the effort. The switchbacked path wends its way through a beautiful mixed hardwood forest with Carolina hemlocks and laurel. The pinnacle (at 3,969 feet) is at Looking Glass Rock, a huge rock dome offering breathtaking views of Pisgah National Forest and the Blue Ridge Parkway. This dome itself is perhaps best seen from the Parkway. This trail is especially lovely in the fall, but is enjoyable and accessible all year round. Bring lots of water for this one!

Directions from Chamber of Commerce, Asheville

Take 240W to I-26. Get off at Exit 9 (Airport exit) and turn right on NC-280 and go to Brevard. Once in Brevard, take a right onto US-276-N towards Waynesville. Follow this scenic road along the Davidson River and take a left turn onto FR-475. Go 0.4 miles to the Looking Glass Rock parking area on your right.

Looking Glass Rock seen from the Blue Ridge Parkway.

Author's Tip

While you are in the area, it is worth visiting **Slick Rock Falls**, **Looking Glass Falls**, and **Sliding Rock**.

Directions to Slick Rock Falls

From the parking area for Looking Glass Rock, continue on FR-475 for about 1.1 mi., then take FR-475-B to the right. Go another 1.1 mi. to a pull-off by the right by the falls. The 200-ft. trail leads to a scenic 35-ft. fall with a small cave behind it.

Directions to Looking Glass Falls

From the Looking Glass Rock parking area, backtrack on FR-475 and take a left onto U.S.276-N , go 0.3 mi. to a large parking area on your right. There are stairs leading down to the base of this popular 80-ft. fall. If you decide to swim in the pool, and the light is just right, a rainbow may appear around your head as you swim.

Directions to Sliding Rock

From Looking Glass Falls, go another 2.1 mi. on U.S.276-N to a parking area on your left. This is a popular recreational area with a fabulous slide into a frigid 6-ft. green pool. It is almost as much fun to spectate as it is to brave the 60-ft. slide. There are changing areas, toilets and lifeguards from Memorial Day to Labor Day. Just the thing after a sweaty hike up Looking Glass Rock.

Slick Rock Falls, Pisgah National Forest

Gems of Geological Wisdom

Snow, ice, sleet, and frost are minerals, according to UNC-Asheville geologist Dr. Bill Miller. He firmly states that "Igneous is bliss" but as a matter of fact, snow is a kind of ice.

Snowflakes are dendrites of ice formed directly from water vapor (a gas) in the atmosphere. The process by which this occurs is called sublimation. It's a slightly different reaction than the simple freezing that creates sleet from raindrops.

Professor Miller explains that Looking Glass Rock, like most of the rocky knobs around here, is made of a granite-gneiss that formed two or three million years ago. Metamorphism transformed it from granite into granite gneiss, giving it a distinctly glassy look which shines like a mirror on a clear, sunny day.

Horsepasture River Trail

Lake Toxaway Area
Transylvania County, Nantahala National Forest

Map reference: USGS Quadrangle: Reid
Difficulty level: moderate to strenuous. Initially easy, the trail
deteriorates after Rainbow Falls, with some fairly dangerous
parts as you near Stairway Falls and Windy Falls.
Miles: 2.8 miles round trip.
Driving time from Asheville: about 1 1/2 hours.

Some background information

The Horsepasture River was saved by grassroots environmental action in 1986, when a power plant threatened to destroy its fabulous waterfalls. Local conservationists, together with legislators, state and federal agencies won the battle to preserve this unique area. The 435-acre tract is now protected as part of the National Wild and Scenic River System.

Trail description

This trail features a series of dramatic waterfalls. The first is the **Drift Falls**. Sliding down these 80-ft. falls is not recommended. The locals call it "Bust-yer-Butt Falls" for obvious reasons. If the name alone doesn't put you off, perhaps this will: makeshift crosses are often planted at the base of the falls as memorials to unfortunate sliders. The next waterfall is **Turtleback Falls**. Swimming in this pool seems a bit safer, but the swirling white water is not for everyone. Swimmers have fun standing behind the falls and popping out through the spray. The *pièce de résistance* of the Horsepasture River has to be **Rainbow Falls**, so called for the rainbows that form from the tremendous spray it generates. At 150-ft high, this vertical sheet of white water makes quite a spectacle. If you still have energy, and fancy a bit of a scramble, go on another 0.8 mile to **Stairway Falls**, which has 7 "steps." If you feel very adventurous, proceed another 0.8 mile to **Windy Falls**. Use extreme caution for the latter two falls. If it has rained, the path can be treacherous. Sometimes the latter part of the trail is impassable due to downed trees.

Directions from Chamber of Commerce, Asheville

Take 240W to I-26E. Take Exit 9 towards Brevard on NC-280. Go through Brevard and follow signs for US-64 towards Highlands / Cashiers. Follow this winding mountain road past Toxaway Falls and turn left at Sapphire onto NC-281S. Go about 1.8 miles to a parking area on the left and follow the trail from there. This is the "easy" way to get there. This trail puts you out at Turtleback Falls. You will have to turn left to go to Drift Falls, then backtrack to Turtleback if you go this route. Alternatively, drive on a little further to a very obvious, but unmarked widening in the road with ample parking on the right. Cross the road and scramble down one of about four unofficial paths to get to Drift Falls. This can be a bit strenuous, so if you value your ankles, take the first route.

If you have time, it's worth driving the extra 6.8 miles down NC-281S to take in Whitewater Falls.

Turtleback Falls on the Horsepasture River

Whitewater Falls Trail
Transylvania County

Map reference: USGS-FS MAP: Cashiers. USFS #437.
Difficulty level: easy walk,
Miles: 2 miles round trip or 0.4 mile to just the overlook.
Driving time from Asheville: about 1 hour 45 min.
Special considerations: Whitewater Falls parking area has restrooms. The 0.2 mile trail to the overlook is well-paved and wheelchair accessible.

Trail description

The first paved section offers a pretty view of Lake Jocassee and leads to an overlook of the spectacular 411- foot high falls. For a better vantage point, descend the stairs to your right to a rocky outcrop. This trail is part of the Foothills Trail (an 85.2-mile trail). Unless you feel like being gone for a very long time, backtrack up the stairs and take the path to the left for 0.6 mile to the river. If the river is low enough, ford it and continue upstream for another 0.4 mile, then backtrack.

Directions

Same as for Horsepasture River, except go 8.6 miles on NC-281S and then turn into the parking area on the left. It is well sign-posted.

Big Creek Trail
Great Smoky Mountain National Park

Map reference: USGS-FS Luftee Knob. OR:
Hiking Map and Guide, Great Smoky Mountains
National Park (Earthwalk Press), map area 11-B.
Difficulty level: easy to moderate.
Miles (round trip): whole trail -10.6 miles. 4.0 miles to
Mouse Creek Falls and back.
Driving Time (from Asheville): about 1 hr 15 min.

Trail description

This trail follows the imaginatively named "Big Creek" from the campground of the same name. Along the way, don't miss **Midnight Hole**, a gorgeous 6-ft dark green pool with a small cascade where the foolhardy swim. The 2-mi. gentle walk to the enchanting **Mouse Creek Falls** makes a pleasant trip, with the option of walking further if you feel inspired. Camping is possible at Upper Walnut Bottom campsite at the end of the trail (5.3m). If you feel like making this hike into an overnight affair, this trail joins up with Swallow Fork Trail (after 5 miles) then with Mt. Sterling Ridge Trail and Baxter Creek Trail to form a loop. Check a map for details on these.

Directions from Chamber of Commerce, Asheville

Take 240W to 40W. Get off at the Waterville exit, which is just over the Tennessee border. At the end of the exit ramp, turn left to get to Waterville Road, on your left. Follow this 2.1 miles (past the hydro-electric plant) to a crossroads. Go straight to enter the National Park. Park at the end of the road, about 0.8 mile from the crossroads. The trail is a graded Jeep road that starts a few feet from the parking area.

Eco-Hiking

Consult a Park Ranger Station (like the one at the Folk Art Center near Asheville) for books, pamphlets, and advice on ecological hiking. Keep in mind that wild animals aren't in the habit of recycling our plastic bottles, aluminum cans, and cigarette butts. They expect us to do it ourselves. So if you carry anything like that into the woods, carry it out. And stop along the way to pick up litter. It will help you respect yourself in the morning.

TICKS
LOVE BUGS
& FUZZY HUGS

(AND HOW THEY RELATE TO YOUR FASHION STATEMENT)

When walking in the woods, beware of ticks. They are especially attracted to pinestraw, so keep that in mind if you're hiking a pine forest. And they tend to jump at light and bright colored clothes. Dark khaki and army green are good colors to wear in the woods, as long as it's not deer hunting season. (During deer season, wear blaze orange and a pair of bulletproof longjohns.)

Like the proverbial *Love Bug*, ticks are much easier to manage before they bite you than afterwards. After a hike, undress and check your clothing and body for the little culprits. Otherwise you might have a fluid-exchange bonding experience with a six-legged vamp.

Don't underestimate the power of poison ivy. One fella we heard of had a visitor from the city who couldn't identify it. They were walking across some farmland, and the visitor was chewing on a piece of straw, getting into the whole country culture. But it wasn't straw; it was poison ivy. He might have been better off chewing tobacco, because in most cases

chaw (not to be confused with *chai*) only makes you turn green and wretch all weekend, whereas poison ivy ingested makes your insides itch like they're wrapped in ragwool.

Especially if you are a tree-hugger, beware that brown fuzzy rope on tree trunks, even though it might look lovable. That's how poison ivy looks sometimes, especially after winter...like a hairy dark brown vine.

We heard about some kids who made a campfire with it. One piece of firewood had poison vine fuzz on it, which they didn't recognize. The smoke got in their lungs and they had serious complications for a while, which required hospitalization.

Jewel Weed is considered a natural antidote for poison ivy and it often grows in the immediate vicinity of poison ivy. People who know the woods can spot it and rub some on their skin after contacting poison ivy. The rest of us carry store-bought meds. Ask an area pharmacist to recommend something. If you think you've contacted poison plants, wash thoroughly with soap and water as soon as possible.

225

Trails of the Panthertown Valley

Jackson County

Map reference: USGS-FS MAP: Big Ridge.
Difficulty level: moderate.
Miles (round trip): the route described below is about 5 mi.
    (other options possible).
Driving time from Asheville: about 1 hour 45 min.

Background information

Panthertown Valley is a little known wonder of Western North Carolina that brims with biological treasures. After changing hands several times, narrowly avoiding irreparable damage by Duke Power company, this unique tract of land presently belongs to the U.S. Forest Service. Thankfully, the area's eight globally endangered plant species still survive today in its 6,295 acres. The valley is criss-crossed with old RR grades and logging roads from the 1800s, and has many unofficial trails that connect these roads, making loop trails. For a detailed description of all the trails in the area, check out "North Carolina Hiking Trails" by Allen de Hart.

Directions from Chamber of Commerce, Asheville

Because of restricted parking spaces elsewhere, the western access to Panthertown Valley is recommended. This is how you get there. Take 240-W to I-26E. Take exit 9 (airport) and go to Brevard on NC-280. From Brevard, take US-64W towards Cashiers. You will pass the turn-off for N.C. 281S and go a further 8 miles before turning right onto Cedar Creek Rd (S.R. 1120). Go 2.2 mi. to Breedlove Rd. (S.R. 1121). Take a right and drive 3.5 mi. to where the road deadends at the parking area. The road can be muddy and rutted for the last mile or so if there has been a lot of rain, so make sure your vehicle can handle this or you may need to walk a bit to get to the trail head.

Skinny Dipping

(It's one way to find out the difference between "naked" and "nekkid.")

Skinny dipping with a love interest is pretty romantic as long as you both enjoy fooling around in water so cold it can make a Maine lobster blush.

Whenever you go hiking (whether you plan to do a striptease water ballet or not) the possibility for drastic changes in temperature exists. Always take extra clothing or blankets along in case you get caught in the cold. Nothing tests the warmth and sincerity of a relationship like fighting over one thin blanket or a single windbreaker.

Trail description

From the western access parking area, take the gravelly Salt Rock Gap Trail 0.3 mile to a lovely view of the granite walls of Big Green Mountain (nearest you) and Little Green Mountain. Continue this trail to Deep Gap Trail (right) at 0.6 mile. It is worth following this trail 1.1 miles until the trail ends at a locked forest gate. Along the way you may enjoy discovering pink lady's slippers, galax, tall hardwoods and a small waterfall. Backtrack to Panthertown Creek Trail on your right. Rock-hop Panthertown Creek at 0.3 mile, then take a 0.4 mile shortcut to your left through the rhododendrons to a tranquil spot with interesting rocks in shades of pink, orange and yellow and a large swimming pool with white sandbars. In summer, the water temperature here can be fairly tolerable. Follow this shortcut to Hogback Mountain Trail and take a left. This will take you to an intersection with Greenland Creek Trail. Take a right onto this and take time to wade or swim in the lovely pool at 0.8 mile. (There is a small shed near the pool). Go another 0.1 mile, cross a bridge over Panthertown Creek and follow the right hand trail 0.4mile upstream until you cross another bridge. Then take a right onto Schoolhouse Falls Trail (0.1 mi.) and spend some time skipping stones and admiring this small but magical waterfall. To return to your car, backtrack along Greenland Creek Trail, which intersects with Salt Rock Gap Trail, which leads uphill to the parking area.

How To Skip A Stone On Water

Dense, smooth, disc-like stones and glassy-surfaced water make for the best skipping. To skip a pebble, make a pistol shape with your fingers. Lay the stone on top of the curled fingers and then move the forefinger back to grasp it. Lower the thumb to hold it in place. Use a sidearm throw with a little Elvis-pelvis action. He was probably an ace at this business. Be sure to release the stone parallel to the surface of the water, not at a downward angle.

Joyce Kilmer Memorial Loop Trail

Graham County, N.C.
Slickrock Wilderness Area

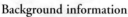

Map reference: USGS-FS MAP:
    Santeetlah Creek.
Difficulty level: easy
Miles (round trip): 1.9 mi.
Driving time from Asheville: about 2 1/2 hours.

Background information

This 17,394-acre wilderness is the only example of virgin forest in North Carolina. The Memorial Loop Trail, while heavily used, has the most impressive examples of ancient trees. Words cannot describe the awe-inspiring experience of gazing up at a towering 400-year-old poplar. Some trees are over 20-feet in circumference and stand 120-feet tall. The forest consists of poplar, oak, hemlock, basswood, sycamore, birch, beech, and maple. A lower canopy of rhododendron, laurel and flame azalea make for a magical blaze of color in spring and summer. Don't forget to look down! It is all too easy to become mesmerized by the primeval trees and miss the trillium and iris beneath your feet. The forest's namesake, Joyce Kilmer, was a soldier and poet killed in WWI and author of the poem "Trees". There are myriad trails in Slick Rock Wilderness area. A topographical map and compass are essential for these trails as there are few blazes or markers. Depending on your phobias, you may be blessed or unlucky enough to encounter some of Slick Rock Wilderness's residents: copperheads, timber rattlers, wild hogs and bears.

Directions from Chamber of Commerce, Asheville

Take 240-W to I-40W, exiting towards Waynesville at exit 27. Take 23/74 towards Sylva. After Sylva, take 441 towards Bryson City until it turns into 19, then 28 towards Stecoah or Robbinsville, then take a left onto 143 towards Robbinsville. While in Robbinsville, it may be a good idea to pick up a brochure and map of Joyce Kilmer Memorial Forest at the Nantahala National Forest / Cheoah Ranger District office (828.479-6431). 143 will deadend into129. Take a right onto 129. A short way out of Robbinsville, the signs to Joyce Kilmer Memorial Forest will begin, and simply follow these for the14-mile trip. You will take S.R.1127 around Lake Santeetlah until you turn off to the left onto 416, which leads to the Memorial Loop Trail parking lot. There are numerous camping areas nearby with bathrooms, some within easy walking distance of the trail. We recommend Horse Cove Campground. Go straight out of the parking lot, cross S.R.1127, and get on S.R.1134, which you will see in front of you. The map indicates that this is a gravel road, but it is in fact now paved. The campground is on your left after less than a mile.

This road will also take you back to 129 and Robbinsville

Trail description

Follow trail signs from the Joyce Kilmer Memorial Forest parking area. Start the trail by ascending alongside the charming Little Santeetlah Creek. Follow the Poplar Cove Loop Trail and complete a figure-of-eight by taking a right on the trail at the memorial plaque. The outstanding feature of the trail is a grove of giant yellow poplars.

Mushrooms and Emergency Rooms
(one can lead to the other)

If you forage for wild mushrooms, you might find some precious delights like the prized common morel, (a.k.a. *morchella esculenta*). Morelle mushrooms sell for around $100 per pound, making them the Appalachian equivalent of French truffles. Most mushroom gatherers won't sell their morels for any price; they save the rare and flavorful morels for their own kitchens. Once in a great while American Indian traders will supply them to Spirits On The River Restaurant and they'll wind up in dishes served to lucky customers (For more information, see our write-ups in the restaurant section or American Indian section of this guidebook).

But don't pick and eat wild mushrooms or plants unless you are an expert at identification and are absolutely sure of what you are eating. To underscore the gravity of this advice, we offer the following examples:

If you ingest Poison Hemlock, it can destroy the central nervous system within a matter of minutes. Because it resembles Wild Carrot (Queen Anne's Lace) it has killed more than its share of wannabe-naturalists.

Water Parsnip is sometimes confused with Water Hemlock, and for that reason alone it is best to altogether exclude the tasty wild parsnip vegetable from your diet. A single forkful of Water Hemlock can kill faster than a copperhead snake.

HOT SPRINGS

The town of **Hot Springs** is on the western edge of **Madison County**, which neighbors Asheville's Buncombe County. It is an ideal location for a day or weekend trip. Only a fifty minute drive from downtown Asheville, Hot Springs offers a combination of historical houses, mountain views, and varied outdoor pursuits. As the name suggests, the primary draw to the town is its wonderful mineral baths, a popular tourist destination since Victorian times. There are also opportunities for whitewater rafting, horseback riding, and mountain biking.

Dining

Hot Springs is the only town in an otherwise dry county where you can enjoy a glass of wine. We suggest you do this at any one of the inns mentioned below or at the **Bridge Street Cafe and Inn** (828.622.0002). Their covered deck overlooking Spring Creek offers a peaceful spot for enjoying fresh organic Mediterranean dishes and pizzas from a wood-fired oven. Call ahead for opening hours and reservations.

Accommodations

There are many options in this small town for renting cabins or houses. Camping is available at the Hot Springs Spa and Pisgah National Forest's Rocky Bluff site. Hostel-type accommodation is also available, catering mostly to Appalachian Trail hikers. Contact the Information Center for details.

For luxurious lodging, try the **Mountain Magnolia Inn and Retreat** (828.622.3543). This recently renovated historic 1868 treasure offers wonderful views, period decor, massage therapy, and fine dining by reservation (Fri-Sun; one seating at 7:30pm). If you think rail

Grits

(all you need to know about grits but were afraid to ask)

Is grits singular or plural?

Grits is plural. I mean grits are plural (laughter).

Is grits party food?

Of course grits is party food. Anything good is worth celebrating.

(Craig Claiborne, food critic for the New York Times, in the R. Stan Woodward film documentary "Grits")

Mountain Magnolia Inn and Retreat (the historical Colonel James H. Rumbough House)

travel is romantic, you'll be charmed by the noise of the passing trains, but if you are a light sleeper, the Inn's Garden House may be a quieter option. It can sleep families, groups, or individuals, and has front porch rockers, a gorgeous back garden, and kitchen and laundry facilities.

Another attractive B&B is the Duckett House Inn and Farm (828.622.7621), a circa-1900 farmhouse on the banks of Spring Creek. A great secluded spot for relaxation, this B&B has six well-appointed rooms with shared bathrooms and a cottage available for families with children. The Inn offers picnic baskets and mountain bike rental. Delicious homemade breads are featured on the breakfast menu and a set vegetarian evening meal is available on the weekends. Call the friendly staff a few days in advance for dinner reservations.

Hiking

Hot Springs is the nearest access from Asheville to the Appalachian Trail, the fabled 2000 mile path leading from Georgia to Maine.

Don't miss Max Patch, an easy hike on a grassy bald near Hot Springs that affords a fantastic 360-degree mountain view. Take Hwy 209 for 7.6 miles, turn right at the Meadow Fork/Max Patch sign onto a gravel road for 5.4 mi. to Route 1181. Turn right and follow signs from there to Max Patch. For more detailed information about hiking in the area call or visit the Forest Service office (next door to the Info Center). After your hike you may want to take a dip in Hot Springs' famous mineral baths.

Directions to Hot Springs from Asheville's Chamber of Commerce

Take a right out of the Chambers and get on I-240 West. Take 19/23 North towards Weaverville. Get off at the Marshall exit and follow route 25/70 West to Hot Springs. Journey time: about 50-60 minutes.
Distance: about 34 mi.

Hot Springs Spa and Campground
828.622.7676 or 1.800.462.0933

Adored by locals and visitors from this century and the last, Hot Springs Spa is indeed the "sweet and restful spot" that Daniel Fowle (Governor of NC) wrote of in 1889. Discovered for the first time (at least by white men) in 1778, the springs have been used as a spa since the 19th Century. The modern Jacuzzi tubs come in various sizes and are located in secluded outdoor settings. The most coveted tub seems to be No. 5, which is nestled at the confluence of the lovely French Broad River and Spring Creek. The many grateful testimonials by afflicted visitors can't *all* be coincidental. If you want the full pampering program, go for "the works" and get a massage from their on-site therapist.

Spa Hours: In Season: (Mid-Feb to Nov 30) 9am-11pm. Off Season: (Dec 1- Mid Feb) Weekends only 11am-11pm, weather permitting. Call in advance during winter schedule. Reservations are recommended. Full hook-up RV camping available all year. Seasonal tent camping with partial hook-ups and hot showers available.

Hot Springs Information Center
828.622.7611
Open Mon-Thu 8:00am-3:30pm

Forest Service Office
(Hot Springs) 828.622.3202.
Open Mon-Fri 8:00am-4:30pm

Whitewater Rafting
Blue Ridge Rafting 1.800.303.7238
USA Raft 1.800.USA-RAFT
Nantahala Outdoor Center 1.800.232.7238
Adventures Out 828.622.7550

BASEBALL

BICYCLING

ROCK CLIMBING

WHITEWATER RAFTING

SNOWBOARDING

SNOW SKIING

OUTDOOR RECREATION

Asheville Tourists Baseball Club and McCormick Field
828.258.0428

McCormick Field is home to the *Asheville Tourists Baseball Club*, a minor league baseball team affiliated with the *Colorado Rockies* franchise. Call for schedule of games and information about group discounts and special events.

Directions to McCormick Field from the Chamber of Commerce: Follow Interstate 240 East to the Charlotte St. exit south, go one mile and turn left on McCormick Place.

McCormick Field is big enough to create the larger-than-life thrill of the traditional baseball stadium experience, but small enough to preserve the hometown Casey-at-the-bat excitement of the game.

Babe Ruth, who is considered the greatest baseball legend of all time, played in several exhibition games at this ballpark. He stayed at the famous Battery Park Hotel downtown and allegedly enjoyed chasing Asheville's women and drinking their moonshine whiskey. One day Lou Gehrig (another baseball hall of famer who played at McCormick Field) helped carry a drunk Babe Ruth into the hotel. A few hours later, Ruth played and hit a home run.

Apparently, one of the balls he homer'd over the back fence has never been recovered. If discovered, it would likely fetch millions of dollars in today's market, as a collector's item. But don't waste your time looking for it because it would have decomposed by now. In fact, some old-timers we interviewed claim that a gigantic hickory tree now stands at the spot where the baseball landed.

The folklore seems appropriate because, after all, George Herman Ruth used a bat made of hickory wood when he slammed Asheville deep into the left center field of American baseball mythology.

President Franklin D. Roosevelt gave a speech here in 1936 during his successful second-term election campaign.

Jackie Robinson, the first African American to play major league baseball, played a game here during his controversial rookie season with the Brooklyn Dodgers. It was a 1947 pre-season exhibition game scheduled on the spur of the moment because the cities of Jacksonville and Atlanta refused to host the event. City officials in those towns were afraid that his presence would create violent racial tension. Robinson was a second baseman with a reputation for stealing bases. He won fielding and batting awards and was the first African American admitted to the Baseball Hall of Fame.

If you're an Asheville tourist, you might enjoy an afternoon of cheering your namesake team.

CYCLING IN ASHEVILLE & SURROUNDING AREAS

Bent Creek

Named for a horseshoe-shaped bend near the French Broad River, Bent Creek flows through the Pisgah National Forest, a short drive from Asheville. It is an excellent area for first timers or experts. Trails of varying degrees of difficulty abound.

Directions to Hardtimes Trailhead (where our suggested rides begin) from Asheville. Take I-240 west to I-26 east and take exit 2 onto N.C. 191. Turn left, go past the Biltmore Square Mall, and head south on N.C. 191 for 2 miles. Turn right at stoplight, following the brown signs to the Lake Powhatan Recreation Area (bear left after 0.2 miles on this road). The signed trailhead parking is approximately 2 miles down this road on the left.

Suggested rides at Bent Creek:

1. **Single Track Sampler:** An easy/moderate ride; great as a first ride at Bent Creek. A good ride to take when you don't have a lot of time and want some great singletrack, or a nice addition to other rides or trails. The small climb is done on both gravel roads and singletrack.

2. **South Ridge Road/ Lower Sidehill Trail:** A long moderate/difficult ride; climbing is done mostly on gravel roads. Gravel road cruising and fast, technical singletrack downhills.

3. **The Top And Back:** This is a difficult ride; climbing is done mostly on singletrack with steep uphills and fast, technical singletrack downhills.

Other notable rides at Bent Creek:

1. **Homestead:** 1.0 mile in length. Seasonal use only. Starts at Lake Powhatan beach, follows lakeshore and passes the dam. Goes along Bent Creek. Technical in spots.

2. **North Boundary:** 3.8 miles. Gravel road alternative to "The Top." Easy.

3. **Sleepy Gap:** 1.8 miles. More difficult. Short, steep climb.

4. **Little Hickory Top:** 1.8 miles. Starting from Ingle's Field this old road, now singletrack, leads down the mountain to Laurel Branch. Great downhill cycling.

Mills River

Just over the ridge from Bent Creek, Mills River is another popular riding area. There are trails on both the North and South Mills River. There are over twenty trails to choose from. Some, like Cantrell Creek, are difficult to follow. This particular trail's upper section is overgrown so that the trail sometimes becomes the creek.

Pilot Rock, which is 3.6 miles and steep with sharp switchbacks, has a section with boulders which is nearly impossible to ride and which intersects Blue Ridge Parkway property. There are a few easier sections such as Bear Branch (1.3 miles) and Fletcher Creek (2.4 miles). The North Mills River trail is fairly level but the many river crossings make it more difficult and require lots of wading.

Other trails: Spencer Branch (1.6 miles) is hilly and somewhat technical. South Mills River is long and has many river crossings and some rooty and rocky areas. It becomes quite scenic where the Mills River drops out of the Pink Beds. Turkey Pen Gap trail (5.5 miles) is one of the most strenuous.

Turkey Pens

This is on the road to Brevard. Get off at the Airport exit 5 miles before Brevard. Look for a large green sign. Turn right at Turkey Pens. Go about one mile until the road deadends. You can bike to Pink Beds from there. Be cautious because the road is shared with horses.

Black Mountain

Take I-40 east to the Ridgecrest exit. Turn left and go back over the highway. Go to the stopsign. Take a right at the Ridgecrest Conference Center. Go past it to the next stopsign. Go through the stopsign and across the intersection. The entrance to the trailhead is at the parking lot. At the end of the trail take a hard left onto Old 70. Creekside trailhead / Twin Falls sidehike / Buckhorn Gap. Incredible views, caves, rock outcroppings, and a very fast 1900-foot vertical downhill ride.

Tsali

The popular Tsali Recreation Area is reached by following U.S. 19/74 from Bryson City (Great Smoky Mountains Expressway) to its intersection with N.C. 28 North. Follow N.C. 28 north a few miles to the sign for Tsali Campground on your right. The gravel road will take you to the trails.

The Recreation Area is located on a peninsula reaching into beautiful Fontana Lake. Four long trails wind along the lakeshore and into the wooded interior hills. The trails are well-maintained and lots of fun.

Trail use alternates between horseback riding and mountain biking on different days, but two are always open to mountain biking. There is a two dollar trail use fee for the day. All of the trails are rated as difficult. The surface is generally hard-packed, with some mud, rocks, and gravel. Speedy singletrack is the rule, with roaring downhills and gradual, fun uphills. Occasionally you will encounter a really steep one. Banked turns are frequent. A cold dip in clear blue Fontana Lake is an essential part of the ride.

There is a nice campground at Tsali where the trails meet. It offers plenty of wooded sites, water, hot showers, and flush toilets for about $15 per night. Camping is also allowed for free on National Forest land except in designated wildlife fields and trailhead parking lots. For those who require more civilized amenities there is a hotel located just a few miles from Tsali on NC 28. Incredible views, fast trails, hard-packed, gradual climbs, and drops with some steep, technical sections.

Bike Shops

Hearn's Cycling and Fitness 828.253.4800 (downtown)
Liberty Bicycles 828.684.1085 (Hendersonville Hwy.)
Pro Bikes of Asheville 828.253.2800 (Merrimon Ave.)
Ski Country Sports 828.254.2771 (Merrimon Ave.)

Guided Bike Trip Info

William "Wally" Wallace 828.696.7955
Steve Longenecker 828.254.9726

ROCK CLIMBING

Western North Carolina is blessed with some of the best hard granite climbing in the Southeast. We have everything from the blank face pure friction bolted routes of Stone Mountain to the gnarly crags with deep pockets and grueling overhangs of Devil's Court House off the Blue Ridge Parkway. It's all within about an hour's drive of downtown Asheville. Looking Glass, Cedar Rock, and Linville Gorge are just a few of the other popular climbing areas in WNC. Rock climbing is not a sport to try on your own without the proper training and instruction. Asheville has several guide services that are happy to take beginners out to the rock for a fun and safe adventure.

Four notable guide services that keep folks coming back for more are listed below.

Falling Creek Camp's Coed Adventure Programs
Tuxedo, NC
828.254.9726

A living legend works here. Steve Longenecker is responsible for the first ascent of Looking Glass rock in the Pisgah National Forest. This seasoned professional brought climbing to the Southeast more than thirty years ago and since that time has been instrumental in promoting safety, environmental awareness, and good climbing etiquette.

Mountain Adventures
Hendersonville, NC
828.696.7955

William "Wally" Wallace has been teaching rock climbing and wilderness guiding for more than thirty years. One of the pioneers of climbing in the Southeast, he specializes in working with beginning climbers to teach proper, safe, environmentally aware techniques.

Climbmax Mountain Guides
43 Wall St.
828.252.9996

Located in downtown Asheville on Wall Street, Climbmax sports an outdoor forty foot competition-class climbing wall. They also have an indoor climbing gym with almost all the features of any rock you might encounter in the wild. Climbmax offers instruction and climbing at their facility as well as guided tours to local rock climbing sites.

Black Dome Guides at Black Dome Mountain Sports
140 Tunnel Road
828.251.2001

Black Dome Mountain Sports of Asheville has a huge selection of outdoor equipment as well as informative books, maps, and services. They cover everything from ice climbing to mountain biking. Rock climbing guides are available. Call to speak with one or get more information.

For more information on outdoor recreation in general, check with the Asheville Chamber of Commerce. It has information on white water rafting, mountain biking, climbing, hiking and more.

WHITEWATER RECREATION

With the Nolichucky, Nantahala, Ocoee, Chattooga, and French Broad rivers all flowing through Western North Carolina, Asheville makes a great starting point for paddlers and rafters of all levels. From relaxing float trips on the French Broad that drift past the Biltmore Estate, to rough, technical, Class IV water on the Ocoee, there's something for everyone. But before getting in the water, make safety a priority. The outfits listed below can help you enjoy your whitewater outings.

Southern Waterways
521 Amboy Rd.
828.232.1970
1.800.849.1970

Just a stone's throw from downtown Asheville, Southern Waterways has trips for all ages and abilities ranging from a couple of hours to two days. They offer guided or self-guided float trips that border the Biltmore Estate property. This undeveloped land, once home to Cherokee hunters and traders, is ideal for viewing wildlife and getting away from the city.

On New Year's Eve, 1924, a fellow known as "The Human Fly" climbed the side of the thirteen-story Jackson Building in Pack Square without ropes or nets. Better yet, he made it all the way back down to live and tell about it.

French Broad Rafting Company
Marshall, NC
828.649.3574
1.800.842.3189

Located about thirty minutes from Asheville in the small town of Marshall, the French Broad Rafting Company offers morning, afternoon, and evening sunset raft trips on the French Broad River. They also provide whitewater or calm water rafting trips and boat rentals.

Nantahala Outdoor Center
Bryson City, NC
828.488.2175
1.800.232.7238

They have outposts on all the most popular whitewater river spots in the area. Nantahala Outdoor Center has been the headquarters for paddlers in WNC for years. With more services and trips than you can shake a paddle at, they have plentiful options for serious water lovers and casual rafters alike. Call for programs that suit your particular needs.

SNOW SKIING & SNOWBOARDING

Slopes near Asheville

Wolf Laurel
Mars Hill, NC
828.689.4111
1.800.817.4111 winter only

Wolf Laurel, in Madison County, NC, is the closest ski resort to Asheville. It's a favorite of local ski buffs, especially because of the convenient location. They offer 54 acres of skiable terrain, slopes from beginner to expert, a double and quad lift and a ski school with clinics for all levels.

Check out their newest attraction, the lift-assisted Snow Tubing Park. Four tubing chutes over 350 ft. long zoom you along and then you can get a ride back to the top on the lift. It even operates at night. Great family fun.

Wolf Laurel has its own cozy lodge, or you can stay nearby. It's about 45 minutes from the town of Hot Springs, NC, which is a popular tourist destination in the western part of Madison County. We recommend an overnight stay in Asheville or Hot Springs coupled with a day of skiing at Wolf Laurel, for a great excursion. Refer to the section of this book which covers half day, full day, and overnight hiking for our write-up about Hot Springs.

Cataloochee Ski Area
Maggie Valley, NC
828.926.0285
1.800.768.3588
1.800.768.0285 snow report line

About an hour from Asheville, Cataloochee is the oldest and one of the favorite ski resorts in North Carolina. Established in the early 1960s, Cataloochee was the catalyst for a rapid proliferation of ski businesses in Western North Carolina. They offer beginner slopes as well as the 5400 ft Moody Top, with a 740 foot vertical drop. This is home to some of the most challenging terrain in the region.

While in the vicinity, you can also visit Cherokee, NC, which is described in our section about special excursions. Take a cultural and historical tour of Cherokee and learn about the earliest Americans whose contributions to the region are extraordinary. The Museum of the Cherokee Indian is especially wonderful, and is a great place to take the whole family for an exciting and educational adventure. You might want to combine skiing and sightseeing for an overnight excursion to the Maggie Valley / Cherokee area.

Overnight Destinations

Other slopes in Western North Carolina, which are generally considered for overnight excursions from Asheville, are worth checking out if you love to ski. The following are some of the most popular ones within comfortable driving distance.

Beech Mountain Ski Resort

Beech Mountain, NC
828.387.2011
1.800.438.2093

The resort is located atop Beech Mountain at 5,506 ft. above sea level. Peak elevation: 5,506 ft. Base elevation: 4,675 ft. Vertical rise: 830 ft. Lifts: 1 High Speed Quad, 6 doubles. 1 J-Bar and 1 rope tow. Lift capacity: 8600 skiers per hour. Snowmaking capability: 100% slope coverage. All slopes have lighted night skiing. Ski Beech is the highest ski resort in this part of the country.

Hawksnest Golf and Ski Resort

Banner Elk, NC
828.963.6561
1.800.822.HAWK

Fourteen slopes, peak elevation 4819 ft. Two beginner, six intermediate, and six advanced. Vertical drop: 619 ft. Their "Top Gun" slope may be the best in the entire region. They offer a program called Kiddy Hawk for children and one called Night Hawk for grown-ups who want to stay up past midnight skiing by moonlight.

 Skateboard Parks

There is a skateboard park located on top of the Civic Center parking garage. During the summer it attracts 50-60 skateboarders a day, who range in age from 12 to 30. Asheville Parks & Recreation plans to open a new one at the corner of Flint and Cherry Streets, in the near future.

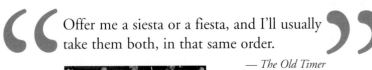

> Offer me a siesta or a fiesta, and I'll usually take them both, in that same order.
>
> — *The Old Timer*

ANNUAL
FESTIVALS

MEET THE MAYOR

BELE CHERE

GOOMBAY

MOONLIGHT OVER ASHEVILLE

DOWNTOWN AFTER FIVE

RAMP FESTIVAL

243

Asheville Mayor Leni Sitnick has done her best to take the formal stuffiness right out of city politics. Employing an "open door" policy, Leni welcomes Asheville residents— from people living on the streets to people who have streets named after themselves—to sit a spell and chew the fat. Make that chew the chocolate, actually, from a perpetually filled candy dish that holds a place of honor in her office, alongside an autographed photo of Southern country-rocker Charlie Daniels.

Mayor Leni actively supports local artists and her encouragement meant the world to us while we worked to complete this book. It meant even more to us when she agreed to speak to our readers. Here's what she had to say.

What do you think is your most admirable quality?
I'm honest.

What quality do you value most in others?
Honesty and integrity.

What historical figure or other person do you admire most?
The peacemakers: Gandhi, King, Kennedy, Lincoln...all the ones who were shot. John Lennon. But if I had to choose one person, it would actually have to be my mother, an absolutely remarkable human being.

If you could have any question answered, what would it be?

How to create peace in the world.

If you were to create a holiday in Asheville, what would it celebrate?

Are you sure you don't want to know what kind of tree I'd like to be? It'd be a Japanese red maple. As for the holiday, I would create a day of understanding and a day of mindfulness and a day of tolerance.

When you want to show off Asheville to visitors, what are the one or two places you make sure to take them?

The first thing I do is take them up on a mountain so they can look down and see the configuration of the entire area. Most of the time that's up to the Grove Park Inn or to one of the overlooks up on the Blue Ridge Parkway. And the second place is downtown, because I think we have a wonderful, exciting downtown.

If you had to live on a deserted island for two years, what three things (besides food and water) would you take along?

I would take Richard Gere and my two grandchildren. [Laughs] That might not work, though. Actually, I would take my glasses, Richard Gere, and a mattress.

What makes Asheville home to you, as opposed to just a place to live?

Twenty-one years ago when I drove through this area, it was the first time I felt connected to a place, to a people—the first time I'd felt at home anywhere. I fell in love and that was that. I can't put it into words. I can only tell you Asheville is the right size, the right make-up, the right visual experience. I wake up every day and look out the window and thank God I'm here.

Asheville Citty Hall

245

ANNUAL FESTIVALS

Asheville is a festive town; during any given month, there are about two dozen festivals within driving distance. We have events to celebrate wild garlic, toy trains, Shakespeare's plays, ghosts, motorcycles, and even an annual event entitled *Bogs, Bugs, and Beavers*.

By all means, find out what's cooking while you're in this neck of the woods. It could be pumpkin pie at the nearby *Pumpkin Festival* or you might be here in time for the *Krazy with Kudzu!* event. Of all the annual festivals we've heard about, the most curious-sounding one has got to be the *BYOB: Bring Your Own Bed* fest. We have no idea what it's all about, but it sounds like fun.

Music festivals which attract both local and international performers have earned this region a world-class musical reputation. **The Lake Eden Arts Festival** (828.68.MUSIC), which is held in spring and fall, and the **Brevard Music Festival** (828.884.2011) are but two examples which come to mind.

Check the arts and entertainment listings of our local papers or call the **Chamber of Commerce** (800.257.1300) for up-to-date information, ticket prices, and schedules regarding festivals in the vicinity during your visit.

The following is a sampling , to whet your appetite for festival-going, of some of the free-to-the-public festivals which are among our personal favorites

*The Southern Appalachian Cloggers perform at the 67th annual **Ramp Festival** in Waynesville, N.C. Some of the dancers have been clogging for more than thirty years.*

Bele Chere

828.259.5800

This is the biggie that everyone gears up for all year long. This event began with one stage on Haywood St. back in 1979, and now ranks as one of the biggest citywide festivals in the whole country. Nearly 350,000 people attend this three-day extravaganza, to enjoy over 100 different acts performing music, storytelling, and dancing on half a dozen stages.

Kat Williams

It's also a major multicultural food fair with block after block of food and drink, to give you enough caloric fuel to browse amongst hundreds of vendors selling everything from Teriyaki and t-shirts to handmade furniture and sterling silver jewelry. This event lasts for three days, but even if it lasted a month, you could never catch all the acts and all the action. Bele Chere is a mega-festival and a sure bet for the whole family's ongoing entertainment.

Brian Vasilik brought his face paints to the festival during Downtown After 5.

Downtown After Five

828.251.9973

Downtown After Five is the best old-fashioned block party you can imagine. It's free, it's fun for all ages, and it flat-out rocks the normally stoic Pack Square. Great bands, great boogie, and a perfect way to celebrate the end of the work week. Best of all, it happens several times per year.

It's our favorite example of the fact that in at least one modern American city, neighbors do indeed get out and meet each other, while dancing up a storm. Bring a neighbor, make a friend, let your hair down and shake off the work week to some Cajun, Rockabilly, Funk, or Jazz. And did we mention the best people-watching opportunities in Western North Carolina?

Goombay

828.252.4614

This late-summertime festival is held in the historic Eagle St. district of downtown. Goombay, Asheville's second-largest street festival, is an award-winning event which has been providing soulful entertainment for the whole family for decades.

The festival's historical roots derive from Bermuda, where it began as an annual day of freedom and celebration for slaves. Today, Asheville's Goombay is an uplifting, colorful festival complete with live music, exotic food, and some of the most interesting browsing and shopping for clothing, jewelry, and handicrafts that you could hope for.

This writer found arts and crafts from artisans as far away as Kenya, juxtaposed with the cool creations of local artists. And after sampling the delicious food offered by street vendors, he wore

off a few pounds while dancing to jazz, hip-hop, funk, and gospel music. This is an event not to be missed, which lasts for three days.

*The "Mud People" perform in Pack Square during the festive **Gay Pride Parade**.*

*Ramp seller Jack Hefner at the 67th annual **Ramp Festival** in Waynesville, N.C.*

*The Southern Appalachian Cloggers from Canton, N.C. kick up their heels at the **Ramp Festival**.*

Rampant Rampers and the Annual Ramp Festival

The national plant of Scotland is the thistle, the English have their rose. Some would say the plant of Western North Carolina must be the rhododendron. We beg to differ. The elusive and stately *ramp*, with its distinctive aroma, surely deserves the title.

A member of the leek family, this pungent vegetable grows wild in damp shady groves of the Southern Appalachians in April and May. The flavor is somewhat akin to garlic and onions mixed, and can produce startling breath odors for days after consumption.

Die-hard "Rampers" claim that long afternoons of happy ramp digging make up for being socially ostracized afterwards. Ramps are considered by some to be a form of contraception, as birth records indicate that no woman in Haywood County has conceived within 3 days of her husband eating ramps. In days of yore, school children who had eaten ramps the night before were sent home from classes so the other children could concentrate on their school work.

Nowhere is the ramp more revered than in Waynesville, where connoisseurs (of dishes like ramp scrambled eggs, ramp meatloaf and ramp taters) come from all over to enjoy the "Allium Tricoccum" (the Latin name for ramps) during the annual Ramp Festival. Started in 1931, this unique event involves a ramp-infused brunch, local entertainment and a ramp-eating contest. The current record is 123 ramps eaten in a 5 minute period.

Contact 828.456.8691 (Haywood County American Legion Post 47) for more information about the annual Ramp Convention held in early May.

249

What do you admire in a person?
A sense of humor. Tolerance.

What do you think is the most important historical event in your lifetime?
Being a Scot, it would have to be Scotland getting its own parliament for the first time since 1707.

If you were going to a deserted island for two years, what three items (besides food and water) would you take with you?
Antibiotics (Hey, I'm a Virgo!). I wouldn't want to stub my toe or get a toothache and die from an infection. A lover. Only easy-going conversationalists with great survival skills need apply. And any musical instrument. I don't play any but reckon I would actually find time on a deserted island to learn how to play at least one. Pencil and paper for writing a journal...whoops, that's four. Oh well, let's go ahead and live dangerously. Ditch the antibiotics.

What makes Asheville home to you, as opposed to just a place to live?
Tom Kerr, open-minded/friendly people, mountains, unusual buildings, and the music scene.

What's one place you would be sure to take a first-time visitor to Asheville?
Riverside Cemetery because it is a great place to combine fresh air, nature, and history.

If you could declare a holiday in Asheville, what would it celebrate?
I'd like to have a Politically Incorrect Day, when all the spiritually elevated crowd can let their hair down and say what really bothers them.

What's the most unusual thing that ever happened to you in the woods?
One time on the Appalachian Trail, I had a haunting. My boyfriend and I were camping, and after dark, as we sat around the fire, a sort of mini-whirlwind blew up from nowhere. It had been calm all night, and it returned to calm afterwards.

The "wind" picked up my friend's hat, then picked up the full kettle of boiling water off the fire and emptied its entire contents over my friend's head, scalding him. We later found the kettle about twenty feet away, and his hat another twenty feet away, in the opposite direction. Oddly enough, a nearby bag of potato

chips and several pieces of lightweight plastic tableware were left untouched. It was so strange we were both convinced it was a haunting, particularly because of my friend's job at the time.

A company wanted to extend their power plant and the law required that archaeologists dig the area first. He was one of the archaeologists they hired, and he had recently exhumed the body of an American Indian shaman.

What historical personality would you like to meet and what would you do with them?

If she really existed, I would like to meet Morgaine the Fey, King Arthur's fairy sister. I'd ask her to take me to Avalon. A close second would be Vincent van Gogh while he lived in Arles. I would just cook him a decent dinner (Well, he *was* a starving artist.), buy him some paints and check him out of the asylum when he needed it. Perhaps even try to talk him out of that nasty ear episode.

AUTHOR TOM KERR

What do you admire in a person?
Empathy and self-awareness.

What's the most important historical event in your lifetime?
It must have been the birth of the so-called Hippy Movement, which in my estimation was simply an amalgamation of all the other socio-political movements which the 1960s represent.

Or the night President Nixon officially ended the Vietnam military draft, two weeks before I was required to report to the Army for my medical examination. My sister Mary Margaret delivered the news to me in person late at night and had to grab me by the shoulders and yell at me before I believed what she was saying. It happened at a party. We were having a party for this

251

guy who was going in the military the next day. I think the war ended before he got to Vietnam. I hope so.

And then there was the night I walked into some beer joint and met Gail Forsyth. Since then my life has been like one of those artistic foreign films with subtitles.

What book would you like to publish?
A scratch and sniff book about flowers.

What's the most unusual thing you've ever discovered in the woods?
The complete skeleton of a man, sitting in a lotus posture, in this narrow space between some humongous boulders on a riverbank.

And when I was about seven years old I had a vision of the ocean in the middle of a pine forest. I believe it was actually just a flooded field after a thunderstorm. But I didn't realize that at the time so to me it was a miracle. All through my childhood I just figured I had discovered an ocean in the woods near my parents' house. I kept going back to look for it again and again, but it had evaporated like a mirage. Part of me still looks for it, I suppose.

If you were going to live on a desert island for two years, what three things (besides food and water) would you take with you?
Bob Dylan and two powerful Muses. Number four was going to be an assortment of musical instruments. But I think between me and Bob and the two Muses I have in mind, we could figure out a way to smuggle in some instruments.

Wait, I'm picking up a signal from one of the Muses. She wants to know if the island has chocolate on it.

If you could declare a holiday in Asheville, what would it celebrate?
Without hesitation I would declare a holiday to celebrate the hard-working and heroic woman named Bonita who manages the Windsor Hotel at 36 Broadway. The individual efforts of this one awesome person contribute more to our community than we could ever possibly imagine. She is an ideal role model as a parent, teacher, social worker, psychological counselor, friend, and citizen. I could write a whole book about the reasons she deserves our respect, admiration, and heartfelt thanks. She deserves the Key to the City.

And I'd like to celebrate children by letting them run the city for a day while the so-called grown-ups listen and learn.

What historical personality would you like to speak to and what would you talk about?
Marilyn Monroe and we'd just whisper sweet nothings.

What question would you like to be asked and how would you answer it?
I'd like for Terry Gross to ask me if she can interview me on her radio show *Fresh Air*. Or for Marilyn Monroe, after we got done whispering, to ask me to help her with her zipper. I'd say, "Alrighty, oui, si-si, yah, aye-aye, yes-sirree-bob, uh-huh, indeedy, okay, sure, yeah."

What makes Asheville home to you and not just another place to live?
There are folks here who let me live inside their hearts without paying rent.

INDEX